# Marketplace Lifestyles in an Age of Social Media

# Marketplace Lifestyles in an Age of Social Media
## Theory and Methods

Lynn R. Kahle
and Pierre Valette-Florence

*M.E.Sharpe*
Armonk, New York
London, England

The EuroSlavic fonts used to create this work are © 1986–2012 Payne Loving Trust.
EuroSlavic is available from Linguist's Software, Inc.,
www.linguistsoftware.com, P.O. Box 580, Edmonds, WA 98020-0580 USA
tel. (425) 775-1130.

**Library of Congress Cataloging-in-Publication Data**

Kahle, Lynn R.
  Marketplace lifestyles in an age of social media : theory and methods / by Lynn R. Kahle
and Pierre Valette-Florence.
    p. cm.
  Includes bibliographical references and index.
  ISBN 978-0-7656-2561-8 (pbk. : alk. paper)
  1. Lifestyles—Psychological aspects. 2. Imagery (Psychology) 3. Internet marketing.
4. Social media. I. Valette-Florence, Pierre. II. Title.

HQ2042.K34 2012
658.834019—dc22                                                          2010040054

Printed in the United States of America

The paper used in this publication meets the minimum requirements of
American National Standard for Information Sciences
Permanence of Paper for Printed Library Materials,
ANSI Z 39.48-1984.

∞

IBT (p)   10   9   8   7   6   5   4   3   2   1

To Alix and Rita, and in memory of my parents. PVF

To my sons, Kevin and Kurtus. LRK

These people have taught us much about

lifestyles—past, present, and future.

# Contents

# Preface

In an increasingly turbulent marketing environment, savvy marketing managers need to maintain a firm grip on the ever-changing attitudes and practices of consumption. Among the available approaches to achieving this goal, lifestyle studies are a viable way of gaining insights into a special and often privileged place in the human psyche. Indeed, one might argue that the very character of our fellow human beings is revealed in part by tapping into this stream of information.

No longer viewed solely as a business-related concept, marketing in the twenty-first century is more aptly described as a new branch of the social sciences. Several investigations into varied lifestyles and their effects on consumption are now available. We believe that an analysis of different lifestyle approaches stimulates constructive reflection on and genuine interest in their contribution to the study of marketing as a social science. While one chapter of this book is devoted to an analysis of the French lifestyle, the main focus of the volume is bringing to light little-known research on purchasing values and patterns of consumption for an English-speaking audience. We offer minimal coverage of North American lifestyle approaches because so many sources already exist on that aspect of the topic (e.g., Shimp, 2010; Solomon, 2009).

This book covers the historic development of academic and applied research, but it also includes a chapter on promising new techniques that might lead to improvements—both methodological and conceptual—in how we study traditional lifestyles and patterns of consumption.

Our aim is to help readers understand this new field of study while simultaneously pointing out the limitations of the research methods that are available today. We hope that our readers will gain a clearer and more objective awareness of the contribution of lifestyle to a better understanding of social practices and consumption. One might ask: Have other, more constructive investigations been conducted on this topic? That is our wish. A discipline must be able to withstand scrutiny in order to preserve its significance. "Chance favors only the prepared mind," said the French microbiologist and chemist Louis Pasteur. We sincerely hope that reading this book contributes to a further appreciation of this discipline.

## ACKNOWLEDGMENTS

Pierre Valette-Florence (1994) wrote a well-received book in French about lifestyle research in marketing. This book updates his arguments and presents them in English. Crafting the arguments accurately requires vigilance and care. Both of us have devoted much of our scholarly careers to capturing and disseminating the issues discussed here. We have benefited from the helpful efforts of Katja Glühr, Kevin Kahle, Jackie Cooper, Kurtus Kahle, and Debi Eisert, who worked tirelessly and sacrificed much to maximize our efforts. We wish to thank as well the many students, collaborators, and colleagues who have provided us with wise insights and beneficial criticism over the years. In addition, we acknowledge support from the Pat and Stephanie Kilkenny Foundation through the Warsaw Sports Marketing Center at the University of Oregon. Finally, we wish to thank Harry Briggs and his colleagues at M.E. Sharpe for showing the confidence, patience, and guidance needed to complete this project.

Lynn R. Kahle and Pierre Valette-Florence

# Introduction

*The main cement between societies and humans is indifference.*
—André Malraux (1951)

"Lifestyles are dead." Such was the laconic line penned by J.L. Swiners in his *Stratégies* article of 1979. However, more than three decades later, lifestyles still seem to be thriving. Recent books on this subject (Cahill, 2006; Cathelat, 1990; Michman, Mazze, and Greco, 2003; Tambyah, Tan, and Kau, 2010; Wang, 2010) testify to the resilence of lifestyle even if they form part of the domain extension. Moreover, companies engaged in the study of societal trends—COFREMCA and the CCA (translated as the Center for Advanced Communication) in France and VALS of SRI (Strategic Business Insights) in the United States, to name a few—are apparently flourishing. The fad has even spread to traditional countries like Japan, where two research organizations on lifestyles were created in the late 1980s and early 1990s. The Japanese advertising agency DENTSU created the Sogo-kenkyu (General Research Institute) in 1987, and in 1981, the Hakuhodo agency created HILL (Hakuhodo Institute of Life and Living).

It is true that attitudes about lifestyles are an attractive topic for research. The interest generated is actually twofold. Their simplicity of representation allows for something akin to viewing a photographer's snapshot of the latest trends in a given area; Figures I.1a and I.1b offer examples of this idea in the areas of leisure and vacations. More important, these approaches shed new light on the relevance of consumption practices. By replacing the traditional criteria of analysis of sociodemographic variables, attitudinal approaches attempt to explain the new behavior patterns and forms of consumption that have emerged in recent years and, in the process, reveal an alternative explanatory framework about modes of purchase.

Yet even a watchful and knowledgeable eye can become lost in the sea of data available on fads and fancies. All of the information hurled at marketing managers resembles "an obstacle course to juggle employees between terms" (Lhermie, 1984). Business practitioners find themselves caught up

Figure I.1a    **Styles of Life (CCA) and Leisure**

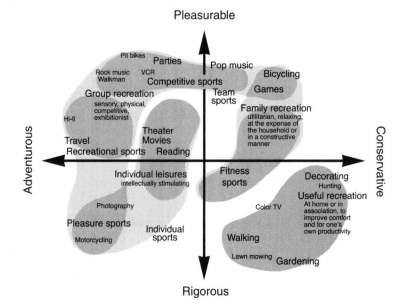

Figure I.1b    **Styles of Life (CCA) and Vacations**

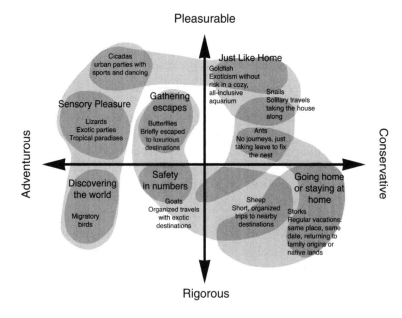

*Source:* Mermet (1985), p. 404 (1.1a), p. 402 (1.1b).

in a difficult dilemma: Are they obliged to follow every new sociocultural trend that presents itself, or can they safely return to decision making based on more tangible economic criteria and conventional demographics? Whom should they believe? What about successful actors in the "research show" (Bernard-Becharies, 1985). Are practitioners "after a new method of enlarging the scope of knowledge" (Burke and Cathelat, 1980) or are they "gurus of a colorful bazaar of sociology" (Benguigui, 1980)?

These concerns are very real, but the answers to them are far from obvious. In truth, for more than forty years, the consumer society has been changing, and it is now entering maturity. The demographic criteria of gender, level of education, or degree of social and professional status, which were traditionally used to identify markets and characterize consumer behavior, no longer seem to tell the whole story. Consumer behaviorists mainly concern themselves with the emergence of single status, the increased purchasing power of households, and the reduction of disparities between socioprofessional categories. However, income dispersion within each socioprofessional category is broad, making the meaning of the categories less definitive or helpful in explaining the inequalities. In addition, lifestyle concepts may obscure a marked improvement in living standards, salaries, and disparities.

Patterns of consumption tend to reinforce private and individualistic concerns, especially because this orientation corresponds to the emergence of an increased single status and a greater feminization of the workforce. Does this new social distribution call into question the use of socioeconomic criteria for defining strategies of segmentation and positioning?

"Certainly," say the enthusiasts of lifestyle studies! The ramifications are not clear-cut, though, and new strategies must be developed with great care. Indeed, recent studies have shown that the aforementioned criteria are still important for the analysis of certain markets such as housing (Herpin, 1986a), as well as sales of automobiles, manufactured goods, and magazines (Munson and Spivey, 1981). We can therefore say that in the analysis of behavior, socioeconomic criteria are always necessary, but their value may fluctuate from one case to another. Therefore, it seems that we should also consider other indicators such as values and lifestyles when looking at consumer trends.

The emergence of "a new consumption" is, above all, about rediscovering consumers at a time when the usual standards of age, income, gender, or mode of living inadequately predict their buying behavior. As researchers and (especially) practitioners have tried to develop innovative approaches to revealing patterns of consumption, the identification of values seems paramount. Consequently, a return to the frenzied worship of individualism at all costs has replaced the socialization of values. Scardigli (1976), in his prospective study, focuses on "the exacerbation of hedonic aspirations and individualization."

Baudrillard (1986b) did note that everything happens against a background of total indifference to the social system.

Faced with increasing isolation, the disarming prospect of more accessible but less discriminating consumption, and a slight attraction to the activities of society, individuals must forge for themselves both a personal and a social identity. And so they search not only for a *reason* to live but also for a *way* to live. As Baudrillard notes, "He negotiates at the time both his individuality and his indifference to everything else."

The cult of narcissism resurrects (Lasch, 1982), as stated by Weil (1986), the "anguish of an individual alone with his conscience." Named for Narcissus, the self-absorbed youth of Greek myth who falls in love with his own reflection, narcissism is characterized by an overblown display of one's own importance, an extreme need for admiration, and a striking absence of empathy. A search for one's "image" in narcissistic terms becomes a complicated experiment steeped in multiple models of behavior and experiences. These models are then perceived as assets. "Prestige is a person who is plugged into the circuit of more potential," writes Baudrillard (1986b). Before the mirror reflects his or her personality, the individual seeks to explore the various scattered facets. The advent of polysensualism, according to COFREMCA, can be seen in the scattering of behavior, the dissolution of interests, and the collapse of cultural values.

It is precisely this identification of values and their evolution that characterizes lifestyle approaches. Thus, COFREMCA detected fifty underlying sociocultural attitudes and behaviors representative of lifestyle trends, among them openness to novelty and change, rejection of authority and order, polysensualism, and reactions against social constraints. Likewise, the CCA has developed a list of thirteen sociocultural flows (Matricon, Burke, and Cathelat, 1974) that highlight the rise of individualism, the importance of symbolism (i.e., image), the mosaic and metamorphosis of people's roles, and the simultaneous but contrary strengthening of certain conservative values such as passivity, focus, and modeling. As Scardigli (1976) puts it, the 1976 CREDOC study (translated as the Research Center for the Study and Observation of Living) focused on "the exacerbation of hedonic and individualistic aspirations." Interest in these approaches may foreshadow lifestyle choices: The identification of dominant values in the society and individuals' identification with those values should enable researchers to better define purchasing behavior and matching consumption patterns.

Seductive as this proposal may seem, the viability of lifestyle analyses is questionable for several reasons:

Swiners (1979) points out in his article for the French periodical *Stratégies* that valid conclusions about lifestyles are somewhat obscured by the proliferation and contradictory nature of so many different studies. For instance, fourteen sociotypes exist for the CCA. (see Chapter 4). COFREMCA identifies nine sociocultural forms. IPSOS, the global survey-based research firm whose motto is "Nobody's Unpredictable," defines five psychological types: the familial altruist, the traditional rigid, the mobile seducer, the mass organizer, and the introverted dreamer. In the United States, confusion also abounds. For Yankelovich, Skelly and White (1981), there are six types; for Leo Burnett, nineteen; and for Needham, ten, and nine study groups in VALS (Values and Life Style Survey) ( Mitchell (1983). The abundance and the disparity of classification hinders decision making and signals the need to proceed with caution.

The low predictive power of these approaches has been highlighted repeatedly in academic research (Kapferer and Laurent, 1981a; Valette-Florence and Jolibert, 1985, 1990). Indeed, some experts feel that lifestyle approaches are still far inferior to the sociodemographic approaches they intended to displace.

In some cases, the failure to launch products has been tied to the analysis of lifestyles. An example is the magazine *Living is an Illustration*. Launched in October 1976 by the Hachette Group, under *Fonne Weekly*, then from March 1977, under *Fonne Monthly*, it stopped publishing in July of that year. Sales did not exceed 30,000 copies, while 60,000 were needed to reach the necessary threshold of profitability. Publication quickly ceased for lack of buyers. The target audience was local working women between the ages of thirty and forty. If the need for such a news magazine existed, it was not compelling enough to translate into a money-making venture.

Magie Noir by Lancôme (Black Magic perfume) is an example of a successful launch (see B. Dubois, 1987, p. 49). Some targets are sensitive to lifestyle, while others are not. In the first case, COFREMCA preferred to speak modestly of porous or poorly defined targets.

Two related issues concerning the effectiveness of lifestyle approaches remain:

- the lack of conceptual consensus and appropriateness of the definition of lifestyle
- the inability to compare the various approaches and make meaningful generalizations about their value

Among the objectives of this work are clarifying the concept of lifestyles and showing that the French approach (or, alternatively, the American approach) is just one example of many possible methods of investigation. Additionally, this book aims to provide a constructive yet critical review of the field through an unbiased presentation of diverse perspectives. The ten chapters in the book are best viewed as four main groups or parts—Chapter 1, Chapters 2–5, Chapters 6–7, and Chapters 8–10. These chapter groupings are complementary and can be approached sequentially.

The first chapter of this book attempts to reconstruct the historic origins of the concept of lifestyles and to clarify the different definitions of its components. It also presents underlying conceptual foundations, which are seldom touched on in other book-length treatments of current lifestyles.

Chapters 2 through 5 discuss the different methods of investigating lifestyle-based behavioral science and marketing. Chapter 2 examines the concepts of values. Chapter 3 looks at AIO inventories (lists of activities, interests, and opinions), mostly of American origin. Chapter 4 deals more specifically with typically French approaches to lifestyle studies. Chapter 5 focuses on the identification and measurement of consumption patterns.

Chapters 6 and 7 deal with lifestyles in practice. The former illustrates the various applications of lifestyle studies, including their use in advertising as well as in distribution, market segmentation, new product design, and sales force management. The latter offers a critique of the field to facilitate a better understanding of the contribution of lifestyle studies to the science of marketing. It seems necessary—indeed, essential—to be concerned about the reliability and validity of measurement tools in the study of lifestyles.

Chapters 8 through 10 summarize the overall outlook for the lifestyle concept, both methodological and conceptual (Chapter 8). Recently, in fact, new and original methods of investigation have emerged. The simplicity of these methods makes them both promising and noteworthy. Chapter 9 attempts to identify and synthesize the main characteristics of lifestyle studies. Chapter 10 presents a theory and method for going forward.

# Marketplace Lifestyles in an Age of Social Media

# 1

# Origins and Definitions

For many years, researchers and practitioners have shown increasing interest in the concept of lifestyles. This phenomenon can be explained in part by the shortcomings of traditional demographics such as socioeconomic variables to predict buying trends, as well as by the sometimes misleading results furnished by motivation-based studies of consumer behavior.

In practice, the concept of *lifestyle* encompasses a variety of elements. Its definition is quite broad, ranging from easily and directly observable behaviors to more hidden aspects of a person's life—including values, attitudes, and opinions—that may function as determinants of his or her behaviors (Hustad and Pessemier, 1974).

The objective of this first chapter is to synthesize the diverse concepts inherent in the study of lifestyles. Taking into account their distinctive origins, these concepts will be presented first in a historical perspective (section 1). We will then retrace their evolution in the domain of marketing (section 2).

## EVOLUTION OF THE CONCEPT

Lifestyle concepts were used in other domains of the human sciences long before they were applied to marketing. Historically speaking, the concept of lifestyles is ancient. As a field of study, it can be traced back to the very first Greek philosophers. Aristotle (384–322 B.C.E.), in his *Rhetoric*, already spoke of "ethos" (or *habitus* in Latin), which allowed for the characterization of manners of being, ways of living, status, and the character of the individual. He inspired his disciple Theophrast (372–287 B.C.E.) to explore the topic further. In his *Characters,* Theophrast described thirty psychological profiles of his time.

Closer to the present day we find portraits of Gidon and of Phedon in *The Characters, or the Manner of the Age* (1688–1694) from La Bruyère (1645–1696). The first citation of the term *style* appeared in the work of the

English philosopher Robert Burton (1577–1640): "It is most true, *stylus virum arguit*—our style betrays us." A century later, the French naturalist Georges-Louis Leclerc de Buffon (1707–1788) wrote: "Style is man himself." Finally, the first appearance of the term *lifestyle* came in the preface of William Wennington's English translation of *Moralische Geschichten* (title means "Moral Tales"), from the work of a German, Adlerjung (1811).

In the twentieth century, it was the German sociologist Max Weber (1864–1920) who popularized the term *lifestyle*. He defined it as "a means of affirmation and differentiation of social status" (1922, 1948), following the idea of *life scheme* proposed in 1899 by Thorstein Veblen. In his book *The Theory of the Leisure Class*, Veblen refers to the life scheme as the state of belonging to a group, along with the choice individuals have to differentiate themselves from groups to which they do not belong. The concept of lifestyle, according to the Austrian physician and psychologist Alfred Adler (1870–1937), differs from the idea presented by Weber and Veblen. Adler (1919, 1929) used the term to describe the system of rules of conduct developed by individuals in order to attain their goals in life.

Adler is best known for his theories of personality and individual psychology. It makes sense, then, that his views on lifestyles would focus on an individual's method of response to the environment. The analysis of lifestyle represents, in fact, the masterwork of Adlerian psychology, because we can trace its influence on his writings for a span of more than forty years. Note that the term *lifestyle* did not appear in his works until 1926, but variations on the word can be found as early as 1912 as "line of direction" (*leitlinie*), "life plan" (*lebensplan*), and "directional image" (*leitbild*), this last expression having been suggested by Ludwig Klages in 1906. The principal concerns of psychologists and sociologists follow the definitions offered by Adler and Weber.

Following in Adler's footsteps, experts in sociology and psychology have preoccupied themselves with the concept of lifestyle as a reflection of personality. Contrary to Freudian theory, which insists on the role of impulse in the formation of personality and behaviors, these theorists explain personality development as a process that blends various aspects of social influence and interpersonal relationships (Hall and Lindzey, 1970; Wells and Beard, 1973).

In the domain of sociology, few works followed Weber's approach. Especially in France, the majority of published works discuss lifestyles of very particular social groups such as the inhabitants of a city or suburb (Kaes, 1963), the members of a profession (Boltanski, 1982), or students (Bourdieu and Passeron, 1964; Baudrillard, 1970). These approaches show that lifestyles are determined not only by demographic or economic criteria, but also by psychological or sociological criteria—for instance, personal interest, taste, level of education, and adherence to certain moral values.

This diversity of work on lifestyles in social sciences, as well as the varied approaches that correspond to them, explains the variety of definitions used in the field of marketing. These definitions are presented in the following section.

## DEFINITIONS OF LIFESTYLES USED IN MARKETING

The history of lifestyle studies follows two major paths: One holds that attitudes determine consumer behavior; the other stresses personality as a primary motivator in purchasing decisions. Paul F. Lazarsfeld (1935) tried to understand consumer behavior by studying the interaction of three groups of variables: predispositions, influences in the form of social connotations, and qualifiers attributed to products. These criteria became the forerunners to the approach based on attitudes and activities, from which we derive the better-known term AIO (an acronym for activities, interests, and opinions), widely recognized in the United States.

Other authors based their approaches on the links that exist between personality variables and the choice of certain kinds of products. Gottlieb (1959), Koponen (1960), and Bernay (1971), for instance, pioneered the incorporation of personality-based variables in more generalized studies of lifestyles. These studies, thus, take on the name of psychographic approaches, which—like studies of the AIO type—are also centered on personality and its relation to economic and social status. However, the majority of research on personalities has proved inconclusive at best (Kassarjian, 1971a), explaining only a small percentage of the variation in consumer behaviors.

It is interesting to note the essentially empirical character that the studies of lifestyles have borrowed from these two orientations (Peltier, et al., 2002; Bolton, et al., 2008). This effect is made apparent in marketing through ongoing efforts to define lifestyle. Many suggestions have been made, both in France and in the United States. Some remain quite general; others are more pragmatic and centered on the individual; still others introduce explicitly the notion of social influence.

Lazer's definition (1963) of lifestyle is very general. It straddles the line between individual and aggregate elements of behavior: "Lifestyle is . . . the result of forces such as culture, values, the symbolism of certain objects, moral values, and ethics. In a certain sense, the aggregate of consumer purchases and the manner in which these purchases are used reflects the lifestyle of a society." This definition is linked to the idea of a system whose process can be schematized, as shown in Figure 1.1.

Figure 1.1    **Hierarchy of "Lifestyles" as Proposed by Lazer**

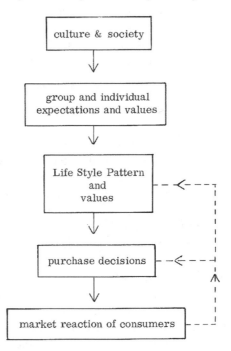

*Source:* Lazer, W. (1963), Life-Style Concepts and Marketing. In S.A. Greyser (ed.), *Toward Scientific Marketing* (Chicago: American Marketing Association), 130–139.

Wind and Green's definition (1974), which is less theoretical than Lazer's and focused more on the individual, defines different levels of lifestyle identification. It falls into the second category of definitions. Wind and Green identify three levels of lifestyle study:

- values and personality traits
- activities, interests, and attitudes
- consumption behaviors

Finally, the concept of lifestyles proposed by Reynolds and Darden (1972b and 1974) and Bernard-Becharies (1980) stresses the importance of social influence. They use ideas founded on George Kelly's theory of *personal constructs* (1955). Kelly believed that a major goal of humans is to predict and control events and experiences. We develop personal constructs to describe our views about the connections between events and experiences. Each person's unique collection of constructs is the basis of personality, in this view.

Reynolds and Darden's approach conceives human behavior as being directed:

- on one hand by the group of cognitive structures that are organized in a system of *personal constructs*
- and on the other hand by the process according to which an individual changes conceptual structures of the universe.

The lifestyle of an individual refers to the system of constructs she or he elaborates and develops personally. In this sense, lifestyle is composed of subsystems built from personal constructions (dimensions or schemas) about the connections between events and experiences. These mental subsystems are ordered, giving the resulting system a pyramid-like allure. The subsystems can also be used in a fragmented way, which is why incomplete information regarding lifestyle is hardly illuminating. We are not capable of understanding the entire person—only certain aspects of the lifestyle. However, it is possible to "group" people according to the similarity of their personal constructs.

The formation of groups of people based on individual similarities of personal constructions is an interesting prospect, but considerable difficulty lies in the measurement of these constructions. The group view of lifestyle rests on a composite concept—one that describes related types of cognitive behavior among members of a sociocultural subgroup. The main problem posed by this definition is its lack of a sufficiently precise operational framework, which leads to ambiguity.

Bernard-Becharies's study (1980) looked at how individuals place themselves in a social group. As a scholar in the field of lifestyle studies, he defined lifestyle as the way of life particular to one group as compared to society as a whole, or of one family as compared to one group, or of one person as compared to one family. According to Bernard-Becharies, lifestyle is really a form of communication, and the concrete manifestations of lifestyle choices—clothes, manners, languages, habits, education, etc.—can be viewed as a system of signs. It would be by such a system that a community communicates its attachments, its norms, and its ways of perception to others.

Bernard-Becharies and Pinson (1981) introduced a distinction between the individual and collective levels of lifestyle. At the collective level, lifestyle—which they call "the way of living"—refers to a great collection of people's cognitions, but with socially differentiating attachments, which they call social values. This represents "the ensemble of types of production of individuals by themselves in a considered hyper-group." At the individual level, lifestyle is the personal expression of a group's way of living and communicating. This definition, too, lacks a precise operational framework.

Figure 1.2    **Integration of the Constituent Elements of Lifestyle**

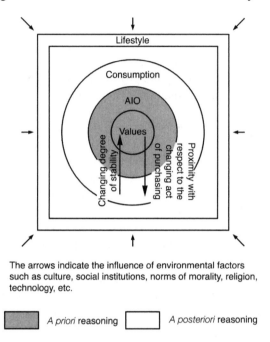

The arrows indicate the influence of environmental factors such as culture, social institutions, norms of morality, religion, technology, etc.

A *priori* reasoning        A *posteriori* reasoning

It is difficult to find any sense of convergence among these definitions. In terms of measuring and describing lifestyles, Wind and Green's definition (1974) appears to be the most complete, because it divides the act of purchasing into three levels. Thus,

- at the most stable and anchored level, we find individual values and personality traits.
- at the intermediate level, we find a collection of attitudes and activities specific to the individual; less stable than values, these are, however, closer to the act of purchasing.
- at the peripheral level is a collection of products purchased and consumed, making this less concrete than the other two levels.

Valette-Florence (1985, 1986) defines lifestyle as an interaction of the three preceding levels: the set of people having a similar lifestyle (ways of behavior analogous to each of the three levels) constitutes a homogeneous group having an identical way of life. The term *way of life* refers to the group's commitment to shared but socially differentiated ideals known as social values. Figure 1.2 depicts this definition of lifestyle as an integration of values and AIO indicators with consumption patterns. Note that often in research values are defined *a priori* and AIO variables are sorted and classified using *a posteriori* methods that statistically cluster the AIO variables along with the consumption behaviors.

The works of Valette-Florence and Jolibert (1985, 1987a, 1988, 1990) expanded on this definition, showing that individuals who display identical behavior in one of the components could, nevertheless, differentiate themselves in the other two. A measure of lifestyle based on the study of just one of the components would lack any sense of depth.

In spite of the limits, researchers typically rely on systems of measure and lifestyle descriptions that integrate only one component, rarely more. In American and French literature, it is therefore possible to list five specific traditions:

1. The first one deals with consumed goods and services: It is based on the principle that a consumer's lifestyle is reflected in the goods and services she or he buys and in the way that she or he consumes them (Levy, 1963; Wells, 1968a; Le Maire, Evrard, and Douglas, 1973).
2. The second tradition deals with a person's primary system of values (Rokeach, 1968a; Kahle, 1983).
3. The third is based on the idea of personality traits (Cohen, 1967; Koponen, 1960) and the concept of "self" (Dolich, 1967; Green, Maheshwari, and Rao, 1969).
4. The fourth tradition focuses on the study of activities and attitudes. Certain activities and attitudes reveal more about an individual's feelings toward a class of products than others (Haley, 1968). A more general approach is based on an inventory of activities, interests, and opinions, hence the acronym AIO (Pessemier and Tigert, 1966; Tigert, 1973; Wells, 1968b; Wells and Tigert, 1971).
5. The fifth approach is more specifically French, dealing with the works of COFREMCA and the CCA. Relying on an analysis of sociocultural trends in development in French society, these organizations' approaches are more dynamic than the others. They place more emphasis on social values and appear somewhat more anchored in thoughtful empirical evidence than the American AIO methods.

The development of these studies has varied widely. The American AIO inventories and the French systems have gained considerable attention, but the other studies have not. Thus, the study of values and their influence on consumption has seen only limited research and development.

Interpreting personality tests and explaining the phenomenon of consumption can be challenging; many practitioners avoid using such exclusive methods (Kassarjian, 1971a). Their usefulness is debatable, as is that of certain personality-like AIO inventories (Wells, 1974). The other approaches will be discussed in subsequent chapters—values in Chapter 2, AIO in Chapter 3, French approaches in Chapter 4, and consumed goods and services in Chapter 5.

CONCLUSION AND SYNTHESIS

This chapter examined the origin of the concept of lifestyle and the difficulties in finding a definition for it that can be applied to the domain of marketing. Generally speaking, a lifestyle is *the integration of an individual's system of values, attitudes, activities, and consumption methods.*

An analysis of literature shows that the absence of a practical and precise conceptual framework for the notion of lifestyles has led researchers to develop faulty definitions and methods of measurement—methods that integrate only one of many components. Among the proposed methods, however, the following distinctions can be made:

- *A priori* studies (those based on deduction) are centered on values or the variability of activity, interest, and opinion (AIO). They attempt to predict a consumer's likely pattern of consumption.
- *A posteriori* studies (those based on induction) are articulated around the definition of types of consumption. These allow the characterization after research on the consumers in the functions with their real or declared consumption.

This distinction corresponds to the three levels of the lifestyle definition we have proposed, which are symbolized in Figure 1.2.

Lifestyle studies offer a wealth of information for commercial research on consumption patterns. A marketer launching a new product will be interested, for example, in identifying the *a priori* values most representative of his or her targeted clientele. Knowledge of these values can be used to define marketing and advertising strategies, taking into account the sociocultural profile of consumers, the most effective media outlet through which they can be reached, and the best buying options for the targeted customer (for instance, in-store or online purchases). By applying *a posteriori* specific modes of consumption, this other approach, although less defensible in a philosophy of science that prizes prediction, has proved itself to be interesting for the research of complementary goods or for an entire range of products.

Recent advances in methodology, theory, and technology have changed the context in which we can discuss lifestyles. Scholars have become more sophisticated, but perhaps more important, lifestyles themselves have changed and become more accessible to researchers *a priori*. Perhaps most noteworthy is the proliferation of social media, which allow for clustering of lifestyle groups through a natural process (common interests) rather than artificial *a posteriori* statistical aggregation. Today, lifestyle groups exist in cyberspace—a reality that previous generations could hardly imagine. For example, "people who love strawberries" may have been an elusive concept for a marketing researcher in a previous generation, requiring extensive survey research and artificial statistical clumping of people into clusters of dubious meaning. Today a Google search of "people who love strawberries" yields over 40 million hits, many of which are blogs and Facebook pages of people who self-identified as belonging in that category. Thus, the time is ripe to revisit the concept of lifestyle in the context of what has been learned over the past generation and what is transpiring today.

In subsequent chapters we will explore the complex choices in deciding how to study lifestyles. One can see that the choice of a method for investigation is a function of scientific philosophy, availability of information, financial constraints, commercial traffic to stores and Web sites specific to each enterprise, and many other factors. Choices depend on the specific characteristics of each study, which is why it is important to examine and understand each method in more detail.

# 2

# Methodological Approaches Centered on Values

In the first chapter, we defined the concept of lifestyles and listed principle ways of investigating them, one of which is the approach centered on values. Although its roots can be found in ancient Greek philosophy, the values approach has received limited attention from researchers and practitioners in the lifestyle field.

Yet, it is the position of values that has created so much interest in recent marketing studies (Dutta-Bergman and Wells, 2002; Kahle, 1983, 1986, 1996; Kahle and Xie, 2008; Sun, Horn, and Merritt, 2004) and in previously mentioned French studies of lifestyle (De Vulpian, 1974; Matricon, Burke, and Cathelat, 1974). Nonetheless, this trend toward values should not constitute a *deus ex machin* for the researcher or practitioner eager to better explain the evolution of and precedent for certain behaviors. After tracing the development of the values concept in the science of behavior, it is important to give a precise and operational definition that applies specifically to the field of marketing.

In order to determine more accurately the contribution of values to the studies of lifestyles, we will dedicate an entire chapter to this idea. The dual objectives of this chapter are: (1) to synthesize the principal historical approaches using the values notion in social sciences and then rank the legitimacy of their theoretical foundations, and (2) to highlight the use of this concept in marketing, presenting evidence of what it has helped to accomplish.

The lengthy discussion of values is justified first of all by the central position that values occupy in our definition of lifestyles, and second by the importance they are given in leading commercial studies of lifestyles, be they of North American, Asian, or European origin.

## HISTORIC DEVELOPMENT OF THE IDEA OF VALUES AND THEIR CHARACTERISTICS

For centuries, values have sparked the interest of researchers and scholars. In fact, it is possible to trace their influence all the way back to the first Greek philosophers (Socrates, 468–400 B.C.E.; Plato, 427–347 B.C.E.; and Aristotle, 348–322 B.C.E.). Various philosophical, anthropological, sociological, and psychological studies follow this influence as well. Given their importance, these philosophers and their views on values will be discussed first.

### Historic Evolution

#### Philosophic Legacy

Beginning in ancient Greece, philosophers were intrigued by the study and analysis of values, as is evident in writings from Aristotle to Kant on aestheticism, and from Plato to Rousseau on the subject of founding governments and the responsibility of citizens. Nevertheless, as noted by Werkmeister (1967), not one of these philosophers elaborated on the general theory of values. All the same, it is possible to track certain points that mark the evolution of value-based arguments in history.

Aristotle emphasized the intrinsic capacity of certain objects to furnish pleasure to people who possess them. He referred to the intangible aspect of values and underlined their conceptual essence (Haney, 1936). For instance, the notion of peace is an important value in itself, but it can also be broken down into more concrete aspects such as the absence of wars and social conflicts. According to Aristotle, ownership and hospitality are the most important values a human can hold.

After Aristotle's pioneering examination of personal values, a great number of philosophers from Plato to Rousseau to Hegel wrote about the values that govern institutions. Others such as Bentham (1815, 1825) and Buridan (1300–1358) focused on the more tangible human preoccupations. Bentham studied the hedonistic and instrumentalist aspect of behavior. He theorized that cultural values are acquired by "re-enforcement or inhibition," referring to what he termed "the principle of utility." This principle stipulates that individuals will acquire only those values that help them attain well-being or avoid unwanted situations. According to Buridan, however, the value of goods is based on their ability to satisfy the desires of those who possess them. By linking the concept of value to real situations and physical objects, he helped form the definition of values that the economic sciences use to this day ("variable characteristic of an object, susceptible to being desired.")

The philosophic concept of values adds an abstract component to the mix. It was not until the beginning of the nineteenth century that this rather challenging aspect of values presented itself for the first time as a unique and specific subject for such German philosophers as Meinong, Ehrenfels, and Scheler. The branch of philosophy that deals with this issue is called axiology, or the study of values (Hartman, 1967). In this approach, the principle debate centers on the objectivity or subjectivity of values. The school of objectivity suggests that values exist independent of their subjects; proponents of the subjective opinion state that it is the individual who gives values their existence. The problem of the objectivity or subjectivity of values was pursued by numerous philosophers, particularly Bertrand Russell in his work from 1925, which was subjectivist, and Friedrich Nietzsche (1872), an objectivist; however, the majority of late twentieth and early twenty-first century philosophers have adopted the objectivist thesis, making the distinction between value and evaluation. For them, if the process of evaluation remains eminently subjective, then the value remains independent of the subject. Values, therefore, are the very things being evaluated in the process of evaluation. In other words, as noted by Frondizi (op. cit., p. 82), "It is before all [the] knowledge of values and their evaluation, which are relative, not the values themselves" (see Frankena, 1967).

The economic concept presented above can be classified as subjectivist because, according to it, the value of goods is solely and essentially linked to the capacity of the goods to satisfy the desires of those people who possess them. For example, the value of a Picasso painting depends almost exclusively upon the subjective importance that it brings to the buyer. On the other hand, the modern, philosophical approach tends to recognize the objective character of values. Thus, it seems the interest of philosophers focused on the analysis of social values that regulate and structure our societies. Sartre, for example, wrote: "A society's system of values reflects its structure." Besides, Boudon and Bourricaud (1982) were correct in underlining that there is no place to treat values as noncontextual Platonic ideas that govern the sublunar world of institutions. On the contrary, values should be considered as collective preferences that appear in an institutional context, and that, by the manner they form themselves, contribute to the regulation of a social group. It is in fact this scheme of reflection that served as the basis for present-day anthropological, sociological, and psychological contributions to knowledge.

*The Anthropological Contribution*

Anthropologists contributed to the examination of values by observing lifestyles. Very early on, they showed that a culture could be viewed through systematic study of its institutionalized motivations and values (Boas, 1911;

Radcliffe-Brown, 1922; Benedict, 1934). Clyde Kluckhohn (1951) gave an operational definition of values as internal motivators, distinctive characteristics of an individual or group that influence actions and possible behaviors.

Florence Kluckhohn (1950), for her part, envisioned values as hierarchically structured, certain ones being considered more important by the individual than others. Thus, the holding of certain dominant values is desirable and commands stature in the social reference group. Prohibited or ostracized beliefs are viewed as deviant because they marginalize those people who adhere to them (for example, criminals and political dissidents). Between these two extremes, Florence Kluckhohn proposes variant values that provide room for maneuvering and allow individuals to exercise their liberty without assessing the system of values itself. Following this lead, Florence Kluckhohn and Strodtbeck (1961) put forward four types of fundamental orientations when facing existence: the link to nature, to time, to others, and to personal activity. Each link triggers different forms of behavior, but they exist in all societies and, according to Kluckhohn and Strodtbeck, allow us to identify cultural variations and orientations.

Lee (1959) stated that values of a culture have nothing to do with the efficacy of work but that they are respected because they reflect the feelings of the community. A society requires its members to conform to certain norms; furthermore, a society generates a system of values to which those individual members are bound. Anthropologists like Becker (1941) consider values critical to the determination of what is good/bad, correct/incorrect, superior/inferior, and usable/unusable, and invaluable to the setting of the goals of human existence.

*The Sociological Contributions*

The sociological take on values is significant but simultaneously diverse and controversial. Very early on, sociologists (Small and Vincent, 1894; Sumner, 1907; Thomas and Znaniecki, 1921) saw the generation of values as a process occurring within the context of concrete social situations. In particular, Thomas and Znaniecki mixed the objective and subjective approaches, considering a value as "everything having empirical content accessible to the members of a social group and a significance regarding what is or can be considered an object of activity." For these researchers, values represented unknown phenomena whose nature needed to be studied in situ (by empirical analysis).

On the contrary, Parsons (1939), when critiquing Spencer's evolutionist views of values, viewed them as fundamental elements governing social systems. The thesis of Pareto (1848–1923) and his concept of residuals, and that of Durkheim (1858–1917) and his interest in "Protestant ethics" or "the spirit of capitalism" (1893), revive values to show that cultural values, particularly those having a moral component, are the determining and differentiating elements of social existence. This functionalistic orientation of values underwent a period of development until the 1950s; viewed as a sine qua non for the stability of society, values were systematically structured and unwavering. Since then, however, the Parsonian approach has been criticized for several flaws, including its overall abstractness (Blake and Davis, 1964), its lack of empirical validity, and the problem of deductive imposition or overreliance on logic (Smelser, 1959; Wrong, 1961).

Other sociological studies on values had shortcomings, as well, either because they were based on idiosyncratic works or because the specific definitions used in the studies (Mukerjee, 1946; Becker, 1950; Morris, 1956, 1964, and his thirteen principal orientations; Catton, 1954, 1959, and his six hypotheses from his theory of values) were equally criticized (F. Adler, 1956, 1960) and had only modest implications. Ideas initiated at the beginning of the twentieth century by such authors as Durkheim (1893) returned in the late 1950s. Thus, Tönnies (1957) envisioned values as being "the collective conscience" that defines the relations among members of a society. They become essential for the definition of all human activity within one culture or subculture. According to Blau (1964), the main determinant of social conduct is the institutionalization of the system of values in a society: It defines the identity of the group, sets up moral standards, and legitimizes governmental authority. Not until the publication of works by Melvin Kohn (1969) and his collaborators on values and social classes and Rokeach (1973) on the values system did pertinent studies combine theoretical conceptualization and empirical validation. Given their more psychosociological orientations, these topics will be dealt with later in this book.

*The Psychological Contributions*

While recognizing the objective and social character of values, psychologists are often the first group of researchers to show interest in more precise themes such as attitudes and motivations. Spranger, a pioneer in the field, was one of the most important writers on the psychology of values. As of 1928, he had elaborated one typology of individuals according to their values: The typology held that values are reflected in all social behavior, and it is the dominant value's orientation that serves to structure the personality of the individual. Six types of personal orientations emerged from Spranger's works: theoretical, economic, aesthetic, social, political, and religious. His approach was later confirmed by other researchers who put forth corroborating theories. Thus,

Pinter (1933) and Evans (1952) reached the same conclusions and once again emphasized the "learning" of values.

Between 1938 and 1954, few psychological studies on values were conducted. Rather, research was based more on the study of needs—for instance, Murray's clinical analysis of needs (1938) and, thereafter, Maslow's classical but questionable hierarchy of needs (1954, cf. Kahle, et al., 1997). As Levitin (1973) remarked, one of the reasons for this quasi-inexistence (i.e., the dearth of studies during this period) resides in the fact that values are based primarily on feelings or preferences, which are not only difficult to express but also difficult to capture, particularly using the psychometric techniques of the time.

In 1954 Thurstone proposed his method of measuring values with the aid of the comparative judgment technique. He developed a ladder of moral values. Thurstone is credited with opening the way to other researchers, such as Scott (1959), who developed instruments to measure values or ideologies within a culture. Since then, larger developments have been made in social psychology and in the practical fields of investigating values.

*The Contributions in Social Psychology*

The works from Kohn (1969, Kohn and Schooler, 1969), for example, are relative in many cultural contexts to the values of children, such as those children's values that are formulated by their parents. Carefully validated from an empirical point of view, they have been confirmed by several similar studies undertaken by other researchers. They all converge and indicate that people of a higher socioeconomic status allow their children a greater degree of freedom in determining their own values than people of lower socioeconomic status. According to Kohn, this phenomenon is principally due to differences in professional occupation and level of education.

At the same time, the studies conducted by Rokeach (1968a) offer the advantage of reconciling theoretical reflection and empirical validation. His studies fall into the category of reference proposed by Franz Adler in 1956. According to Adler, four approaches account for all conceptual possibilities when defining values, whether they are of philosophical, psychological, or sociological origin. First of all, values can be considered as "absolute," "eternal ideas," or "parts of God's conscience." Second, values can be viewed as the inherent potential of objects to satisfy needs and desires. Indeed, some scholars (e.g., Maslow) use the terms *needs* and *values* interchangeably. Third, values can be seen as an outgrowth of all the learned or innate preferences present within each individual. Finally (and most important, according to

Adler), is the view of values as they relate to a sense of action: In this way, Adler recognized human endeavors would become the only way to pinpoint the system of values objectively.

The majority of social psychologists prefer Adler's third approach, which presents a value as a hypothetical construction—sometimes referred to as a "meta-attitude"—closely linked to attitudes and behavior. Not directly accessible by observation, a "meta-attitude" can be inferred from verbal cues and thus can help in predicting behavior. Without debating which forms of knowledge are gained and which are innate, it seems more important to link values to the concept of preferences and their implications for behavior.

Such an approach, the most commonly accepted by current researchers, was developed by Rokeach (1968a, 1973). According to him, people possess a great number of attitudes toward products, objects, or specific situations, but they have a relatively limited number of values. This difference suggests that values and attitudes are connected in a hierarchical system in which values form the heart. They become more stable and resistant to change than attitudes. Robinson and Shaver (1973) confirmed this study by reviewing evidence that values are derived directly from culture, and maintained and regulated by a social structure that gives them significance, stability, and cohesion.

A value, for Rokeach (1973, p. 5), "is an enduring belief that a specific mode of conduct or end-state of existence is personally or socially preferable to an opposite or converse mode of conduct or end-state of existence." In addition, "a value system is organized along a continuum of relative importance." Given the hierarchy of values, Rokeach nevertheless makes a distinction between two types of values: instrumental and terminal.

When a value refers to modes of conduct, it is an instrumental value; when it refers to end-states of existence, it is called a terminal value. Instrumental values like courage or honesty are ways of being or ways of acting; terminal values like peace or freedom are goals, either for the individual or for society.

In keeping with the hypothesis that the combination of instrumental and terminal values held by an individual differ according to the subjects' social and economic characteristics, Rokeach (1974) developed a test (the Rokeach Value Survey or RVS) to determine individuals' value systems. He began by examining the values of different groups of people according to their age, education, sex, occupation, and religion. From those data, Rokeach came up with eighteen instrumental and eighteen terminal values representing values in contemporary American society (ca. 1974). They are presented in Table 2.1.

Table 2.1

**Rokeach (1973) Value Survey (RVS)**

| Instrumental values | Terminal values |
| --- | --- |
| • Ambitious | • A comfortable life |
| • Broad-minded | • An exciting life |
| • Capable | • A sense of accomplishment |
| • Cheerful | • A world of peace |
| • Clean | • A world of beauty |
| • Courageous | • Equality |
| • Forgiving | • Family security |
| • Helpful | • Freedom |
| • Honest | • Happiness |
| • Imaginative | • Inner beauty |
| • Independent | • Mature love |
| • Intellectual | • National security |
| • Logical | • Pleasure |
| • Loving | • Salvation |
| • Obedient | • Self-respect |
| • Polite | • Social recognition |
| • Responsible | • True friendship |
| • Self-control | • Wisdom |

This study prompted further research throughout the world. Rokeach's work was validated at the level of its empirical implementation (Mitchell, 1976; Rankin and Grube, 1980) as well as at the level of its transcultural application (Feather, 1975, in Australia and New Guinea; Moore, 1975, in Israel; Penner and Anh, 1977, in Vietnam; Sinka and Sayeed, 1979, in India; Cochrane, Billig, and Huggs, 1979, and Searing, 1979, in Great Britain). In fact, it is this more practical and operational orientation that gives the concept of values its interdisciplinary application in the domain of marketing.

*Implementation of the Concept of Values*

The diversity of approaches to the study of values occurs as a result of the implementation of practical procedures of measurement. The previous historical presentation proves that philosophers were essentially content with treating the existence of nature in the same way as that of values—without proposing concrete methods of research or investigation. Anthropologists resorted to observation for identifying and analyzing cultural values, principally in relation to their studies of small tribes (Lee, 1959). The sociological and psychological fields of investigation seem most amenable to incorporating value-based research techniques. With that idea in mind, consider two principal problems:

1. The first problem concerns theoretical order, because it deals with the conceptual distinction made by researchers between what is preferred and what is preferable. This difference between what an individual desires and what he or she should desire affects the way values are measured. A measuring system can address the concept of actual preference, the concept of ideal preference, or both at the same time. Examples of each method will be presented later.
2. The second more practical problem concerns the specific methodology chosen for the collection of information, assuming that results are given in the form of a list (Likert) or a classification by rank reflecting the respondents' preferences.

## A Value as Something That Is Preferred

Regarding a value as something that is preferred, we can refer to the works of Allport, Vernon, and Lindsey (1961). Using the typology of individuals indicated by Spranger in 1928, they studied the actual preference of six different types of activities (theoretical, economic, aesthetic, social, political, and religious). The majority of questions in this test concern the choice of occupation or field of work. For example:

Assuming you had the necessary education, which would you prefer to be:
____ A banker?
____ A politician?

Another illustration of a preferred value study is Gordon's test of interpersonal values (1960). This test aims to measure an individual's desires based on his or her responses to hypothetical psychological situations involving issues of freedom, conformity, recognition, independence, charity, and leadership. The following is an example of a question of this type:

In each group of three phrases, mark the one most important to you with an (M) and then the one least important to you with an (L). You will leave one sentence unmarked:
____ Being able to do everything that I really like to do.
____ Being in charge of an important project.
____ Working for the well-being of others.

*A Value as Something That Should Be Preferred*

Another approach to studying values deals with the moral aspect (that which is good or that which is bad) of questions. Rettig and Pasamanick (1959) devised a test to measure students' views on the justifiability of actions such as cheating on exams, lying under certain circumstances, or using contraceptives. Subjects were asked to judge whether these actions are right or wrong. Here is an example:

> Indicate whether the following situation seems morally upright to you. Circle a [1] if, in your opinion, the situation seems to conform completely to moral standards. Circle a [10] if the situation seems at odds with your concept of morality in action. The intermediate numbers serve as a means to moderate your response:
> Shooting someone in the case of legitimate defense.
> [1]    [2]    [3]    [4]    [5]    [6]    [7]    [8]    [9]    [10]

Another interesting study is that of Scott (1965) and his test of personal values. In a similar manner, as the following example illustrates, his test explores individuals' feelings on what is correct or incorrect, good, or bad.

> For each sentence, indicate whether it describes a characteristic that you always admire in others, never admire in others, or whether your opinion depends on each person:
> Having a strong intellectual curiosity:
> ___ Always admired
> ___ Never admired
> ___ "It depends"

Similar studies were conducted by Wright (1973) in his Value Inventory and by Bales and Couch (1969) in their Value Profile.

*The Mixed Concept of Values*

The third means of measurement of the concept of values deals with the mixed acceptance of values as being desired and desirable at the same time. One illustration of this idea is Perloe's questionnaire of social values (1977), which attempts to measure the dimensions of accepting moral obligations (what should be desired) to the individual preference toward a specific behavior (what is desired). The following question is typical of this type of questionnaire:

> Indicate the number best representing your agreement or disagreement with the following statement:
>     Those people who try their best but do not have the capacity of most normal people have the right to receive help from others (circle one).

> Completely agree    1    2    3    4    5    6    Completely disagree

One use of this mixed conception of values is Rokeach's test of values (RVS). This test asks individuals to rank the eighteen terminal values and the eighteen instrumental values according to their importance as principles of life, thus leaving it up to the individuals to decide what is most important to them—be it their own preference or their ideal preference. In this way, the RVS is particularly interesting because it eliminates the problem of distinguishing values that are desired from those that are desirable. Festinger's work on cognitive dissonance (1957) demonstrates that once people have made their choice as to what is preferred, they are able to find justifications for deeming that choice the most preferable. In addition, given the fact that community values are imposed on people by society and the diverse institutions that compose it, social and individual values may be viewed in tandem. Thus, Rokeach's presentation allows for a global result, generally more representative of social and individual values, by leaving it up to the individual respondent to choose the formulation, consciously or not, between what is desired and what is desirable.

*Methodological Aspects Relative to Measuring Values*

Regarding this topic, one debate seems actually opposed to the partisans of Likert's collection of statements in the form of a list, to facilitate the task of the respondent and to allow an easier approach (Munson and McIntyre, 1979; Rankin and Grube, 1980; Munson, 1984) to classify by rungs considered as leading to a better reliability of the results (Reynolds and Jolly, 1980). In France, one study conducted by Valette-Florence and Jolibert (1991) regarding the same topic tends to prove—by the use of a structural model more reliable than the classic multitrait, multimethod approaches—the superiority of Likert's method to the original work done by Rokeach.

The types of Likert-like questions asked by Valette-Florence are presented in the following form:

Below you will find a list of values. Rate their degree of importance to you and in your life (circle one):

Happiness

Not important at all    1    2    3    4    5    6    Very important

Broad-mindedness

Not important at all    1    2    3    4    5    6    Very important

This approach has multiple advantages. First of all, the questionnaire as it is constructed requires no interviewing or special manipulations. It is also easy to return to the survey-giver via the postal service or e-mail. Filling it out proves to be even simpler than classifying by rank, which can be tedious. Finally, the scale allows for the use of statistical tools (factor analysis, typology, etc.) that are less easily applied to the ranking approach, with its ipsative (forced choice) and interval elements. Recent progress has been made in the interpretation of survey results, however. A model proposed by Kamakura and his colleagues (1991, 1992), based on Thurston's law of comparative judgment, allows for a more realistic reading of an imperfect assessment by adding a term for the margin of error. Applied with success to Rokeach's inventory (Kamakura and Mazzon, 1991), as well as to Kahle's (Kamakura and Novak, 1992), the estimation method based on the logit models also makes it easier to identify groups of individuals sharing identical systems of values. The principal critique of this study is in the hypothesis of homogeneity of the distribution of margin of error; such hypothesizing is necessary to the estimation process but rarely verified in practice, mainly because of the increasing number of values under consideration. One substantial improvement, unfortunately much too complex to use in practice, consists of using a *probit* model under the constraint of heteroscedasticity, which eases the preceding hypothesis. (Consult Walsh [1991] for an illustration.) A second problem is that, in practice, the hierarchical relations among elements rarely cluster in the theoretically specified way.

## Contributions and Specifications of Values

Throughout the historic evolution of the study of values, confusion has existed about the distinction between needs, personality traits, interests, social norms, beliefs, and attitudes. It is therefore important to clarify the differences that exist among these diverse concepts by referring to specificities of values as they are presented by Rokeach.

*Values and Needs*

Many authors, Maslow included (1954), suggest that values and needs are two somewhat equivalent concepts. Maslow speaks in particular of self-actualization as being both a need and a value (of elevated order). While all living beings have primary needs (for example, a tree needs water in order to grow), only humans engage in the quest to fulfill their potential—the quest embodied in self-actualization. If it is admitted in social symbolism that an expensive bottle of wine does not have the same value as a cheap bottle of water, how then can we explain the fact that they are both capable of quenching our thirst? If one considers values as cognitive representations of needs or sanitized needs, it appears that the phenomenon of higher-level inconsistency comes not only from cognitive representations of individual needs, but also social and cultural needs.

It is only after being transformed into values that needs can be expressed and justified appropriately, just as much on an individual level as on a societal level. As Rokeach indicates, "Needs are cognitively transformed into values so that a person can end up smelling himself, and being smelled by others, like a rose" (1973, p. 20). For example, a need for sex may be expressed as valuing warm relationships with others. Human values, then, can be considered as individual and social expressions of underlying needs.

*Values and Personality Traits*

An individual's personality is what makes him or her unique. Personality comprises those characteristics that distinguish one person from another. Because they are acquired principally during childhood, it could be argued that such traits remain fixed in spite of the changing situations with which one is confronted. From a phenomenological perspective—that is, a philosophy that deals with things as they are perceived rather than with things as they "really" are—personality may be viewed as an outgrowth of people's value systems. For example, people perceived as permissive according to their personality traits will likely place a higher value on the spirit of openness and tolerance than on obedience and politeness.

These ideas support Rokeach's notion (1973, p. 20) that personality is more a system of values than a mere group of traits. The incorporation of values into the exploration of personality explains the possibility of personality changes resulting from changes in social conditions. Consequently, a study centered on values will be better able to accommodate fluctuating social constraints than a more rigid study centered on personality traits.

In recent years, the study of personality has emphasized the trait approach, focusing particularly on the empirically derived "big five" traits of openness, conscientiousness, extraversion, agreeableness, and neuroticism (Goldberg,

1993). Interestingly, consumer research on anthropomorphizing products and brands has also focused on five traits, although these five are sincerity, excitement, competence, sophistication, and ruggedness (Aaker, 1997).

*Values and Interests*

Authors such as Perry (1970) believed that a value can represent any object of interest and that these two concepts—values and interests—are identical. According to Rokeach, an interest, like a value, can be seen as a cognitive representation of one's needs that are dealt with on a more abstract level. If we assume that interests can (1) guide one's actions and judgments, (2) serve as a mechanism for social adaptation and self-defense, and (3) function as a source of recognition and actualization, it does not necessarily follow that interests represent an ideal mode of behavior or a desirable state of existence. In fact, individual interests lack the underlying sense of control and moderation needed in any coherent system of conflict resolution and decision making. If interests and values have common attributes, it is because human interests are simply loose expressions of human values.

In comparison to interest-based studies, value-based studies are typically more restrictive. The coherence of values systems for each individual allows us to regroup similar values more easily than those that are more diverse, numerous, and less stable.

*Values and Social Norms*

Rokeach (1973, pp. 21–22), lists three ways in which values differ from social norms. First, a value may refer to a mode of behavior or an end-state of existence, whereas a social norm refers only to a mode of behavior. Second, a value transcends specific situations; in contrast, a social norm is a prescription or proscription to behave in a specific way in a specific situation. For example, moviegoers under a specific age (e.g., 17) are not allowed to see R-rated films in theaters, yet they can watch these same films freely in their own homes. Third, a value is personal and internal, whereas a norm is consensual and external to the person. This third point serves as a starting point for understanding the reactions people have when faced with changing social norms. Batra, Homer, and Kahle (2001) discuss social norms and values more thoroughly.

*Values and Attitudes*

Behavioral scientists often study attitudes and values in tandem. McGuire (1969) offered two definitions of values to help illustrate the relationship between values and attitudes. The first defines values as developed attitudes; the second defines values as components of attitudes. In this sense, an attitude toward a specific situation would be defined as the positive or negative result of valence of all values to which this situation is related. There is effectively a link between value and attitude, attitudes expressing values, and not the inverse (see also Meddin, 1975).

A modern definition of attitudes, such as that of Triandis (1979), suggests that the three components of attitudes (cognitive, conative, and affective) follow the instrumental and terminal orientations that Rokeach applied to values. There is a need, then, to differentiate between the two concepts (Rokeach, 1968a, p. 62). Rokeach (1968a, p. 112) defines an attitude as "a relatively enduring organization of beliefs around an object or situation predisposing one to respond in some preferential manner."

In distinguishing attitudes from values, Rokeach takes certain factors into account, the first being that an attitude evolves from many beliefs related to one project or to one precise situation, while a value remains linked to a single belief concerning general phenomena. From a practical point of view, then, values can be measured directly with a single question per value. On the other hand, an attitude toward an object or situation is the mean result of a diverse measure of representative beliefs, each relative to this same object or situation.

Rokeach then proposes that while an attitude applies to certain objects or situations, a value transcends them. For example, an individual who expresses different attitudes toward public and private schooling will typically hold the concept of liberty as a value.

This perspective brings about Rokeach's third proposition, which classifies values, but not attitudes, as standards for living. Thus, a person can conceivably hold numerous attitudes, both positive and negative, toward objects or situations based on a relatively small number of values. To refer back to the previous example, an individual who identifies freedom as a value would likely hold many diverse attitudes toward issues such as education, religion, politics, and morality.

The fourth difference between values and attitudes as proposed by Rokeach concerns their depth: Values, he states, form the very core of one's personality. One person, if he or she only has a limited number of values (recall that he identified eighteen instrumental and eighteen terminal values) relative to learned beliefs concerning desirable types of behavior or goals for life, will possess, on the contrary, just as many attitudes as direct or indirect relationships with the specific objects or situations, which can amount to thousands.

According to Rokeach, values serve as a driving force in the determination of attitudes and behaviors. Such is the standpoint that Allport takes (1961, pp. 801–803) when he speaks of values, interests, attitudes, and opinions as successive points on the same continuum. Allport considers attitudes in particular to be directly dependent on preexisting values.

Finally, Rokeach traces the effect of values on motivation in the following manner: values influence attitudes, attitudes influence behavior, and behaviors bring either satisfaction or dissatisfaction. If motivation is what brings purpose and direction to behavior, then values are intimately connected to the forces that motivate us.

Homer and Kahle (1988) attempted to disprove Rokeach's theory that values directly cause behavior. They used a structural equation model to demonstrate that values do, indeed, lead to attitudes but not directly to behaviors. They also found, however, that attitudes have a direct causal connection to behaviors. Values provide the abstract context from which the more numerous and specific attitudes can develop (cf. also Maio and Olson, 1994; Torelli and Kaikati, 2009).

## Summing Up

The nature of values has sparked ample research in the social sciences. Table 2.2 lists the principal historic studies on values,.

The philosophic approach toward values lacks an explicitly elaborated theory concerning them. Two principal points, however, deserve further attention. The first one concerns the formulated recognition by Aristotelian thought of their conceptual character, but which does not exclude their concretization by real references whose state can be measured. Measurement should be important from an Aristotelian perspective. The second point is relative to the progressive abandonment of discussion on the Platonic ideas that govern the world, for a study more attentive of the social values that govern our societies' behaviors. It is, in addition, this recognition of objective character of values and their assimilation with the collective preferences that open the door to new perspectives in other behavioral sciences. The "objective" quality of measured values may be overstated by the reification the measurement provides.

Anthropologists were among the first social scientists who observed and followed dominant values in societies. They emphasized the role of values as internal triggers that activate specific behaviors. Furthermore, they pointed to the hierarchical structure of values—certain ones being considered more important than others. Anthropologists make a distinction between central or dominant values, deviant values that marginalize those people who adhere to them, and variant values that give a margin of maneuver or variability to the individual.

Table 2.2

**Representative Approaches to Values**

| Field of investigation | Principal approaches and representatives |
| --- | --- |
| I. Philosophical | 1. Plato (427–347 B.C.E.); Aristotle (384–322 B.C.E.); Buridan (1300–1358)<br>2. Russel (1925); Nietzsche (1844–1900) |
| II. Anthropological | 1. Kluckhohn C. (1951)<br>2. Kluckhohn F. (1950)<br>3. Lee (1959) |
| III. Sociological | 1. Small and Vincent (1894); Sumner (1907); Thomas and Znaniecki (1921)<br>2. Parsons (1939)<br>3. Mukerjee (1946); Morris (1956 and 1964); Catton (1954 and 1959)<br>4. Durkheim (1893); Tönnies (1957); Blau (1964) |
| IV. Psychological | 1. Spranger (1928); Allport (1961)<br>2. Murray (1938); Maslow (1954)<br>3. Thurstone (1954); Scott (1959) |
| V. Psychosociological | 1. Kohn (1969); Pearlin and Kohn (1966); Kohn and Schooler (1969)<br>2. Rokeach (1968a, 1973, 1974); Mitchell (1976); Kahle (1983) |

Of all the social scientists, however, psychologists have probably contributed the most to the knowledge of values by linking theoretic concepts with empirical validation. According to the psychological school of thought, values can be defined as beliefs determining which type of behavior or goal of existence is preferable. In general, values possess four important characteristics (Assael, 1984):

1. Values are acquired by socialization or by acculturation.
2. A system of values consists of a group of norms that govern behavior.
3. Values are typically stable and dynamic, their evolution following a long cycle.
4. Values are shared within the same social cohort.

Additionally, Rokeach (1973) argued for the differentiation of values from other neighboring concepts used in social psychology. Contrary to biological needs, values represent social concepts in relation to individuals. Differing from personality traits, which are much more stable and fixed, values are dynamic and can serve to initiate behavior. Organized in systems, values are more transcendent and less numerous than interests. On top of that, values remain more general, more stable, and more internal to the person than do social norms, which are more external and likely linked to specific situations. Finally, values are fewer in number, more central, potentially more dynamic, and more closely linked to motivation than attitudes are. Transcending objects and situations to which attitudes are linked, values distinguish themselves by their unique liaison with beliefs. More general, in practice more stable, and more fixed than attitudes, values represent preferable types of behavior or goals of existence that can be measured more easily than attitudes, which are, in some sense, too diversified to quantify.

The most significant study of values seems to be the one proposed by Rokeach (1968a). It focuses on five postulates:

1. The total number of values possessed by one person is relatively small.
2. All individuals possess the same values, but to different degrees.
3. Values are organized in systems.
4. The antecedents of human values come from culture, from society and its institutions, and from personality.
5. The consequences of human values are found in almost all phenomena studied in the social sciences.

Rokeach makes a fundamental distinction between two types of values:

- terminal values or goals of existence, which are individual or social objectives, such as peace or freedom
- instrumental values or types of behavior, which are modes of conduct or ways of acting, such as courage or honesty

The Rokeach Value Survey (Rokeach, 1973) was the instrument Rokeach and many others used to measure values. Rokeach found that values generally differ according to social class, age, race, and religion. Furthermore, he identified cross-cultural differences in value systems. It is in fact this more pragmatic orientation that leads to several diverse applications of the RVS in marketing.

Finally, Schwartz (1992) and Schwartz and Bilsky (1987, 1990) offer a constructivist view of values, stressing the totality of experiences that each person brings to the formation of value systems. According to Schwartz and Bilsky, values are extremely important in everyday life; they underpin the goals and objectives that individuals pursue to satisfy their interests (individual, collective, or both). The Schwartz Value Survey (Schwartz, 1992) identifies ten motivational domains.

The innovative aspect of Schwartz and Bilsky's proposition resides in the definition of the motivational domains described in Table 2.3. These domains are modeled after the work of several researchers from diverse spheres in the social sciences (e.g., Bandura, 1988; Berlyne, 1967; Deci and Ryan, 1985; Kluckhohn, 1951; Maslow, 1959; Scitovsky, 1976). In addition, these domains, according to Schwartz (1992), exhibit one circular (quasi-circumplex) structure under the form as seen in Figure 2.1, for which the centers of interest are superimposed. The interest in such a representation resides, on the one hand, in the compatibility of two adjacent domains, and, on the other hand, in the conflicting position of two opposing domains in relation to the origin. Thanks to the inventory of fifty-six values proposed by Schwartz, other studies have empirically validated aspects of this structure in different cultural settings (Schwartz, 1992) and in different contexts, such as environmental preservation (Grunert and Juhl, 1991).

Since their seminal papers (Schwartz and Bilsky, 1987, 1990), Schwartz and his coauthors have extended the study of social values to encompass diverse and broader domains such as managerial behavior (Smith, Peterson, and Schwartz, 2002), environmental concern and conservation behavior (Schultz, et al., 2005), and the inclusiveness of the moral universe (Schwartz, 2007), just to name a few. Finally, very recently some researchers (e.g., Daniel, Scheifer, and Knafo, 2012) have proposed the Values in Context Questionnaire (VICA). The VICQ is an adaptation to life contexts of the aforementioned SVS, where each participant rates the importance of his or her values in a number of life

Table 2.3

**The Motivational Domains Proposed by Schwartz and Bilsky (1990) (and the Items Used to Measure Them)**

- Self-direction    Independence of thought and action—choosing, creating, exploring. [creativity, freedom, independence, curious, choosing own goals]

- Stimulation    Excitement, novelty, and challenge in life. [daring, a varied life, an exciting life]

- Hedonism    Pleasure and sensuous gratification for oneself. [pleasure, enjoying life]

- Achievement    Personal success through demonstrating competence according to social standards. [successful, capable, ambitious, influential]

- Power    Social status, prestige, control or domination over people and resources. [preserving my public image, social recognition]

- Security    Safety, harmony, and stability of society, of relationships, and of self. [family security, national security, social order, clean, reciprocation of favors]

- Conformity    Restraint of actions, inclinations, and impulses likely to upset or harm others and violate social expectations or norms. [politeness, obedient, self-discipline, honoring parents and elders]

- Tradition    Respect commitment and acceptance of the ideas and customs that traditional culture or religion provide the self. [humble, accepting my portion in life, devout, respect for tradition, moderation]

- Benevolence    Preserving and enhancing the well-being of people with whom one is in frequent personal contact. [helpful, honest, forgiving, loyal, responsible]

- Universalism    Understanding, appreciation, tolerance, and protection for the welfare of all people and for nature. [broad-minded, wisdom, social justice, equality, a world at peace, a world of beauty, unity with nature, protecting the environment]

*Source:* Adapted by S. Grunert and H. Juhl (1991), Values, Environmental Attitudes, and Buying of Organic Foods: Their Relationships in a Sample of Danish Teachers. In *Proceedings of the Workshop on Value and Life-Style Research in Marketing.* Brussels, Belgium: EIASM.

contexts, which are social roles or groups in which the individuals lives. On the whole, four main points deserve attention:

1. More recently, Schwartz and his colleagues (Schwartz, et al., 2001) have proposed the Portraits Value Questionnaire (PVQ), a new and different method to assess human values. Basically, the PVQ includes short verbal descriptions of forty different people, gender-matched to each respondent. Each portrait depicts a person's goals, aspirations, and wishes that describe the importance of a value using two sentences. Respondents

Figure 2.1    **Schwartz's (1990) Prototypic Structure of Value Systems**

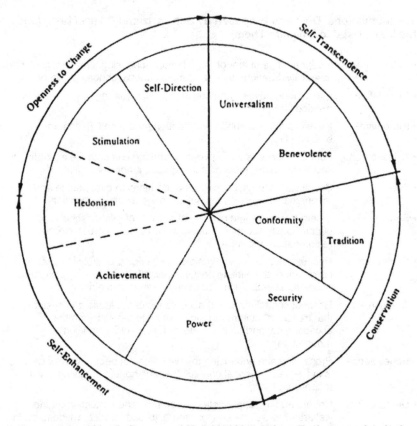

*Source:* Adapted by S. Grunert and H. Juhl (1991), Values, Environmental Attitudes, and Buying of Organic Foods: Their Relationships in a Sample of Danish Teachers. In *Proceedings of the Workshop on Value and Life-Style Research in Marketing.* Brussels, Belgium: EIASM.

report the similarity of the person described to them on a rating scale. Individuals' own values are inferred from their self-reported similarity to people who are described in terms of a particular value. In the European Social Survey (ESS), several studies relying on only twenty-one values derived from the PVQ have shown good reliability indices and factorial invariance of the instrument across countries (Spini, 2003; Davidov, 2008; Davidov, Schmidt, and Schwartz, 2008). Although a recent study has shown partial invariance for most of the ten values and parameters (Steinmetz, et al., 2009), relying on twenty-eight of the forty original items, the PVQ has been criticized (Lindeman and Verkasalo, 2005) because it does not query for self-conscious values; therefore, the respondents themselves are unaware they are answering a value questionnaire. Moreover, as recognized by Schwartz himself, the language level of the PVQ is that of an eleven-year-old child; hence, the PVQ does not seem to be the best value questionnaire for educated adults.

2. On a practical side, a scale with fifty-seven items may be too time-consuming to complete, especially in the context of complex surveys designed to develop meaningful representations of, say, consumer behavior in a particular domain. In a recent investigation, Lindeman and Verkasalo (2005) developed a short scale based on the ten values. The reported results show that the new scale has good reliability and validity and that the values measured by the Short Schwartz's Value Survey (SSVS) were indeed arrayed in a circle identical to the theoretical structure of values; however, this short scale only gives insight into broad values. Hence, if detailed information is still needed, the original SVS remains the best choice.

3. Very recently, Schwartz and his coauthors (Fischer, et al., 2010) have investigated the degree of similarity (or isomorphism) between the structure of values in individual versus country-level data analysis. They found substantial similarity in structure across levels, but the findings did not exhibit a true structural isomorphism. The authors suggest that sampling and individual value fluctuations may be the cause. In addition, method factors or real differences between individual and cultural factors could account for the remaining dissimilarity. Ultimately, hierarchical linear models may be able to explain differences in mean-country levels and individual differences in value levels.

4. Some authors (Perrinjaquet, et al., 2007) have challenged the circumplex structure of Schwartz and Boehnke (2004). This research replicates and refines their confirmatory approach by using two large samples of the Swiss and the French populations, which conform to previous samples used in SVS research. Although the value structure seems to be validated when data are analyzed through multidimensional scaling, the quasi-circumplex structure of human values is not supported when confirmatory approaches are used (i.e., CIRCUM and constrained confirmatory factor analysis).

Table 2.4 presents fit indices for the three different models for the Swiss and French samples. The highly constrained model (Model A) does not fit the data very well. "While GFI is above the conventional threshold for both samples (>.90), AGFI is lower than .90, indicating a lack of parsimony due to the constraints" (Hu and Bentler, 1999; Perrinjaquet, et al., 2007). RMSEAs are too high (CHD.104; FD.114). Removing the equal-spacing constraint (quasi-circumplex model B) leads to an improvement in model fit; however, the RMSEAs are still too high (CHD.102; FD.109). Finally, relaxing the equal communalities constraints (Model C) further improves model fit, but still with relatively high RMSEAs (CHD.089; FD.106).

Goodness-of-fit indices do not provide information as to whether the actual locations of values are consistent with Schwartz's theoretical model. The extent to which value locations depart from the equally spaced and/or equal communalities model has to be established. Figure 2.2 displays three circular representations for each national data set: circulant (fully constrained Model A), communalities constrained to equality with unconstrained polar angles (Model B), and unequally spaced–unequal communalities (unconstrained Model C). Other useful pieces of information provided by CIRCUM are communality indices and polar angles of the measured variables. These indices represent the correlation between each measured variable and its common score (Fabrigar, et al., 1999). When squared, the communality indices represent the amount of common variance in each measured variable. Estimates in Table 2.5 point to measurement error in the ten value types.

In Figure 2.2, *Universalism* was used as the reference variable (location set at 0°). Deviations from the ideal model are consistent with those of the MDS results, where *Achievement* and *Power* already formed a joint domain. Two domains from the MDS, *Stimulation* and *Hedonism* (CHD6°; FD9°) are also closer than postulated by a circumplex structure, that is, equally spaced (see Table 2.5). Figure 2.2 shows that the ordering of values is consistent with Schwartz's theory; however, the differences between the angles of the two unequally spaced models (B and C) and those angles of the equally spaced model (A) are rather important. In the unequally spaced–unequal communalities representation (Model C), *Achievement* and *Power* are near each other in the Swiss data (1°), while *Stimulation* and *Hedonism* (9°) are close in the French data. On the other hand, *Tradition* and *Conformity* are clearly separate from one another for both countries (CHD20°; FD19°). This result contradicts the "definitive" model proposed by Schwartz (1992) and tested by Schwartz and Boehnke (2004).

"Because CIRCUM cannot test the circumplex structure for the latent variables together with the simple factorial structure of the manifest variables, constrained confirmatory factor analyses were conducted. Three different models were tested: two empirical circulant models based on different reference matrices and a quasi-circumplex model. None of these models comes close to an acceptable level of fit" (Perrinjaquet, et al., 2007). In addition, fit indices are likely to decrease and reach unacceptable levels when nesting such a measurement model into a structural model (Anderson and Gerbing, 1988; Fornell & Yi, 1992). Finally, the reliability of the measures, as well as their construct and discriminant validities, were tested. Results show that the measures have low levels of reliability and weak construct and discriminant

Table 2.4

**Summary of CIRCUM Fit Indices for the Swiss and French Samples**

| Model | df | $\chi^2$ | $F_0$ | GFI | AGFI | RMSEA [90% CI] |
|---|---|---|---|---|---|---|
| A. Equally spaced–equal communalities | | | | | | |
| Switzerland | 41 | 667.23 | .446 | .918 | .890 | .104 [.097, .111] |
| France | 41 | 1055.09 | .537 | .903 | .870 | .114 [.108, .120] |
| B. Unequally spaced–equal communalities | | | | | | |
| Switzerland | 32 | 503.79 | .336 | .937 | .892 | .102 [.095, .110] |
| France | 32 | 750.93 | .380 | .929 | .879 | .109 [.102, .116] |
| C. Unequally spaced–unequal communalities | | | | | | |
| Switzerland | 23 | 280.76 | .184 | .964 | .915 | .089 [.080, .099] |
| France | 23 | 513.59 | .260 | .951 | .882 | .106 [.098, .114] |

Table 2.5

## CIRCUM Point Estimates for Polar Angles and Communality Indices for the Swiss and French Samples

|  | UN | BE | TR | CO | SE | PO | AC | HE | ST | SD |
|---|---|---|---|---|---|---|---|---|---|---|
| **Swiss Model** | | | | | | | | | | |
| *A. Equally spaced–equal communalities* | | | | | | | | | | |
| Polar angles | 0 | 36 | 72 | 108 | 144 | 180 | 216 | 252 | 288 | 324 |
| Communalities | 0.7 | 0.7 | 0.7 | 0.7 | 0.7 | 0.7 | 0.7 | 0.7 | 0.7 | 0.7 |
| *B. Unequally spaced–equal communalities* | | | | | | | | | | |
| Polar angles | 0 | 40 | 78 | 111 | 128 | 195 | 196 | 264 | 276 | 309 |
| Communalities | 0.72 | 0.72 | 0.72 | 0.72 | 0.72 | 0.72 | 0.72 | 0.72 | 0.72 | 0.72 |
| *C. Unequally spaced–unequal communalities* | | | | | | | | | | |
| Polar angles | 0 | 38 | 78 | 98 | 118 | 188 | 189 | 257 | 263 | 310 |
| Communalities | 0.62 | 0.75 | 0.56 | 0.85 | 0.76 | 0.8 | 0.76 | 0.59 | 0.71 | 0.77 |
| **French Model** | | | | | | | | | | |
| *A. Equally spaced–equal communalities* | | | | | | | | | | |
| Polar angles | 0 | 36 | 72 | 108 | 144 | 180 | 216 | 252 | 288 | 324 |
| Communalities | 0.75 | 0.75 | 0.75 | 0.75 | 0.75 | 0.75 | 0.75 | 0.75 | 0.75 | 0.75 |
| *B. Unequally spaced–equal communalities* | | | | | | | | | | |
| Polar angles | 0 | 24 | 60 | 79 | 103 | 178 | 189 | 243 | 252 | 280 |
| Communalities | 0.75 | 0.75 | 0.75 | 0.75 | 0.75 | 0.75 | 0.75 | 0.75 | 0.75 | 0.75 |
| *C. Unequally spaced–unequal communalities* | | | | | | | | | | |
| Polar angles | 0 | 19 | 64 | 83 | 106 | 175 | 201 | 242 | 251 | 273 |
| Communalities | 0.73 | 0.75 | 0.71 | 0.87 | 0.76 | 0.79 | 0.8 | 0.61 | 0.67 | 0.76 |

Figure 2.2 **French and Swiss CIRCUM Results** (1996)

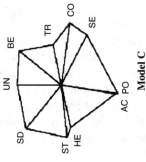

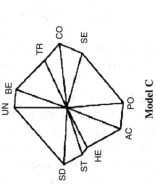
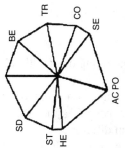
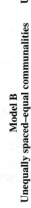

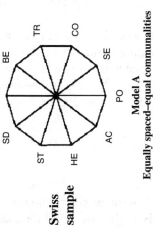

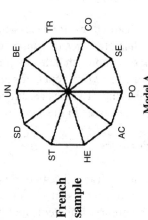
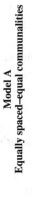

**Swiss sample**

Model A
Equally spaced–equal communalities

Model B
Unequally spaced–equal communalities

Model C
Unequally spaced–unequal communalities

**French sample**

Model A
Equally spaced–equal communalities

Model B
Unequally spaced–equal communalities

Model C
Unequally spaced–unequal communalities

*Source:* Fabrigar et al. (1999).

validity, resulting from multicollinearity between value types. Thus, the present findings show that while exploratory approaches to test SVS quasi-circumplex structure provide acceptable results, confirmatory tests provide weak support.

Ultimately, a possible track for improving SVS is to use a second-order CFA model with higher-order dimensions such as *Self-enhancement/Self-transcendence* (SE-ST) and *Openness-to-change/Conservation* (OC-CO) as suggested by Schwartz and Sagiv (1995). Value types as first-order dimensions relate to higher-order dimensions, that is, *Power* and *Achievement* to SE, *Universalism* and *Benevolence* to ST, *Self-direction* and *Stimulation* to OC, and *Conformity-tradition* and *Security* to CO. Such an improved measurement tool should provide a better foundation for the testing of the circumplex structure of human values.

## VALUES AND APPLICATIONS IN MARKETING

Values have been applied to the marketing field in three main ways (see Table 2.6):

1. The first and earliest use of values in marketing dealt with locating, identifying, and selecting values.
2. The second use of values in marketing focuses on behaviors, which are studied by linking values to such concepts as motivations, attributes of purchased goods, and cultural differences.
3. The third use concerns studies of lifestyles, using values as factors in the study of segmentation and identification of potential markets.

These distinctions are necessary in order to understand more clearly the specific characteristics of studies corresponding to the third orientation. In addition, this approach helps highlight the complementary relationships that exist among these different paths of investigation. Thus, recent developments in the clarifying of values (Kahle and Xie, 2008; Schwartz, 2007) may lead to new perspectives in the study of lifestyles.

### Locating Values

As indicated in Table 2.6, two important periods can be identified. The first, marked by the works of Copeland and Clawson at the beginning of the twentieth century, was dedicated essentially to the origin and formation of existing values. However, this path offered few insights into the significance of values in marketing, leading instead to the production of long lists of

Table 2.6

**Early Utilizations of the Concept of Values in Marketing**

| Types of Application | Principal Approaches | Major Representatives | Significant Implications | Comments |
|---|---|---|---|---|
| I. Location of values | 1. Earliest research (1924–1948) | Copeland (1924) Clawson (1946) | Revealed two key motives for buying: <br>• Emotional motivations (twenty-three of them) <br>• Rational motivations connected to the principle of choice in products | Reiterates the distinction between economic and philosophical concepts of values. <br>Leads to long lists of values of little use in practice. |
| | 2. Newer research (beginning ca. mid-1970s) | Vinson, Scott, and Lamont (1977) | Creation of a list of 128 values, the first six categories of which correspond to Spranger's six types. Two kinds of values: <br>• Global values (terminal and instrumental) <br>• Values connected to the attributes of the purchased products | Reaffirms the economic and philosophical character of values. |
| | | Kahle (1983 and 1996) | Approach founded on the theory of social adaptation, which stipulates that individuals adapt to certain roles in life according to their values. <br>• Empirical brand validation <br>• Reasoning versus RVS and VALS (Beatty et al., 1985; Kahle et al., 1986) | Outlines the individual character of values as opposed to the more societal nature of certain values described by Rokeach (Valette-Florence 1988). |
| | | Schwartz (1992) | List of fifty-six values belong to ten specific motivational domains. | Model still holds true in more than twenty countries. <br>*(continued)* |

Table 2.6 *(continued)*

| Types of Application | Principal Approaches | Major Representatives | Significant Implications | Comments |
|---|---|---|---|---|
| II. Values and performance of consumers | 1. Transcultural studies | Munson and Mc Intyre (1978)<br>Kanter (1977)<br>Ng et al. (1982)<br>Scott and Lamont (1973) | All the studies indicate the primary differentiator of values between multiple ethnic groups or nations. | Character is more descriptive than explanatory in this research. |
| | 2. Descriptive analysis | Vinson and Munson (1976)<br>Henry (1976)<br>Vinson, Scott, and Lamont (1977)<br>Grube et al. (1982)<br>Pitts and Woodside (1983)<br>Evard and Tissier-Desbordes (1985) | • All of this research engages in creating evidence the "profiles" of values corresponding to the performance of specific consumption such as cars or media.<br>• Only the Henry study (1976) uses the anthropological method of Kluckhohn and Strodtbeck (1961)' the others worked with the approach employed by Rokeach. | Character is essentially descriptive in these studies, but do not explain the differences in the performance studies. |
| | 3. Explanatory research | Bozinoff and Cohen (1982) | The interest of an approach of interaction, the values and the variables of the situation did not explain the doubling in variance that were separately envisioned. | Arellano's study (1983)* evidenced the absence of relations between the real performance and the declared performance. |
| | | Arellano (1983)* | The values of Rokeach explain more than 20 percent of the real performance of energy economies. | |

| | | | |
|---|---|---|---|
| | Homer and Kahle (1988) Roehrich and Valette-Florence (1991); Kahle, 1996; Kahle and Xie 2008 | These approaches of "conceptual" order studied the average models of causality of values and other concepts nearing diverse consumption such as new products or domestic energy. | For each type of consumption studied, values create proof for a explicative power of significant performance, although somewhat weak. Valette-Florence's research (1991)* demonstrates connections between "values" and "implication" and outlines the interest in their joint contribution on the study of methods of consumption. |
| | Gutman (1982, 1986) Reynolds (1985) Perkins and Reynolds (1987) | Analysis according to "chains" as a means to an end. An essentially qualitative approach makes connections between "values" ← "consequences" ← "attributes." | Complex procedures and character qualifying changes that limit the reach of this study a priori. |
| | Valette-Florence and Rapacchi (1989, 1990b, and 1991b)* Aurifeille and Valette-Florence (1992a and 1992b)* Roehrich and Valette-Florence (1992)* | "Qualitative" treatment of information evidenced by cognitive changes. | Immediate managerial implications in terms of segmentation and the definition of "communication styles." |
| III. Values and lifestyles | Jacoby (1971) | Characterization of a "profile" of the values of innovators. | The Valette-Florence study (1987b) confirmed the impact of values on the performance of the innovator. |
| 1. Specific studies | Arellano (1983)* | Determination of the profile of the values of 3 groups of consumers of domestic energy: frugal, static, and spenders. | |

*(continued)*

Table 2.6 *(continued)*

| Types of Application | Principal Approaches | Major Representatives | Significant Implications | Comments |
|---|---|---|---|---|
| | 2. Commercial methods | Yankelovich (1971): Monitor | Known methodologies and following publications characterized these approaches derived from the United States. | Strongly criticized in France for the lack of theoretical fundamentals (Bernard-Bechaires, 1980; Peninou, 1980).* |
| | | Mitchell (1980, 1983): VALS | French commercial approaches for lifestyles according to the location of values in a worrying place. | |
| | | De Vulipian (1974)*: COFREMCA Matricon, Burke, and Caskelat (1974)*: CCA | Predictive quality of very weak consumption in the few dispensable studies on this subject (Kapferer and Laurent, 1981; Valette-Florence, 1985 and 1988b).* | |
| | 3. Conceptual approaches | Kahle (1986) Beatty et al. (1985) Kahle, Beatty, and Homer (1986) | Kahle's work utilized the LOV approach (Kahle, 1983) and compared its impact against the performance in regard to the RVS and VALS methods. These appeared to be better in every case. | In France, Valette-Florence (1988b)* outlined the ties between the RVS and LOV methodologies. |
| | | Kapferer and Laurent (1981b and 1985)* | This research evidenced the superiority of the values approach on methods of lifestyles in France for the study of methods of consumptions. | Valette-Florence and Jolibert (1988)* demonstrated interest in utilizing the components of systems of values, more so than simplistic typologies. |
| | | Valette-Florence and Jolibert (1985, 1987b, and 1988)* | The Valette-Florence study indicated the interest of the combined contribution of "values" and "implication." | |

*The asterisks reflect research carried out in a French context.

values and their implications with very little practical use. The second, more recent period involves a surge of empirical studies associated with the List of Values (LOV) by Kahle (1996; Kahle and Xie, 2008) and his colleagues, along with another proposed by Schwartz (1992). Let us briefly specify each of these traditions.

## The First Developments

According to Clawson and Vinson's article (1977), the first two academic contributions to marketing in terms of consumer values came from Copeland in 1924 and Clawson in 1946. After the analysis of 936 advertisements appearing in American magazines in 1923, Copeland concluded that all motivations for purchase can be classified according to two dimensions. The first relates to the type of decision being made; it groups the motivations that influence the buying choice by class of product, brand name, and store. The second dimension—considered more fundamental—concerns *emotional* motivations, as opposed to the *rational* motivations of the previous dimension. Copeland identified twenty-three motivations that originate from human emotions and instincts. In addition, these correspond to the instrumental and terminal values that would be proposed by Rokeach several years later. Copeland's (1924) work can therefore be considered a forerunner to that of Rokeach. Copeland first proposed a connection between human values and product attributes, which points to a similar relationship between philosophic and economic values.

Clawson also analyzed hundreds of advertisements, leading him to a list of 128 values. The first six categories correspond to the six types of people identified by Spranger and to which he added two more classes consisting of twenty-nine physical values and seven general values. Clawson assigned three levels to each of these values: the level of accomplishment, the level of ideality, and the level of expectation; however, the research that grew out of his study proved to be of little use in value-based marketing work.

## Recent Contributions

It was not until the 1960s that Rokeach introduced a less specific view of values, which is still accepted today. In 1977, Vinson, Scott, and Lamont stretched Rokeach's paradigm by considering values on only two levels. The first, conceived as global values, includes both instrumental and terminal values. The second refers to values that are tied to attributes of desired products and to behaviors during buying transactions. It seems that these authors do nothing but combine the philosophic and economic studies that have already been introduced; nonetheless, their conclusions are interesting. Given the potential impact that the knowledge of personal values and of the change of value orientation have on marketing strategies, they think that the most interesting applications of these studies are the analysis of the markets, the segmentation of these markets, and the planning of products and promotional strategies.

Kahle and his collaborators took an innovative look at the identification of values. Their methodology, referred to by the acronym LOV (List of Values), developed from the works of researchers at the University of Michigan (Veroff, Douvan, and Kulka, 1981). Based in part on the earlier studies of Maslow (1954), Rokeach (1973), and Feather (1975), LOV draws on the theory of social adaptation (Kahle, 1983, 1984), a process by which individuals adapt themselves to certain roles in life, partly in conjunction with their values.

From an operational point of view, the LOV methodology consists of condensing Rokeach's terminal values into a smaller list of nine person-oriented values, as opposed to some of Rokeach's values that are oriented toward society (national security, for example). Values included in the LOV relate plausibly to each of life's major roles: work, leisure, marriage, and parenting. This LOV is presented in Table 2.7.

A comparison of Kahle's List of Values (LOV) with that of Rokeach (RVS) reveals the following:

1. Certain items are identical: a *sense of accomplishment* and *self-respect*.
2. Others from Rokeach's list have been combined in the LOV into a more general item: the concept of *security* (LOV), for instance, includes both *family security* and *national security* (RVS). Such is also the case with *excitement (an exciting life), fun and enjoyment in life (pleasure), warm relationships with others (true friendship),* and *being well-respected (social recognition)*.
3. Certain items in Rokeach's list have disappeared altogether: *a world of peace, a world of beauty, happiness, mature love, inner beauty, salvation, wisdom*.
4. Finally, certain terms are specific only to the LOV: *a sense of belonging, self-fulfillment*.

The LOV, then, is more concise than Rokeach's list (nine items instead of eighteen), it uses more generic terms, and it contains an orientation almost exclusively to the individual with regard to terminal values. As indicated by the research of Valette-Florence (1988b), which contrasted these two methods at an empirical level, it is above all this reference to personal character that leads to the choice of one method over another. The LOV has a more purposeful tie to the theories of Maslow than does the RVS (Kahle, et al. 1997); it also has

Table 2.7

## The List of Values (LOV) Used by Kahle (1996)

The following is a list of things that some people look for or want out of life. Sometimes, you have to give up a little of something important because something else is more important to you. Please study the list carefully and then rate each choice based on how important it is in your daily life, where 1 = important to me, and 9 = extremely important to me.

|  | Important to me | | | | | | | | Extremely important to me |
|---|---|---|---|---|---|---|---|---|---|
| 1. Sense of belonging (to be accepted and needed by your family, friends, and community) | 1 | 2 | 3 | 4 | 5 | 6 | 7 | 8 | 9 |
| 2. Excitement (to experience stimulation and thrills) | 1 | 2 | 3 | 4 | 5 | 6 | 7 | 8 | 9 |
| 3. Warm relationships with others (to have close companionships and intimate friendships) | 1 | 2 | 3 | 4 | 5 | 6 | 7 | 8 | 9 |
| 4. Self-fulfillment (to find peace of mind and to make the best use of your talents) | 1 | 2 | 3 | 4 | 5 | 6 | 7 | 8 | 9 |
| 5. Being well-respected (to be admired by others and to receive recognition) | 1 | 2 | 3 | 4 | 5 | 6 | 7 | 8 | 9 |
| 6. Fun and enjoyment in life (to lead a pleasurable, happy life) | 1 | 2 | 3 | 4 | 5 | 6 | 7 | 8 | 9 |
| 7. Security (to be safe and protected from misfortune and attack) | 1 | 2 | 3 | 4 | 5 | 6 | 7 | 8 | 9 |
| 8. Self-respect (to be proud of yourself and confident with who you are) | 1 | 2 | 3 | 4 | 5 | 6 | 7 | 8 | 9 |
| 9. A sense of accomplishment (to succeed at what you want to do) | 1 | 2 | 3 | 4 | 5 | 6 | 7 | 8 | 9 |

Now reread the items and circle the one thing that is *most important* to you in your daily life.

greater reliability (Beatty, et al. 1985), does not confuse individual values with societal values that often have little impact on daily life (e.g., *a world at peace*), and is methodologically easier to use in surveys (Kahle, 1996). The higher reliability may result from the less strenuous cognitive challenge of comparing and contrasting nine items (within the range of the "magic number" of 7 +/– 2) rather than eighteen items.

It is equally important to highlight Schwartz's (1992) proposition, which used between forty-four and fifty-six items (Schwartz Value Survey, SVS) belonging to one (or more) of the ten motivational domains, which were described and presented respectively in Table 2.3 and Figure 2.1. This approach has been used with some success (e.g., Grunert and Juhl, 1991; Schwartz, 1996), especially in international research. We have done research on the LOV and the SVS. Although the main selling point of the SVS (i.e., quasi-circumplex model) is not supported by our data, it seems that both the SVS and the LOV do an equally good job of explaining most dependent variables. Moreover, values from the LOV and values from the SVS are correlated in a meaningful way. However, because the SVS includes more values than the LOV (forty-four items to represent ten values in SVS vs. nine items/values in LOV), it is more demanding for participants.

A few marketing scholars have used Hofstede's (1980) cultural dimensions of power distance, uncertainty avoidance, masculinity/femininity, and individualism in their work. Other researchers have studied a single value, such as materialism (e.g., Richins and Dawson, 1992) or collectivism (e.g., Sun, Horn, and Merritt, 2004).

### Using Values in Consumer Behavior

The development of an instrument for measuring values led to multiple uses of the concept of values in marketing. Of the studies listed in Table 2.6, the only exception, which did not use a new measurement instrument, concerns the research of Henry, who used Kluckhohn and Strodtbeck's anthropological study. The table deals with:

- cross-cultural studies
- descriptive analyses of specific behaviors
- more explicit research on behavior

### Cross-Cultural Studies

These studies attempt to link values with consumer segmentation in different cultures. A good illustration of this approach can be found in the work of Munson and McIntyre (1979), which reveals more about the anthropological domain than that of marketing. It uses the RVS in order to highlight differences among consumers from Thailand, Mexico, and the United States. The authors find that the discriminatory functions built from answers to Rokeach's test permit one to classify 65 percent of the individuals according to their cultural tradition.

Along the same line of thinking, Kanter (1977) indicates that technological, environmental, governmental, and economic changes in the United States fueled a change in instrumental and terminal values among Americans. This growing American trend—consisting of a skeptical view of newly proposed products—is closer to that of European consumers, who have a somewhat more fatalistic attitude of life and are less enthralled by the virtues of individual effort. Also worthy of note is an increased appreciation for natural simplicity and sensuality among American consumers.

More recently, Ng, et al. (1982) used Rokeach's test for differentiating human values in nine countries (Australia, Bangladesh, Hong Kong, India, Japan, Malaysia, New Zealand, New Guinea, and Taiwan). While not making an explicit distinction between instrumental and terminal values, their analysis seems to explain more than half of the cultural variations in the groups. This study remains, nevertheless, rather descriptive, as opposed to theoretical, in the sense that it presents profiles of different values without explaining them.

Finally, the study by Jolibert, Nique, and Velasquez (1987) examines the influence of culture and values on the results of professional negotiation in France and in Brazil. Their results, in spite of remaining ambiguous regarding the study of negotiation, allow us to differentiate the profiles of values in these two countries. Brazilians, much more than the French, value a life at ease and a sense of accomplishment, whereas the French value ambition and logic.

Because these illustrations rely more on a descriptive aspect than on the explicative power of values, their practical use in marketing is limited.

*Descriptive Analyses*

Much of the research on values in marketing is descriptive in the sense that it does not attempt to explain specific consumer behaviors but rather draws up profiles of values that might correspond to buying decisions. One notable exception, however, is Ritchie's study (1974), which used Rokeach's test of values to measure subjects' opinions about twelve leisure activities. The author found no perceptible link—taken individually or associated with sociodemographic variables—between individuals' values and their feelings about these activities.

Let us cite several examples that are representative of these types of studies. Various works (Scott and Lamont, 1973; Vinson and Munson, 1976;

Henry, 1976; Vinson, Scott, and Lamont, 1977) have shown the relationships existing between personal values and the attributes of various automobiles. Henry's study is one of the rare applications of the anthropological method developed by Kluckhohn and Strodtbeck (1961) to analyze the four principal orientations of values in American society. In other domains, Grube, et al., (1984) came up with distinctive profiles of values of smokers and nonsmokers, while Pitts and Woodside (1984) demonstrated the link between values and the criteria for choosing a product and brand name for cars, deodorants, and travel. Finally, in the realm of media, Becker and Connor (1981) examined the values of American readers and television viewers, while in France, Evrard and Tissier-Desbordes (1985) studied the relationship between value systems and reading in the family.

*Explicit Behavioral Research*

There are three main behavioral approaches that deal with values and purchasing patterns. The first concerns the direct influence of values on consumption. The work of Bozinoff and Cohen (1982) illustrates this connection. These authors examine the impact of values on the evaluation of automobiles. Their results offer an interesting perspective because they show an interest in a linked study (Punj and Stewart, 1983; Kahle, 1984), the values and variables of the situation explaining together the doubling of variance only while they are seen separately. Another pertinent illustration is that found in the research of Arellano (1983) on the consumption of energy in France. This study indicated that Rokeach's values explain almost 20 percent of real behavior as it pertains to the economics of energy.

The second behavioral approach is based on the analysis of causality models. Thus, the work of Homer and Kahle (1988) tests and validates—by means of a Lisrel model (that is, a linear structural relations model)—the structurally hierarchical and simple relationship between "values → attitudes → behavior" as it applies to natural food choice. In France, many works of this order have been undertaken using the PLS model (partial least squares). The conclusions of these projects show the significant impact that values have on consumption, whether they deal with new products (Roehrich and Valette-Florence, 1987b), with domestic energy (Arellano, Valette-Florence, and Jolibert, 1988), or with high-involvement products, such as cars (Valette-Florence, 1988b, 1991). Numerous studies have followed this method and are reviewed elsewhere (Kahle, 1996; Kahle and Xie, 2008). Topics range from financial decisions (Vitt, 2004), to natural health (Thompson and Troester, 2002), to sports (Kahle, Duncan, Dalakas, and Aiken, 2001) and fashion (Rose, et al., 1994).

Finally, the conceptual approach offered by Gutman (1982, 1986) and his collaborators (Reynolds and Gutman, 1984; Reynolds, 1985; Reynolds and Olson, 2001) gives a more qualitative explanation of the links between purchased products and the central values held by the purchasers of those products. Their methodology, completely innovative, consists of an analysis and a means-end chain analysis, which is hierarchical and can define, as the connection between instrumental and terminal values of individuals, the consequences of psychological order or consequences of using a product and the nature of its different attributes:

$$values \leftarrow consequences \leftarrow attributes$$

Figure 2.3 gives a partial illustration of this study (Gutman, 1986). Coffee's attributes (e.g., caffeine) lead to consequences (e.g., the ability to study longer), which in turn lead to the achievement of core values (e.g., success). Note the similarity to Homer and Kahle's finding that values (e.g., a sense of accomplishment) lead people to develop attitudes (e.g., staying awake aids studying, which in turn contributes to accomplishment) that drive behavior (e.g., purchasing and consuming highly caffeinated coffee).

Gutman's interest resides in the possibility of isolating the chaining—the connections between a person's values and his or her product choices—which appears the most pertinent for increasing awareness of or characterizing the potential of a given product to the user. To compensate for the limitations inherent in behavioral-based marketing research, Valette-Florence and Rapacchi (1989, 1990b, 1991b) proposed a purely quantitative approach based on the joint application of the theory of graphs and the factorial analysis of correspondences. The theory of graphs allows for the automated construction of hierarchical maps, while the analysis of correspondences furnishes both a graphic and global representation of individuals and of the different elements of chaining in a common perceptual space; above all, however, it offers the possibility of carrying out a typology of consumers according to the links they have evoked.

This study, applied with success in a European context (Valette-Florence and Rapacchi, 1990b), was subjected to methodological improvements—improvements that called for a return to multidimensional analysis and constrained typology (Aurifeille and Valette-Florence, 1992a, 1992b) while using semantic research indicators (Aurifeille, 1991; Roehrich and Valette-Florence, 1991, 1992). The openings in research sparked by the analysis of cognitive chaining are extremely promising and will without doubt uncover numerous practical applications in the future. They allow for overlap of consumption styles and practices (Roehrich and Valette-Florence, 1992), as well as the

Figure 2.3   **Gutman's (1997) Means-End Chain for Coffee Consumption**

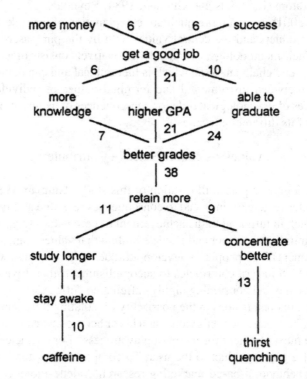

*Source:* Gutman (1997). This material is reproduced with permission of John Wiley & Sons, Inc.

prediction of consumer styles that traditional approaches using an inventory of very general values (Aurifeille and Valette-Florence, 1992b).

## *Values and Lifestyles*

Interest in the use of cultural factors to explain consumer behavior has largely expanded; in France, much commercial success was won by the classifications of CCA and COFREMCA on marketing studies. Nevertheless, it is still relatively rare to find explicit uses of the concept of values in a study of lifestyles oriented toward the analysis or segmentation of markets (for an example of this subject, see Valette-Florence, 1985). Table 2.6 lists the studies of values in this sense. It is possible to make a distinction between three types of approaches:

- more specific studies that have worked, from a less theoretical angle, on values
- global commercial studies that incorporate values into their identification of evolving cultural tendencies in society
- conceptual and more solid methodological approaches established in the United States around the works of Kahle and his colleagues, then developed in France, principally by the research of Valette-Florence and Jolibert.

A discussion of each of these three approaches follows.

*Specific Studies*

In the first category, Jacoby (1971) is without doubt the first to use the values of Rokeach as an indicator of innovative character in individuals. He showed that the values of an open mind, of sociability, and—on the other hand—of withdrawal are good criteria for identifying innovators. Another researcher, Romana (1975), used a Rokeach-inspired method to reveal the profiles of American women preoccupied (or not) by their health. It demonstrated that the women of the first category prioritized happiness and responsibility, but gave less priority to wisdom, indulgence, and imagination than did members of the second group. From a marketing perspective, the results of this work allowed for the better positioning of certain hygiene products and some vitamins.

In France, Arellano (1983) demonstrated the explicative power of Rokeach's values on the real and declared saving of energy. He classified people as cost-conscious consumers, wasters, or static consumers, according to their energy-saving practices. Such a result thus allows us to target the specific segments while defining a strategy of adapted communication for each segment.

In another domain, Budillon and Valette-Florence (1990) came up with a profile of hang gliding enthusiasts according to the sociocultural values proposed by the CCA (see Figure 2.4). While the study developed by the CCA measured sociocultural category with a long list of interview questions, Budillon and Valette-Florence developed a study that measured each sociocultural orientation with one question alone. In spite of being much reduced, their method allows for the very accurate characterization of three specific practices of hang gliding to which relatively stereotypical behavior types correspond. Shoham, Rose, and Kahle (2004) reported similar findings with the LOV.

*Commercial Studies*

In the United States, many commercial studies focus on values as a tool for analyzing sociocultural changes (Yankelovich, 1971, 1974; Mitchell, 1983).

Figure 2.4    **Classification of Sociocultural Value Orientations of People Who Practice Hang Gliding**

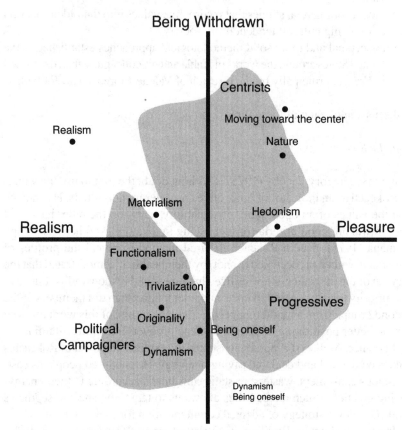

*Source:* Budillon and Valette-Florence (1990).

On the basis of an annual study of 2,500 people, Yankelovich identified thirty-one sociocultural values, listed in four categories, which are presented as key indicators of social currents and important markers for understanding behaviors. These categories are presented in Table 2.8.

The VALS (Value and Lifestyle Survey) approach, developed by Mitchell, is based on the theory of needs according to Maslow (1954) and the concept of social character (Riesman, Glazer, and Denney, 1950). VALS includes thirty-four questions—each carefully worded and validated at a statistical level (Holman, 1984)—on the basis of a survey of 1,635 Americans and

Table 2.8

**Social Trends Measured in Monitor by Yankelovich**

**Personal and Egocentric Orientation**
- Personalization
- Physical improvement
- Well-being
- Social and cultural self-expression
- Personal creativity
- Ostentatious religion
- Significant work
- Introspection
- Hedonism
- Sexual liberalism
- Feminine careers
- Preservation of private life

**Environmental Orientation Favoring Personal Expression**
- Mysticism
- Sensuality
- New romanticism
- Novelty and change
- Beauty at home
- Return to nature
- Science and technocracy
- Preservation of the environment
- Search for community

**Simplistic and Reassuring Environmental Orientation**
- Simplification
- Antihypocrisy
- Anti-enormity
- New cynicism

**Destruction of Lifestyle**
- Antimaterialism
- Rejection of ownership
- Rejection of authority
- Living from day to day
- Unisex trend
- Tolerance for chaos and disorder

*Source:* Yankelovich, Skelly & White (1981), Social Trends Measured, Yankelovich Monitor, #3.

Table 2.9

**The Nine Groups of Lifestyles Used in VALS 1**

| Name | Percentage |
| --- | --- |
| The survivors | 4 |
| Those who maintain themselves | 7 |
| Those who belong to a group | 35 |
| The imitators | 9 |
| The winners | 22 |
| The I-am-me types | 5 |
| The experimentalists | 7 |
| Those concerned with society | 9 |
| The integrated (ones) | 2 |

*Source:* Adapted from Leon G. Schiffman and Leslie L. Kanuk (1991), *Consumer Behavior,* 4th ed., Englewood Cliffs, NJ: Prentice-Hall, pp. 136–137.

their spouses. Unfortunately, the methodology is not considered scientifi-cally sound (Kahle and Kahle, 2009). The nine types of lifestyles are pre-sented in Table 2.9. One should take equal note of the recent development of a typology called VALS2, which classifies Americans into eight groups distributed into three categories based on the priorities of (1) action, (2), social recognition, or (3) their own beliefs (see Table 2.10). The VALS2 typology accords one important place in its results to sociodemographic characteristics: The groups are organized according to potential revenue. Many companies have used the Yankelovich Monitor and the VALS surveys to predict buying patterns.

The formation and evolution of values has always been considered carefully in French lifestyle studies. Consequently, COFREMCA has detected about fifty (underlying) sociocultural trends that lead to certain attitudes and behaviors, among which one can reveal authenticity, confusion, emotional experience, openness to change, rejection of authority, and accession to polysensualism, among others (see Table 2.11). Similarly, the CCA developed a list of thirteen measurements for socioculture (Matricon, Burke, and Cathelat, 1974), more or less similar, as presented in Figure 2.5. Each is defined in a bipolar manner (for example, passiveness in comparison with dynamism), and they mirror the more classic "socio-styles" of the AIO inventory.

*Comparison and Contrast of Methods*

One innovative methodological and theoretical orientation developed recently in the United States around Kahle's LOV. On this subject, two comparative studies deserve mention:

- The first (Beatty, et al., 1985) compares and contrasts Rokeach's RVS with Kahle's LOV, applying them to different choices of leisure activ-ity and media. According to Beatty and his colleagues, both show a convergent validity and useful discrimination for the study of consumer behavior, and the LOV view seems preferable for the study of individual behavior. Similar conclusions resulted from research by Valette-Florence (1987), who contrasted at a conceptual level these two studies with the use of a structural model (PLS). The LOV method, which is centered on the individual, seems preferable for the analysis of behavior responding to personal rather than social needs. On the contrary, Rokeach's method corresponds more to the analysis of societal values.
- The second study (Kahle, et al., 1986) compares VALS1, which had just been discussed, with the List of Values. The study of their respective predictive power on a list of seventy-three opinions or activities shows the superiority of the LOV method, which is likely attributable to its rapidity and facility of administration.

Table 2.10

**The Eight Groups of Lifestyles Used in VALS2**

Innovators
Thinkers
Achievers
Experiencers
Believers
Strivers
Makers
Strugglers

*Source:* Schiffman and Kanuk, pp. 138–139.

Table 2.11

**List of the Trends and Dimensions Identified by COFREMCA, by Their Abbreviated Ranking (1992)**

- Achievement #16N
- Anti-accumulation #13
- Personal appearance #30
- Authenticity #59
- Need for sense #56
- Need for national superiority #12
- Open citizenship #54B
- Competition #23N
- Connectivity #49
- Personal creativity #5
- Confusion #45
- Marginal differentiation #2
- Collective emotions #37
- Professional development #7
- Ethnicity - Folklore #24T
- Emotional experience #47
- (Sensitivity to one's) figure #34
- Pleasure management #62
- Hypernatural #44N
- Harmony #61
- Personal expression #3
- Uncertainty and complexity #41

- Intraception #26N
- Irrational #27T
- Playing with signs #57
- Sexual liberalism #17
- Less attachment #10
- Differentiation between sexes #28B
- (Openness to) globalization #63
- (Sensitivity to) nature #21T
- (Search for) novelty #8A
- Strategic opportunism #53B
- Openness to change #8B
- Polysensualism #25T
- Gregariousness #18N[JC1]
- Rejection of authority #9
- Reprioritization #60
- Risk #35
- Sociable #58
- (Worry for one's) health #31A
- Social spontaneity #52
- Standing #1N
- (Sensitivity to) violence #33
- Vitality #51B

*Source:* COFREMCA (1992). See Chapter 4.

The result of the second study is related to those found in France by Kapferer and Laurent (1981b, 1985), who proved the weak predictive power of lifestyles classification by both the CCA (which focuses on preconscious values) and COFREMCA (which focuses on the study of present values). Kapferer and Laurent's study consisted of a series of questions on about forty

Figure 2.5    **CCA List of Thirteen Measurements for Sociocultural Trends**

| | |
|---|---|
| Passivity (tranquility) | 1. Dynamism (conflict) |
| Realignment (your home) | 2. Extension (elsewhere) |
| Transcendence (belief in something) | 3. Interchange (living in the here and now) |
| Individualism (the deprived) | 4. Integration (the collective) |
| Symbolism (that which we feel) | 5. Realism (that which we observe) |
| Hierarchy (the leader) | 6. Cooperation (participation) |
| Modeling (that which normalizes) | 7. Originality (that which disturbs) |
| Discipline (order) | 8. Liberalism (flexibility) |
| Mosaic (society) | 9. Monolithism (coherence) |
| Nature (natural) | 10. Technique (technology) |
| Hedonism (pleasure) | 11. Functionalism (utility) |
| Let it be (be what they think) | 12. Materialism (that which we do and that which we have) |
| Permanence (that which is stable) | 13. Metamorphosis (that which moves) |

*Source:* Dubois (1987).

food, hygiene, self-care, and cosmetic products. Also, Valette-Florence and Jolibert (1985a and 1987a) showed superiority of using Rokeach values over a method like COFREMCA regarding the study of consumption of a series of 140 products in current use. They also underline the interest of work at a level of components of the values system of individuals (more than that of an excessively reductive typology), the predictive power of consumption finding itself notably improved by improved accuracy (Valette-Florence and Jolibert, 1990). Finally, one study of 1,500 people validates these results by extending them to the consumption of more symbolic products (fine wines) (Valette-Florence, 1988a, 1991).

Together, these studies highlight the implications of value-based research in the global study of consumer behavior, activity choices, and/or opinions. These studies exhibit, as much in France as in the United States, a superior explicative power in analyzing classic lifestyles. Although they do not pretend to be a substitute for sociodemographic methods, they are nevertheless capable of furnishing valuable information for defining strategies of segmentation and public communication.

## CONCLUSION AND SYNTHESIS

This chapter looks at the philosophical, anthropological, psychological, and sociological origins of values. It appears that the psychological aspect is the most important in the application of values to the marketing domain (Kahle, 1983; Rokeach, 1973).

The influence of culture (in an ethnological or anthropological sense) on consumer behavior has been widely recognized for more than 50 years (for more on this subject, see Dubois and Douglas, 1977; Dubois, 1987). The analysis of cultural values consists of an axis of privileged research, defined by Rokeach (1973) as "durable beliefs, determining that a type of behavior or goal of existence is preferable to another." Values can also be distinguished from other concepts such as attitudes, social norms, needs, personality traits, and interests.

The implementation of Rokeach's values—leaving it to others to debate between the concept of actual preference and ideal preference—allows for three principal types of marketing applications. The first is concerned with the identification and selection of values. It is principally thanks to the work of Kahle and Schwartz that two innovative fields of investigation were developed, relative to their identification. The second ones, the more numerous, center on cross-cultural studies and the descriptive analysis of specific consumption practices. Among these marketing applications, it is important to recognize the innovative approach of Reynolds (1985; Reynolds and Gutman, 1984; Reynolds and Olson, 2001), based on the study of value linking, which allows us to cognitively link the purchase of a given product. In addition, the methodological developments recently proposed by Valette-Florence and his colleagues allow for a quantitative and more structured approach to the collection of information, thus making the study much more easily accessible to all.

The results of the LOV work on values, just as much in France as elsewhere, tend to show their interest in the considerable provision that they can furnish descriptions of market segments and definitions of positioning strategy and advertising communication comparable to classical methods. The study of values therefore remains a topic of interest (Allen and Ng, 1999; Florenthal and Shoham, 2000; Kilbourne, Grunhagen, and Foley, 2005; Kropp, Lavack, and Silvera, 2005).

The predictive power of values in the marketing field was neglected for a long time in favor of strictly empirical approaches, better known in the United States under the name AIO inventory. This tradition will be discussed at length in Chapter 3.

# 3

# Traditional Approaches Focusing on Attitudes and Activities

In the previous chapter, we described the principle characteristics of value-based approaches to the study of lifestyles, which have received little attention and seen only limited development. This chapter emphasizes another approach—one that focuses on attitudes and activities and has seen numerous applications. It is perhaps best known by the acronym AIO (Activities, Interests, and Opinions).

The first part of this chapter defines and retraces the history of the AIO approach. The second part examines its theoretical foundations. In particular, we will look at the concept of attitudes and how they function in an analysis of lifestyles. The concept of activities will be discussed in a similar manner.

Finally, the third part presents the different types of approaches that focus on attitudes and activities. Some are quite general in character; others are more specific and therefore lean toward exclusive topics—attitudes specific to a certain type of product or to the variables of different personality types.

## HISTORY AND DEFINITION

This approach derives its essence from the reasoning of Merton (1949), who held that the key to the formation of lifestyles is not established at the broadest level of the society (that of the group as a whole), but at the level of the social groups that form the complex network of a society. From this perspective, the approaches focusing on attitudes and activities developed around the works of Pessemier and Tigert (1966) and Wells (1968b); these researchers sought to determine the lifestyles of individuals by examining, in the most exhaustive manner possible, their diverse activities and attitudes rather than the degree to which they adhere to cultural values and behavioral norms.

As Hustad and Pessemier (1974) noted, these general approaches tend to reveal people's centers of interest, their attitudes, their activities, and some of their personality traits, along with their self-perception and opinions on their social, political, and economic environments. Consequently, the majority of studies of this type are developed in an empirical manner, run by progressively more important questionnaires, but without ever clearly defining the theoretical foundations of their underlying concepts. For this reason, it seems appropriate to justify the use of attitudes and activities in understanding lifestyles.

## THEORETICAL FOUNDATIONS FOR THE CONCEPTS OF ATTITUDES AND ACTIVITIES

We will first define these concepts and then justify their use with regards to the central theme of lifestyles.

### The Definition of Attitudes

The introduction of the concept of attitudes is relatively recent in the study of behaviors. It grew out of attempts to explain the differences observed by behaviorists such as Watson (1925) when different individuals were exposed to identical stimuli. Its use and importance from then on became essential. In 1935, Allport came up with the following definition: "An attitude is a mental and neural state of readiness, organized through experience, exerting a directive or dynamic influence upon the individual's response to all objects and situations with which it is related."

Allport's definition gave way to many other propositions, the most well known among them being devised by Krech, Crutchfield, and Ballachey (1948) from a conceptual point of view, and by Fishbein and Ajzen (1975) from an operational point of view. For Krech, Crutchfield, and Ballachey, an attitude is defined as being an enduring system of motivations, emotions, perceptions, and cognitive responses an individual has to a given aspect of the world. This interpretation emphasizes motivation and emotions as distinctive factors separating attitudes from beliefs. For Fishbein and Ajzen, attitude is "a learned predisposition for responding favorably or unfavorably in a coherent manner to a given object." According to them, attitude is a potential behavioral state attributed to and based on the object—an object that satisfies physical, social, or psychological needs.

Finally, there is Triandis's (1979) definition, which states that an attitude is "an emotionally charged idea which predisposes to a certain action in response to a specific situation with which one is presented." This definition synthesizes the conceptual reasoning of Allport with that of Krech, Crutchfield, and Ballachey. Thus, the guiding influence to the response from Allport corresponds to the *predisposition to a certain action* about which Triandis speaks. In the same manner, the *mental and neural state* can be associated with the *emotionally charged idea.*

Similarly, the *motivational techniques* of Krech et al. can be associated with the *predisposition to a certain action* mentioned by Triandis in the same way that *emotional and perceptual responses* correspond to the *emotionally charged idea.* From a more practical point of view, the recognition of a certain object's attributes, defined by Fishbein and Ajzen, implies the idea mentioned by Triandis. Likewise, the predisposition to respond *favorably* or *unfavorably* is similar to the *emotionally charged idea* from Triandis's proposition.

The modern definition of attitude, according to Triandis, corresponds to the propositions of Hustad and Pessemier (1974). All three researchers suggest that attitudes define individuals' connections to and relationships with the people and objects that surround them. Consisting of their beliefs, opinions, values, and preferences, attitudes allow us to predict people's behavior by revealing their predispositions about things or other people; hence, the central theme is that an individual's collection of attitudes reflects preexisting tendencies toward certain behaviors. In previous definitions, and particularly in Triandis's, it was noted that attitudes are likely to produce different behaviors among individuals depending on the different circumstances that arise.

Lifestyle studies can help explain various types of reactions in a population and therefore identify groups having similar behavioral types. This notion can be understood more easily if one observes attitudes from the point of view of their functions and components.

### *The Functions of Attitudes*

Attitudes serve at least three psychological functions (Kelman, 1958; Kahle, Kambara, and Rose, 1996; Bee and Kahle, 2006). These functions—compliance, identification, and internalization—reflect an ascending level of commitment. Different conditions activate these different functions, and the process of changing attitudes hinges on which function the attitudes follow. Sometimes, people just want to get along, and they comply with perceived social expectations. Other times, people want to understand themselves, and their attitudes reflect the need for identification. Attitudes serve the internalization function when people express their most deep-seated characteristics.

The theoretical foundations for attitudes are rather straightforward: Compliance attitudes tend to follow the predictions of behaviorist theory; identification derives from neopsychoanalytic theory; and internalization follows the edicts of humanistic psychology. Compliance and identification have both a public and a private side, which in some circumstances can have conflicting implications. Practitioners who seek to understand, work with, or change attitudes need to understand which function a particular attitude serves before they can hope to carry out their goals effectively.

## The Components of Attitudes: Their Implications in an Approach Based on Lifestyles

To recap, Triandis's definition of attitudes stresses emotion as a defining element and adheres to the idea that circumstances tend to alter the case. From a classic perspective, there are three principal components to an attitude:

1. a cognitive component (the idea or belief)
2. an emotional component (emotionally charged or evaluative)
3. a conative component (which predisposes one to a type of action)

Our next step is to examine the implications these components have on the study of lifestyles.

### The Implications of the Cognitive Component

The cognitive component, often referred to as "the information" in a perceptual component, represents how an individual perceives his or her surroundings (the objects in those surroundings as well as the overall environment). This component consists of a person's opinions and beliefs about the objects and events with which he or she is confronted. Above all else in the perceptual realm, the cognitive component is the minimal condition composing an attitude. One's awareness of a problem, therefore, has an impact on the behavior that results from it. Hence, many approaches to lifestyle studies use opinions as a means of influencing attitude.

However, in a work on knowledge relativity, Molt (1982) shows that if the cognitive component of an attitude effectively shares a link with the products a person uses, then that cognitive component can be transformed by an individual in a way that makes the product fit with his or her preferences in a system of values. This subjectivity, which can be introduced by influence attempts of self or others, gives way to the second component of attitudes, the affective component.

### The Implications of the Affective Component

Also referred to as the motivational or sentimental component, the affective component represents the degree of emotional response that accompanies an opinion an individual forms about an object or situation. According to the circumstances, the objects are evaluated as more or less favorable or unfavorable, depending on whether they are associated with pleasant or unpleasant events and desirable or undesirable goals.

As a result, the positive or negative value that people assign to objects and situations affects their perception of those objects and situations. The opinions and central interests that result from this confrontation with the outside world are an expression of our own system of preferences and values. Measuring attitudes by opinions and interests in a study of lifestyles, therefore, allows us to distinguish each of the different behavioral types apparent in each individual.

The personal evaluation that stimulates the affective component is very important because, as noted by McGuire (1969), the cognitive and conative components vary according to it. Thus, the more positive the evaluation, the easier it will be to recognize a problem that opposes the important cognitive component. In the same manner, the more intense the affective component, the more likely it is to encourage one to act.

## *The Implications of the Conative Component*

The conative component represents a person's predisposition to a certain behavior or action. This component stems from one's values and from the affective component assigned to either the object or the present situation. The type of behavior that results depends on the intensity of the component. The more important it is, the stronger the corresponding interest and the more likely it is to hold meaning for the individual.

Kassarjian (1971a), for example, showed a link between favorable attitudes toward the environment and the purchase of environmentally friendly products. The measure of attitudes and interests in studies of lifestyles equally recognizes the conative component—the component most directly related to behavior.

The three components of attitudes are inextricably linked. And, together, they create a relation between attitude and behavior. Likewise, opinions and interests, which are often used in the study of lifestyles to verify attitudes, correspond to the three aforementioned components. Because of the narrow links that they maintain with behavior, it seems justifiable to incorporate them into an attitudinal approach to the study of lifestyles.

The nature of the causal relation that exists among the three components has generated some discussion in recent literature. One view (Solomon, 2009) holds that correlation depends upon the level of involvement a person has with the topic of the attitude. For high involvement attitudes, the causal sequence is

cognitive → affective → conative

For lower involvement attitudes, the causal sequence is

cognitive → conative → affective

For even lower levels of involvement, called the experiential sequence, the pattern is

$$\text{affective} \rightarrow \text{conative} \rightarrow \text{cognitive}$$

The importance of the links that tie attitudes together with behavior has fueled interest in activities as an expression of different people's behaviors in diverse fields.

## Activities

The concept of activities is directly linked to the concept of time. Activities represent the actions people choose to engage in during their free time. As with numerous other authors, Jacoby, Szybillo, and Bering (1976) inquired about the implications existing between the use of time and the act of consumption.

Feldman and Hornik (1981) proposed the following categories of activities: work, necessities (e.g., sleep), domestic work, and leisure time. This classification is interesting because it presents the different activities as a sort of ladder, descending in terms of obligations, going from mandatory activities to those actions that are pursued freely as leisure activities. The authors consider the ensemble of chosen activities as corresponding to different behavioral types, which they prefer to call *time styles* rather than *lifestyles*. According to Feldman and Hornik, all human activity results from the following interdependent factors:

- the time aspect (frequency and duration)
- the economic aspect (referring to the cost of the activity)
- the spatial aspect (relative to the location of the activity)

Time is the primary determining factor in choosing an activity (Feldman and Hornik, 1981). Schary (1971) similarly considers the time variable and its impact on one's choice of activities as important criteria for determining their priorities and their schedules. Settle, Alreck, and Glasheen (1978) also see a link between people's lifestyles and their personal orientation to time. As a result of all these studies, one could say that the activities in which people involve themselves are a reflection of both their behavior and their use of time.

In lifestyles research, the activities typically studied are leisure activities—vacations, ways of relaxing in the home, regular attendance at social and cultural events, habits linked to professional work, or exposure to different forms of media—which correspond, in fact, to the categories proposed by Feldman and Hornik.

It is important to note that these approaches are not homogeneous: Some cover activities in all domains; others concentrate on specific sectors such as exposure to various forms of media. A particularly noteworthy study by Kelly (1975) essentially uses leisure activities as an approach to studying people's lifestyles. Activities taken into account by researchers are not always identical and appear to be generated in an empirical manner to satisfy the requirements of specific studies. Research confirms the idea that people's preference of activities is linked closely to their use of time.

## DIFFERENT STUDIES FOCUSING ON ATTITUDES AND ACTIVITIES

The concept of attitudes and activities in relation to lifestyles has led to three types of studies:

- studies that center on interests (these have undergone limited research)
- studies that focus more specifically on attitudes relative to a specific product
- studies similar to AIO, examining a large scale of activities and attitudes (expressed in the form of interests and opinions) that serve as widespread topics of study for researchers and practitioners

### *Studies That Emphasize Interests*

It appears that the interest-based approach was developed in Europe according to the works of Cerha (1974). Cerha demonstrated that social influence is not exerted vertically by opinion leaders as much as it is exerted horizontally within groups constituted on the basis of common interests.

Thus, it became necessary to research the configuration of the most frequent interests and discern how groups of people articulate themselves around these interests in order to better understand the formation of lifestyles. In fact, this method received little attention until recently in present-day marketing. Rarely have diverse interests been studied from the point of view of their relation to consumer behavior. In practice, the researcher determines the interests of individuals—such as local life, politics, television, cuisine, or gardening—and then regroups the individuals in accordance with these interests and a series of other behavioral variables (purchasing characteristics or reaction to the media, for example). One illustration of this approach is a study conducted in France in which the relationships between 81 interests, 30 socioeconomic variables, and 27 supports were examined (Agostini and Boss, 1973). Table 3.1 shows some of the interests chosen for this study.

This approach, however, is still too descriptive and insufficiently able to provide conceptual prediction and understanding, as is indicated by Table 3.1,

Table 3.1

**Some of the Interests Studied in an Inquiry on French Media**

| % Men | | % Women | |
|---|---|---|---|
| **1. Activities that interest at least 60% of the interviewees** | | | |
| 77 | Watching television | 86 | Decorating the house |
| 74 | Decorating the house | 75 | Watching television |
| 67 | Vacationing | 74 | Participating in family gatherings |
| 66 | Driving | 73 | Cooking |
| 66 | Reading the newspaper | 73 | Receiving gifts |
| 64 | Listening to the radio | 68 | Taking vacations |
| 63 | Repairs around the house | 67 | Reading the newspaper |
| 63 | Participating in family events | 66 | Taking care of (the) children |
| | | 62 | Reading books |
| | | 61 | Listening to music |
| | | 61 | Weekends in the country or at the beach |
| | | 60 | (Grocery) shopping |
| | | 60 | Having friends over |
| **2. Subjects for which at least 60% of the interviewees wish to receive information and/or advertisements** | | | |
| 71 | Environmental protection | 76 | Health and hygiene |
| 68 | Health and hygiene | 72 | Women's clothing |
| 63 | Automobiles | 69 | House decor |
| 61 | Child education | 67 | Child education |
| | | 66 | Household linens |
| | | 65 | Environmental protection |
| | | 65 | Cosmetics |
| | | 63 | Maintenance products |
| | | 62 | Furniture |
| **3. Sections of the newspaper that interest at least 60% of the interviewees** | | | |
| 74 | Local news | 77 | Health and hygiene news |
| 74 | Regional news | 72 | Recipes |
| 70 | Health and hygiene news | 71 | House decor |
| 67 | Current affairs | 69 | Regional news |
| 63 | French politics | 67 | Household advice |
| | | 67 | Local news |
| | | 66 | Current affairs |
| | | 66 | Women's fashion |

*Source:* Agostini, J., and Boss, J. (1973), "Classifying Informants in Consumers' Surveys According to Their Areas of Interest," *European Research*, 1, 20–25.

and only vaguely explains consumer behavior and the association of chosen media. This problem is likely tied to the origin of interests. To ensure that results are not skewed, the individual interests represented in the study must be sufficiently diverse , but they also must be fairly mainstream and not overly representative of marginal domains in which only a few people are interested. Analysis of the combinations of interests at an individual level could prove to be more useful than the individual study of each interest.

### Specific Studies on Attitudes Relative to a Particular Product

Studies on attitudes toward a particular product are more specific and based as follows:

- Haley's (1968, 1971) approach deals with the researched advantages of a given product, which allows us to uncover new segments and product opportunities for exploitation.
- Heller's (1970) approach focuses on attitudes developed by an individual in a specific buying situation and looks at ways of increasing the consumption of a given brand within a certain class of products.

### Approaches Based on Researched (Sought) Advantages

This original method, sometimes called *segmentation a priori* or *functional segmentation*, was developed by Haley on the basis of propositions by Yankelovich (1964, 1971). Haley believes that there are six factors involved in the segmentation of the market:

1. product advantages
2. clinical measures of personality
3. measures of attitudes
4. general measures of lifestyles
5. demographic variables
6. beliefs about product categories

Although segmentation is possible along any of these lines, Haley suggests that the *sought advantages* approach remains the most pertinent for differentiating purchases by product classes and specific brands. Effectively, if every consumer searches for the maximum possible number of advantages in the purchase of a product, then the weight attributed to each advantage varies from one group to another, allowing us to differentiate among them. For example, suppose one is seeking speed and economy in the purchase of a car. That buyer cannot rank these priorities equally when choosing the brand. The segment thus defined in terms of sought advantages will be more clearly associated with classic demographic variables or more general lifestyles.

An explicit example of such an approach is given in Table 3.2 (Pras and Tarondeau, 1981). It concerns segmentation within the toothpaste market in the United

Table 3.2

**Segmentation by Sought Advantages—Example: The Toothpaste Market**

| Segment Names | Sensory (types) | Sociable (types) | Worriers | Independent (types) |
|---|---|---|---|---|
| Principal advantages researched | Taste, product appearance | Tooth whitening | Prevention of cavities | Price |
| Demographic group | Children | Adolescents | Large families | Men |
| Particular behavior characteristics | Menthol toothpaste consumers | Smokers | Big consumers | Big consumers |
| Clearly preferred brand names | Colgate Stripe | Mcleans Ultra-Brite | Crest | Any brand |
| Personality trait | Strong personal implication | | Tendency toward pessimism | Strong autonomy |
| Lifestyle | Pursuit of pleasure | | Conservative | Price/quality conscious |

*Source:* Adapted from Haley, R. (1968), "Benefit Segmentation: A Decision-Oriented Tool," *Journal of Marketing,* 8, 3–8, from Pras, B., and Tarondeau, J.C. (1981), *Comportment l'acheteur*, Paris: Sirey.

States. Note that the implications of segmentation by sought advantages apply just as well to the strategic product attributes as to the media choice or the channels of distribution used to market the product. For example, if worriers are the target segment in the toothpaste example, their principle criterion of choice is cavity prevention: It would be in the brand's best interest to use forms of advertising media that attract large families, namely, television. Furthermore, advertisements expressed in a moderate, classic tone (according to the conservative lifestyle of these clients) can put an emphasis on the preventative quality of the toothpaste by including the opinion of experts such as dentists or pharmacists.

Segmentation by sought advantages is therefore very important. As noted by Pras and Tarondeau, segmentation allows for the discovery of new segments or new product opportunities ripe for exploitation. In this sense, Engel, Blackwell, and Kollat (1978) insist upon the fact that the success of new products is largely due to segmentation by sought advantages.

*Approaches Based on Attitudes Developed by the Consumer in a Specific Buying Situation*

This approach, proposed by Heller (1970), asks how a consumer's attitude toward a product is linked to its purchase without determining whether attitude is the actual cause or effect of the purchase. This last point seems particularly open to criticism, because a consequence variable might be utilized as a segmentation criterion. Instead of preceding the purchase, it actually could result from it.

On the other hand, this type of approach requires long lists of about 400 to 600 items before extracting by factor analysis the 150 to 200 key variables for the considered study. It is easy to see how this approach could be prohibitively expensive to implement. Finally, food products (such as water, oil, eggs, and fruit) hardly allow for such an approach because they do not typically generate strong attitudes or (in the case of Haley's approach) significant sought advantages.

Conversely, as noted by Heller, products with too strong an image or status mask their intrinsic characteristics and, as a result, may conceal the advantages gained in using them. Heller illustrates these two points of segmentation by sought advantages with coffee (a product characterized as either too commonplace or too social to use the attitudinal approach).

This approach may have some merit when the investigation is limited to a certain class of products (Hustad and Pessemier, 1974). Contrarily, a more general approach is recommended if it concerns the evaluation of what causes the increase of consumption as a whole.

### Studies of the AIO Type (Activities, Interests, Opinions)

The most exhaustive and eclectic approach, which is known as the AIO approach, was developed in the United States to study lifestyles. It was later replaced to some extent by the VALS approach (Mitchell, 1983), which was discussed in the previous chapter. VALS was constructed under the same scheme but purportedly gives greater weight to the role played by values.

Two principal orientations have been identified in the different AIO perspectives:

- The first one uses, in particular, variables of personality and is called psychographics (Wells, 1974).
- The second, which is much more vast, attempts not only to determine individuals' interests but also their self-perceptions and their opinions on the economic and social environment (Hustad and Pessemier, 1974; Wells and Tigert, 1971).

#### Psychographic Studies

In psychographics, one studies personality traits—independence or aggressiveness, for example—and their association with different types of behavior,

Table 3.3

**Personality Traits Pertinent to Characterizing Consumption of Cosmetic Products**

Narcissism
The need for fantasy
Exhibitionism
Sociability
The importance of appearance
Reference
Impulsiveness
Immaturity
Order
Being active
Domination
Liveliness
The search for status

*Source:* Adapted from S. Young (1972), "The Dynamics of Measuring Unchange," in R.I. Haley (ed.), *Attitude Research in Transition,* Chicago: American Marketing Association, 62.

assuming these traits (which make up a person's identity) are what determine the nature of their interaction with others. The goal of psychographic studies is to consider societal trends in personality the way demographic studies may consider factors such as age, income, and education; however, the absence of a theoretically sound method of selecting and measuring key psychological traits has slowed the development of these studies considerably (Goldberg, 1976).

Because of this shortcoming, only several studies have been conducted following this approach. They were based in particular on the relations between traits such as introversion, autonomy, aggression, development, and respect for others, on the one hand, and media choice, on the other (Villani, 1975). Thus, by virtue of example, individuals who spend a significant amount of time listening to the radio tend to be introverts with a lower need for psychosocial interaction than others. Similarly, people who listen to the radio infrequently have a stronger need for psychosocial interaction for dominance over others and stronger resistance to interpersonal influence (Peterson, 1972).

By and large, the historic studies that relied on the measure of personality traits to predict behavior were unsuccessful (Kassarjian, 1971a). These results most likely stem from the unsuitability of a marketing context for general behavior measures initially constructed in clinical psychology (Dubois, 1990). To date, the most promising marketing-related attempts connecting personality and behavior focus on the functions of the products studied or on a class of particular products such as cosmetics (Young, 1972). In order to illustrate this concept, Table 3.3 presents some of these personality types common in marketing studies.

In recent years, the study of personality in psychology has emphasized the trait approach; in looking at situational interactions, the focus is on the empirically derived "big five" traits of openness, conscientiousness, extraversion, agreeableness, and neuroticism (Goldberg, 1993). Interestingly, consumer research in recent years has made use of more sophisticated theory on anthropomorphizing products and brands that has also focused on five traits, but these five are sincerity, excitement, competence, sophistication, and ruggedness (Aaker, 1997). The use of values rather than traits in psychographic studies may hold some promise (Kahle and Riley, 2004; Kim, et al., 2006).

*Taking Inventory of AIO*

The AIO approach, by contrast to other approaches, is much more general than the previously discussed method and assigns far greater importance to the environment of the individual in the process of forming lifestyles. According to this view, individuals in general adopt a lifestyle conforming to the dominant traits of those social groups to which they belong or wish to belong (Baudrillard, 1970). The types of activities people choose, the things with which they surround themselves, and the clothes they wear all denote their belonging or their desire to belong to certain groups (Grubb and Grathwohl, 1967; Laumann and House, 1970).

Studies of the AIO type try to obtain a relatively complete image of an individual's lifestyle by describing the individual's own values as they appear in activities and in interests and attitudes toward leisure, work, and consumption, given the social and societal context in which they evolve. Note that this type of inventory listing is used in studies of French lifestyles.

Because of the ambitious nature of these studies, they involve very comprehensive questionnaires composed of several hundred items that take an empirical approach. It is important to note that each study develops, in principle, its own methodology in collecting given information (Wind and Green, 1974). As a general rule, the items used can be divided into three groups following the different themes presented in Table 3.4.

In practice, the usual procedure is to develop a questionnaire incorporating a plurality of scales in these three areas of activities, interests, and opinions, and then reduce the mass of information thus obtained through conventional multivariate analysis. This procedure occurs in two steps:

Table 3.4

**The Three Categories of Investigation in the AIO Approach**

| Activities | Interests | Opinions |
|---|---|---|
| • Work | • Family | • Self |
| • Hobbies | • Home | • Social questions |
| • Evening parties | • Work | • Politics |
| • Going out | • Local life | • Business |
| • Vacation | • Leisure | • Economy |
| • Clubs | • Fashion | • Education |
| • Community life | • Food | • Products |
| • Shopping | • Media | • The future |
| • Sports | • Personal fulfillment/achievement | • Culture |

*Source:* Plummer, J. (1971a), "Learning About Consumers as Real People: The Applications of Psychographic Data," *Montreal Chapter Conference*, Chicago: American Marketing Association, November 1971.

- The first step aims to construct relatively simple but valid questions. On average, between 300 and 500 items are commonly used. Some studies even go beyond that for the sake of completeness (for instance, over 1,000 for DDB Needham in the United States, and nearly 3,000 for the CCA [Center of Advanced Communication], in its first phase of collection). The corresponding tools are the main factorial analysis component or the canonical analysis, which is more innovative and responsive. (The latter is the solution adopted in France by the CSF [see Chapter 4].)
- The second step is to group individuals according to the dimensions highlighted in the previous step. The statistical method is the corresponding cluster analysis; it can be hierarchical or modal.

Figure 3.1 depicts the corresponding analysis. The impact of lifestyle on consumption can then be appreciated by measuring adherence to respective dimensions from factor analysis, raising the corresponding profile to a given group. Table 3.5 gives the labels of 22 general dimensions of lifestyles from a principal components analysis on 300 AIO items (Wells and Tigert, 1971). Table 3.6 presents the profiles of Customer Credit Agricole from typological analysis and a corresponding second direction.

On what level should one engage attitudes, interests, and opinions? Almost all of the companies using a commercial AIO inventory prefer to use typologies: Admittedly simplistic since the individual can be identified only by the mean distance from the center of gravity of the group, a typology nevertheless has the advantage of being more directly operational for defining

Figure 3.1    **Typical Lifestyle Data Collection and Analysis Process**

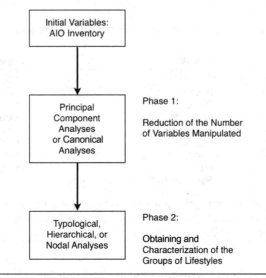

Table 3.5

**General Guidelines for Lifestyles: Examples of Dimensions Obtained by Factor Analysis**

- Sensitivity to price
- The followers of a regimen
- Fashion lovers
- Financial optimism
- Homebody orientation
- The use of credit
- Community orientation
- Sports fans
- Focuses on children
- Cooking
- Stresses order and cleanliness
- Research information
- Self-confidence
- Research on new products
- Leadership of opinion
- Research on new visions
- Tolerant of disorder
- Art lovers
- Enjoys sewing
- Financial satisfaction
- Buys canned food
- Packaging fanatics

*Source:* Adapted from W. Wells and D. Tigert (1971), "Activities, Interests, and Opinions," *Journal of Advertising Research* 2(4), 35.

Table 3.6

## An Example of Use of Lifestyle: The Typology of the Guests of Credit Agricole

1. The Confident

The confident are primarily conservative and fear the uncertainties of technical progress. They are defenders of the institutions: clergy, army, police, and banks. They are very attached to traditions and family.

Money, which represents the value of work is something sacred, and should not be wasted. For this reason, they prefer to pay for their purchases with cash rather than credit card. These are serious customers who have a trusting relationship with their bank. These are mostly older people, who are modest, and living in rural areas. Therefore many of them bank with Credit Agricole.

2. The Dominant

This kind of individual declares a respect for traditions and moral values. Thus, they are very respectful to those who go astray from the straight and narrow. Very ambitious, they want to exercise responsibility, enabling them to impose their ideas. Success for them means earning a lot of money and growing their interests. Moreover, the bank is to offer competent, efficient services. They are very demanding customers, but have a large portfolio. Members of this group are happy people, mature in age, living in small towns. Large farmers belong to this type.

3. Planners

Individualistic in nature, this type is primarily concerned with what benefits themselves and their family. Unambitious, they aspire to a stable job that brings them a steady income. They are very faithful to principles and habits, and relatively repressed especially if it involves money. For the bank, this type of customer is one, that is very difficult, picky, fussy, and tolerates no error. Therefore they prefer to deal with machines, believing that they are more reliable and faster than employees. This group is fairly correlated with objective variables. This group seems composed of rather young people, of middle-income and modest personality.

4. Sidelined

Very attached to individual freedoms, they deny any must indoctrination and everything that creates obligations. Slightly environmental, and rather idealistic, they love to be surrounded by friends, and chat with them to rebuild the world. Full of ambiguities, they also like to enjoy life, even if they lose their income. And this is the problem: frequent adventure, few financial products, except of course the credit card. In this group, there are many senior and middle managers, living in urban areas and rather young in age.

5. Players

These individuals take life at good odds. Very realistic, they know how to use the regulations and laws to their advantage. Money is made to be spent and it's often fun to win. Their ambition is to make the most of life's pleasures, avoiding all possible constraints. For the bank, they represent a friendly customer, even if it is not always easy enough to inform them of bank regulations, they try to enjoy all the services offered by the bank, especially overdrafts and credits, but always with kindness, This group is composed of very young clients, of varied socioprofessional categories. They are found mainly in large cities.

*Source:* Pugnet, Anne, and Jean-Claude Coutin (1982), "Application of a Lifestyle Customer Banking: A specific approach of Credit Agricole," *Revue française du marketing,* No. 90, pp. 55–64.

strategy of positioning or communication. However, individual membership dimensions of lifestyle (that is, the factor score or canonical scores) show an improved predicative quality of consumption as belonging only to a group of lifestyles.

Thus, Valette-Florence and Jolibert (1985 and 1990) showed in two consecutive studies that belonging to a group explained at most 12.4 percent and only once in ten times the nature of ten specific consumption patterns, while adherence to dimensions of corresponding lifestyles could predict up to 14.6 percent of buying behavior, and that result occurred in nine out of ten cases of that kind (see Table 3.7 for more detailed results).

Ultimately, the main interest in AIO studies is the number of relevant dimensions analyzed, which can be adapted to the analysis of specific situations. On the other hand, the diversity of measures employed and the lack of justification for the theoretical foundations on which they are based represent the main criticisms of AIO. In the Anglophone world, there are many AIO and geographic/psychographic segmentation systems maintained by large research organizations and/or large advertising agencies, including VALS2 by SRI, MOSAIC by Experian, ACORN by CACI, Cluster Plus by Donnelly Marketing, RISC, PRIZM$_{NE}$ by Claritas, Global Scan by Backer Spielvogel Bates Worldwide, New Wave by Ogilvy & Mather, and the Lifestyle Study by DDB World Communications Group, Young & Rubicam, Grey, and of course Universal McCann (Shimp, 2010; Solomon, 2009; Weiss, 2000).

## CONCLUSION AND SYNTHESIS

Chapter 3 takes a detailed look at the study of lifestyles based on attitudes and activities.

The use of these two concepts—attitudes and activities—was justified by a theoretical perspective as a criterion for differentiating lifestyles. The concept of attitude has received particular attention given its importance in the behavioral sciences. Research on the three components of attitudes (cognition, knowledge, and emotions) has confirmed the validity of an attitudinal approach to lifestyle studies, particularly because of the implications for understanding behavior. This analysis also helped to justify the use of interests and opinions as a gauge of lifestyles due to their links with the components of attitudes. Similarly, consumers justify the influence of activities in reporting different uses of their time.

Finally, this chapter examines three specific approaches to lifestyle studies that use the concepts of attitudes and activities.

- The first approach focuses primarily on interests but has seen only limited development, given its low explanatory power of purchasing behavior.

Table 3.7

## Comparison of Predictive Power: Dimensions of Lifestyles and Belonging to Groups

| Methods of Consumption* (explained variables) | Dimensions of Lifestyles (explicative variables) | Belonging to Groups (explicative variables) |
|---|---|---|
| 1. Purchases for children | 1. Idealism (4.3%) | |
| | 2. Paternalism and tranquil life (2.2%) $R^2 = 6.5\%$ | |
| 2. Household | 1. Distraction (–) (3.9%) | 1. The taciturn containers |
| | 2. Paternalism and tranquil life (2.7%) $R^2 = 6.6\%$ | $R^2 = 12.4\%$ |
| 3. Modern women | 1. Distraction (7.4%) 2. Fun and easy life (7.2%) $R^2 = 14.6\%$ | |
| 4. Environmentalists | 1. Associative and involving $R^2 = 9.4\%$ | |
| 5. Nonconsumers | 1. Distraction (–) $R^2 = 5.4\%$ | |
| 6. Men's habits | 1. Fun and easy life $R^2 = 4.6\%$ | |
| 7. Hygiene products and maintenance | 1. Aspect Media Information (3.5%) | |
| | 2. Fun and easy life (–) (3.1'%) 3. Distraction (–) (2.7%) $R^2 = 9.3\%$ | |
| 8. Clothes for women | 1. Traditional (–) (4.1%) | |
| | 2. Distractive media (2.7'%) $R^2 = 6.8\%$ | |
| 9. Young men | 1. Traditionalism $R^2 = 3.4\%$ | |
| 10. Young women, low consumption | | |

*Source:* Valette-Florence and Jolibert (1990), "Social Values, AIO, and Consumption Patterns: Exploratory Findings," *Journal of Business Research,* 20(2), 118.

*Please see Chapter 5 for a discussion of the method of obtaining the signification and modes consumption.

- The second focuses on the research benefits and attitudes developed during specific purchase situations and seems too specific to be generalized to larger groups of purchase categories.
- The third, more commonly known as AIO (Activities, Interests, Opinions) approaches, view themselves as the most general and comprehensive ap-

proaches to lifestyle studies. They describe the lifestyle of individuals in relation to their business, their interests, and their attitudes toward leisure, work, and consumption—all within the social and societal environment in which they operate. The generality of AIO suggested they would be a useful tool in a large number of specific tests situations. However, the very same characteristics—AIO's diverse and sweeping nature, along with a lack of clearly defined theoretical foundations for the approach—has led to considerable criticism.

That is why these approaches have been replaced by more sophisticated approaches, mentioned in the previous chapter, that center on the identification of cultural influences. Although AIO inventories have not been abandoned completely, this shift defines the approach of French lifestyles to different features developed in the following chapter.

# 4

# French Approaches

While the preceding chapter has put the emphasis on the lifestyle approachs focused on attitudes and activities so common in North America, this chapter aims to show the specific French approaches that developed around the theme of lifestyle. All of these approaches, although different in their operation, pursue the same objective of furnishing, by the observation of the sociocultural population, an explanatory framework for overall behavior. They stress the importance of identifying cultural values that define each group of individuals. This reference to social values gives the French approach deeper insights into behavior than the present American AIO inventories.

The French approaches come mainly from three organizations: COFREMCA (a French company specializing in market research and lifestyle trends), the CCA (Center for Advanced Communication), and CREDOC (Research Center for the Study and Observation of Living). They differ by the degree of importance they place on values, thus justifying specific presentations. Indeed, COFREMCA (Section 1) seeks to study these values directly through looking at trends, while the CCA (Section 2) is concerned with more inherited and sociocultural values. Finally, CREDOC (Section 3) includes those values relative to living conditions and social attitudes. To conclude this overview of studies of lifestyles, we will present a final section (Section 4), consisting of two other neighboring approaches on a methodological level, followed by the Agorametric in France and the approach used to carry out the *Belgian Socioscope*.

## Section 1: Studies of COFREMCA

The work of COFREMCA was strongly inspired by Yankelovich (1971) in the United States and has revealed thirty-one sociocultural values. After determining that what was published could apply to systems of consumer values, Yankelovich developed a measurement method called the "Yankelovich

Monitor." The study, first conducted around 1970, was repeated following the evolution of the value systems in the United States. A derivative of the "Monitor" has been in use since 1972 in the United Kingdom by the research company Taylor Nelson Sofres (TNS).

In the mid-1960s, the COFREMCA teams in France and Yankelovich's teams in the United States exchanged information on the transformations of Western societies, not only in terms of economic and technological change but especially in terms of the customs and values people shared. This exchange led COFREMCA to make a few changes to its own approach and to consult with the Nelson Company (De Vulpian, 1974). The data in Table 4.1, borrowed from Susan Douglas's research (1978), compare Yankelovich, COFREMCA, and Taylor Nelson. It follows from this comparison that certain trends are common in the United States, France, and the United Kingdom, while others concern only a country or two.

Unlike the Yankelovich study, which had a mainly typological orientation (meaning the classification of types was based on common traits), COFREMCA has sought to highlight the current sociocultural trends, following fifty of them (Demuth, 1978, 1980) according to a system called 3SC (whose full title is COFREMCA: A System for Monitoring Social and Cultural Trends).

Emerging sociocultural trends represent a change of a cultural value in all or part of society. This change in mindset must reflect considerable depth and frequency in areas of social behavior. The 3SC is designed for:

- early detection of sociocultural trends and the eventual emergence of new trends, understanding the meaning experienced (for consumers, workers, etc.) for each of the trends and changes in trends;
- understanding the real-life significance (for consumers, workers, etc.) of each of the trends and modification of trends;
- determining the method that we use to understand events that influence consumption;
- measuring the influence of each of the trends in the different segments of the population;
- identifying threats and opportunities afforded by a particular sociocultural change for consumers.

Overall, each course will measure what sociologists call the "total social" phenomenon, that is, a phenomenon with a certain sociological gravity in terms of importance and evolution. Five levels of analysis are captured in each stream:

1. the evolution of values;
2. the evolution of behavior and attitudes;

Table 4.1

## Comparative Study of Sociocultural Patterns in the United States, France, and the UK: Trends

**1. Attitudes regarding a society of abundance**

Common tendencies
- Concerned about appearance
- Concerned about health
- Expression of personality
- Personal creativity
- Give meaning to professional life

| Trends | Country |
|---|---|
| New forms of materialism | United States |
| Self-expression about the social and cultural world | United States |
| Anti-materialism | France |
| Decline of personal achievement | France |
| Antimaterialism | United Kingdom |

**2. Sensation seeking and signifiers**

Common tendencies
- Sensitivity to beauty in their environment
- Polysensualism
- Introspection
- Openness to novelty and change

| Trends | Country |
|---|---|
| Mysticism | United States |
| Marginal differentiation | United States |
| Self-control | France |
| Openness to others | France |
| Concern about the environment | United Kingdom |
| Neo-romanticism | United Kingdom, United States |

**3. Reaction against modern life**

Common tendencies
- Simplification of life
- Return to nature
- Ethnicity

| Trends | Country |
|---|---|
| Greater solidarity | United States |
| Reaction against manipulation | France |
| Consumer skepticism | United Kingdom |
| Greater confidence in technology than traditions | United States, United Kingdom |
| Place less importance on grandeur and power | United States, France |

**4. Penetration of new values**

Common tendencies
- Less differentiation between the sexes
- Sexual liberalism

| Trends | Country |
|---|---|
| Individualistic religion | United States |
| Return to stimulants | United States, United Kingdom |
| Life oriented to the present | United States, United Kingdom |
| Hedonism | United States, France |
| Moral development | United States, France |

**5. Decline of family-oriented life**

Common tendencies
- Rejection of authority
- Less attachment to order

| Trends | Country |
|---|---|
| Focus on family | United States |
| Decline of rank, status, or standing | France |
| Decline of chauvinism | United Kingdom |
| Chauvinism | United Kingdom |
| Anti-Americanism | United Kingdom |
| Remoteness of the family | United States |
| Female orientation toward careers | United States, United Kingdom |

*Source:* Douglas, S. (1978). "The Analysis of Lifestyle and Current Sociocultural Problems and Future Prospects," *Encyclopedia du marketing.* Vol. 1, *Consumer Behavior.* Editions Techniques, p. 3.

3. the customs, defined as large collective rhythms that shape the lives of a cohort (e.g., the majority of the French rise between 7 A.M. and 8:35 A M.);
4. the "paradigms" or underlying worldviews; and
5. the social fabric, or the patterns of relationships between people (presence or absence of social ties).

COFREMCA further improved its tracking tool of sociocultural trends, which now amount to over fifty-five. From a historical perspective, they are presented in Table 4.2 as being identified either before or after 1970.

The methodology used by the 3SC device deals with the following four elements:

1. a posteriori analysis, somewhat socio-historical, of the needs, aspirations, and motivations of the French in many different sectors. Made by COFREMCA since the 1970s, this secondary analysis is used to identify, understand, and trace the evolution of existing trends until such time as new sociocultural trends emerge;
2. a detailed monograph analysis describing each course and its impact on communication and work;
3. in-depth surveys, performed annually to detect possible changes in trends or newly emerging trends;
4. an annual survey with a representative quota sample of the French population (2,500 French men and women). It aims to describe current social and cultural developments, their penetration in various segments of the population, and the ways in which they are statistically related to phenomena that affect users of the system.

The questionnaire in this last phase uses the AIO type inventory. It consists of five sections totaling approximately 300 items that assess:

1. the position of interviewees on the current measured scales of five items. Each sociocultural trend is apprehended by a series of items that reveal a modern attitude. The same battery, except in cases of adding or deleting the current trends, is used each year.
2. manifestations of common items, which are fixed by the news and interests of members.
3. typical activities, media, and principal supports.
4. through thirty specific questions, the consumption of specific products, asked by companies endorsing the inquiry.
5. sociodemographic characteristics.

Table 4.2

**Identification of Current Sociocultural Trends Before and After 1970**

| Sociocultural trends identified and described before 1970 | | Sociocultural trends identified and described since 1970 | | |
|---|---|---|---|---|
| 1 | Decline of rank, status, or standing | 1 | T | New standing |
| 2 | Marginal differentiation | | | |
| 3 | Self-expression | 4 | | Decline the primacy of economic security |
| 5 | Personal creativity | | | |
| 6 | Self-control | | | |
| 7 | Professional fulfillment | 8 | A | Novelty seeking |
| | | 8 | B | Openness to change |
| 9 | Rejection of the requesting authority | | | |
| 10 | Less attachment to order | | | |
| 11 | Open to others | | | |
| 12 | Devaluation of national supremacy | | | |
| 13 | Decline of materialism | | | |
| 15 | Hedonistic | 15 | N | New hedonism |
| 16 | Reduced need for achievement | 16 | N | Achievement |
| 17 | Sexual liberalism | | | |
| 18 | Anti-manipulation | 18 | N | Publicity hound |
| 19 | Antisocial constraints | | | |
| 20 | Simplifying life | | | |
| 21 | Sensitivity to nature | | | |
| 22 | Sensitivity to lifestyle | 23 | N | Competition |
| 24 | Need solid rooting | 24 | T | Ethnicity-Folklore |
| 25 | Polysensualism | | | |
| 26 | Intraception | | | |
| 27 | Irrational | | | |
| 28 | Less differentiation of the sexes | | | |
| 30 | Worry about personal appearance | | | |
| 31 | Concern for their health and shape | 31 | A | Concern for their health |
| | | 32 | N | Integration of the term |
| | | 33 | | Sensitivity to violence |
| | | 34 | | Sensitivity to form |
| | | 35 | | Desire for risk |
| | | 37 | | Collective emotions |
| | | 41 | | Integration of uncertainty and complexity |
| | | 44 | | Obsessed with the natural |
| | | 45 | | Confusion |
| | | 46 | | Expanded mental abilities |
| | | 47 | | Emotional experience |
| | | 48 | | Instinct-Intuition |
| | | 49 | | Connective |
| | | 50 | | Hierarchical |
| | | 51 | | Vitality |
| | | 52 | | Social spontaneity |
| | | 53 | | Strategic opportunism |
| | | 54 | | Open citizenship |
| | | 55 | | Me-We |
| | | 56 | | Need to feel |
| | | 57 | | Playing with signs |

*Source:* COFREMCA.

Figure 4.1   **COFREMCA's Sociocultural System** (1978)

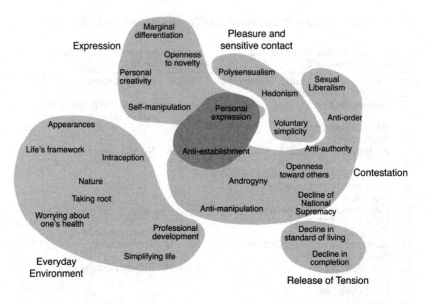

*Source:* Demuth (1978).

On the data collected, COFREMCA performs two types of analysis:

1. For each course, individuals belonging to the advanced quartile are identified. The advanced quartile includes 25 percent of individuals who obtain the highest scores on scales of attitudes that match the sociocultural current and, therefore, show the highest sensitivity to this trend;
2. Factor analysis of multiple matches is then undertaken each year (accession of 2,500 people at the fifty-five streams identified). The multidimensional analysis of similarities (INDSCAL program) was originally used but was replaced by correspondence analysis. It can distinguish between active variables (trends that are well established) and passive or illustrative variables (emerging trends, for example), as well as place the individuals in the perceptual space that was obtained.

In 1976, for example, the projection onto two axes of the twenty-six dimensions taken into account at that time provided the above map (Figure 4.1), which is a structural scheme of sociocultural change in France in 1976 (Demuth, 1978). Note that the search for novelty and a marginal differentiation are very close and oppose the declining taste for completion and standard of living. Figure 4.2 shows the sociocultural map up to 1991.

Regarding this analysis, two minor reservations are worth mentioning. The first, shared by Demuth (1980), is inherent in the method and consists in the projection in two dimensions of a multidimensional reality. The score on each of the trends offsets this loss of information related to the method of correspondence analysis of different segments of the population selected. Thus, the position in each segment returns the equivalent of an axis of correspondence analysis factor, using simplicity to increase understanding. The second problem is the arbitrary choice of the top 25 percent (why not 26 percent?) of individuals with the highest scores on trends. For each course, 75 percent of the information collected about other individuals is thus lost without the use of the segmentation approach developed by COFREMCA.

Initially, COFREMCA also performed a typological, or trait-based, analysis of all scores obtained by individuals on variables in the original survey, mainly on behalf of the French Institute of Demographics. In 1976, nine sociocultural types were identified (Table 4.3). At the time, they were grouped into three broad categories: the innovators, the traditionalists, and the indifferent.

However, the use of cluster analysis for the achievement of the preceding groups raises some problems:

- First, as in all methods of nonhierarchical typological analysis, the approach is heuristic; i.e., we search for good solutions using trial-and-error techniques.
- Secondly, the TYPOL program employed uses the amount of movement between two groups, which depends on the Euclidean distance between the centers of these groups.

However, the variable analyses are correlated—two trends can overlap—and use another metric offsetting correlations between variables, which could lead to the formation of other groups. We should call into account the displacement between groups A and B, where $N_A$ and $N_B$ represent the number of individuals in each group, in the expression:

$$\Delta_{AB} = 2d_{AB} \times \frac{NaxNb}{Na + Nb} \ .$$

This describes the Euclidean distance between centers of groups A and B.

Figure 4.2   **COFREMCA's Sociocultural System** (1991)

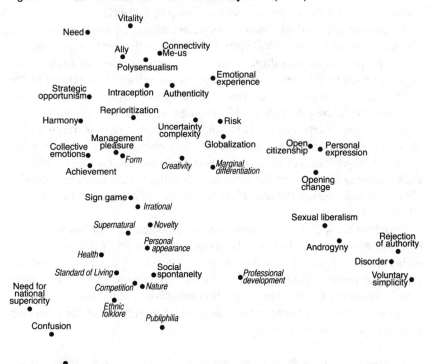

*Source:* COFREMCA.

*Note:* We thank COFREMCA and director Patrick Degrave for allowing us to copy the documents he was kind enough to send us.

---

Table 4.3

**Consolidation of New Sociocultural Types Proposed by COFREMCA**

1. Four types of modernist innovators:
   - The pioneer
   - The innovative egocentric
   - The innovative sociocentric
   - The good consumer
2. A central type:
   - The marshes
3. Four outdated types:
   - The defender of things held together by open mindedness
   - The nostalgic protester (indifferent)
   - The nostalgic moderate
   - The extremist nostalgic (reactionary)

*Source:* Demuth and Neirac (1976).

To level these difficulties, COFREMCA has abandoned the previous un-satisfactory typological approach, focusing instead on measuring people's adherence to different trends in sociocultural analysis. The result is an original and innovative approach, the sociography, consisting of the pro-jection of individuals interviewed on correspondence analyses of the first three axes (a combination of two or three waves of surveys of nearly 10,000 people). The corresponding map is then divided into sixteen squares, each representing 6.5 percent of the sample, which is therefore indicative of the penetration of trends in each population (e.g., those trends at the top of the map in Figure 4.2 have a high level of penetration in any cluster at the top of the map). For a given segment (men, women, youth, etc.) or to a specific question, it is possible to discern the sociocultural leanings in the group by looking at a specific index in each cell penetration. As an illustration, Table 4.4 demonstrates this point with shocking findings on the likelihood of spending money on a whim (9 percent in 1993, restored to a base 100 on the total population). In conjunction with the sociocultural map presented in Figure 4.2, this table displays many contrasts, for example, between the sociography 6 (index 170) and sociography 7 and 11 (respective indices 48 and 96).

Because of the presentation of the sociocultural trends made by De Vulpian in 1974, it has been possible to obtain information on the works undertaken by Demuth (1978, 1980), such as the ones in which David Genzel (1983) refers to the magazine *Elle,* the launch of the newspaper *Football Eleven*, the beer brand George Killian, and the retail company Carrefour. In *Marketing Mix*, Millon (1987) reports a study by COFREMCA of the launch of the card Phox. In the mid-1970s, the observations of COFREMCA on changes in French society distanced it from the other approaches in terms of lifestyles. These other approaches corresponded well to the society of the 1960s and 1970s, when a backlash occurred against the traditions and conventions of the past. COFREMCA turned toward a holistic understanding of lifestyles, emphasiz-ing fewer and finer behavioral changes in the population, particularly through the measure of sociocultural items (over 300) and sociocultural trends (55). The approach of advertising expert Bernard Cathelat, one of the founders of the Center for Advanced Communication, is more fully developed in the next section.

## SECTION 2: THE CENTER FOR ADVANCED COMMUNICATION (CCA)

While COFREMCA detects the current sociocultural analysis through the study of motivation, the CCA seeks to understand through various methods

Table 4.4

**Sociographics* Illustration of the COFREMCA**

**General Sociograph**

|     | 2   | 1   |     |
| --- | --- | --- | --- |
| 6   | 5   | 4   | 3   |
| 10  | 9   | 8   | 7   |
| 14  | 13  | 12  | 11  |
|     | 16  | 15  |     |

**Question Posed**

I find it shocking to spend too much money at this time (9% in 1993 to 100 basis total echelon).

|     | 95  | 106 |     |
| --- | --- | --- | --- |
| 170 | 79  | 60  | 94  |
| 169 | 108 | 30  | 48  |
| 133 | 108 | 105 | 96  |
|     | 113 | 78  |     |

*Source:* COFREMCA.
*The sociography assessed in conjunction with the sociocultural map presented in Figure 4.2.

they call "future latency" (Matricon, Burke, and Cathelat, 1974) to note the evolution of predictable behaviors and products. CCA's methodological innovations, presented below, permit an improved ability to capture these "latent psychological futures."

The CCA analyzes social imbalances more than any other approach. The method is based on the diagnostic of two competing forces: the intensity of behavior, habits, and stereotypes, and dynamic trends revealed by expectations and desires.

Between 1970 and 1973, the CCA's approach evolved relatively empirically. The definition of lifestyle as a stream of ideas, attitudes, and psychosocial values in constant evolution was abandoned due to its lack of precision. The CCA now uses three concepts in its definition of lifestyles:

• cultural trends
• social structures
• sociostyles

The cultural trends lead to dominant forms, ideal product images, or utopian values that are their manifestations (Matricon, Burke, and Cathelat, 1974). This view therefore explains the methods employed to detect cultural trends. In modifying the structure and intensity of a society's value system, CCA defines a culture in evolution.

The social structure is defined as a static configuration, representing a transitory slice of life at any given time in a limited space. The sociostyles represent the transition to reality and the embodiment of cultural trends in terms of attitudes and opinions, whether regarding the product or the consumer.

The CCA system of lifestyles is a multipronged method of inquiry that gathers and interprets information by studying social structures, cultural leanings, typologies, and the dynamic evolution of trends (Matricon, Burke, and Cathelat, 1974).

The centerpiece of this approach articulates the analysis of sociocultural trends directly, along with cultural norms, and dynamically modulates the French society. Cathelat (1977) defines cultural trends as "macrosociological trends, heavy modifying trends which are dynamic in nature, structure and intensity in the value system of the whole culture." For this reason, the sociocultural flow overrides the CCA approach regarding cultural values, giving them more weight.

From a practical standpoint, CCA studies can be divided into two main phases:

- the identification of sociocultural trends most featured in the evolution of French society through qualitative methods
- the constitution of a typology of individuals, called *sociostructure,* describing social structure through the use of quantitative tools. It was established in 1977 and has been updated approximately every two years since.

Let us first identify the sociocultural trends. During several brainstorming sessions (called the "Epsys") between 1970 and 1973, the CCA developed a list of thirteen sociocultural trends. Each trend reflects one of two opposing ends on the ideological spectrum, resulting in the identification of twenty-six cultural values. (See Table 4.5 for these trends and their evaluation over the last ten years). More recently, international studies measuring CCA's now twenty-six values have been divided into thirteen bipolar trends, such as individualism on one hand, and integration on the other hand. These thirteen are presented in Table 4.6. Participants took a test that identified how their conscious desires change with the demands of daily life and social contingencies. We note, however, that the trends and sociocultural identities are

Table 4.5

**Evolution of Sociocultural Trends from 1974 to 1986**

| Percentage of adherence | | | | | | Number | | Percentage of adherence | | | | |
|---|---|---|---|---|---|---|---|---|---|---|---|---|
| 1974 | 1977 | 1980 | 1984 | 1986 | | | | 1986 | 1984 | 1980 | 1977 | 1974 |
| 54.4 | 77.9 | 82.5 | 87 | 88.4 | Passivity (tranquility) | 1 | Dynamic (the fight) | 11.6 | 13 | 17.5 | 22.1 | 45.6 |
| 57.8 | 62.1 | 81.4 | 85.7 | 88.3 | Refocusing (home) | 2 | Extension (outside) | 11.7 | 14.3 | 18.6 | 37.9 | 42.2 |
| 53.5 | 73.5 | 65.9 | 85.6 | 87 | Transcendence (belief) | 3 | Commonality (to live here and now) | 13 | 14.4 | 34.1 | 26.5 | 46.5 |
| 60.5 | 71.7 | 74.8 | 81.1 | 81.3 | Individualism (private) | 4 | Integration (the collective) | 18.7 | 18.9 | 25.2 | 25.3 | 39.5 |
| 50.6 | 52.0 | 69.7 | 61.2 | 69.7 | Symbolism (showing) | 5 | Realism (feeling) | 30.3 | 38.8 | 30.3 | 48 | 49.4 |
| 55.1 | 57.9 | 57.0 | 66.8 | 68.2 | Hierarchy (the boss) | 6 | Cooperation (participation) | 31.8 | 33.2 | 43 | 42.1 | 44.9 |
| 52.6 | 32.7 | 52 | 63.3 | 66.9 | Modeling (normalized) | 7 | Originality (affecting) | 33.1 | 36.7 | 48 | 67.3 | 47.4 |
| 56.2 | 55.5 | 56.3 | 65.1 | 64.7 | Discipline (order) | 8 | Liberals (suppleness) | 35.3 | 34.9 | 43.7 | 44.5 | 43.8 |
| 52.3 | 50.6 | 56.2 | 60 | 64.7 | Mosaic (the company) | 9 | Monolithic (consistency) | 35.3 | 40 | 43.8 | 49.4 | 47.7 |
| 52.0 | 63.0 | 65.7 | 59 | 60.7 | Nature (natural) | 10 | Technique (technology) | 39.3 | 41 | 34.3 | 37 | 48 |
| 42.0 | 60.8 | 64 | 53.5 | 53 | Hedonism (pleasure) | 11 | Functionalism (utility) | 47 | 46.5 | 36 | 39.2 | 58 |
| 44.2 | 59.0 | 60.6 | 51.5 | 50.1 | Being yourself (belief) | 12 | Materialism (owning) | 49.9 | 48.5 | 39.4 | 41 | 55.8 |
| 55.0 | 53.8 | 47.5 | 56.9 | 50.1 | Permanence (stability) | 13 | Metamorphosis (movement) | 49.9 | 43.1 | 52.5 | 46.2 | 45 |

*Source:* Dubois (1987), 50.

Table 4.6

**The Thirteen Cultural Streams Identified by the CCA in France**

 1. Trend toward mosaic, diversification, and differentiation in the personality.
 2. Integration of the trend, participation, solidarity, and acceptance of social life.
 3. Tendency to change, progress toward innovation, recycling.
 4. Trend toward hedonism, pleasure, sensuality, enjoyment, and beauty.
 5. Commoditization trend by everyday interest, toward concrete values.
 6. Tendency to liberalism, tolerance, permissiveness, the relaxation of customs, freedom to debate.
 7. Trend of cooperation, sharing of power, responsibilities, benefits, freedom to debate.
 8. Trend toward nature, simplicity, rusticity, and authenticity.
 9. Refocusing trend, turning in on itself (into a cocoon) toward security, homecoming, and life in a small circle.
10. Trend to be passive, quiet, peaceful, nonviolent; movement toward disengagement and simplification.
11. Trend toward symbolism, dreams, evasion, subjectivity, and consumption of imaginary visual representations.
12. Trend toward modeling, the absorption of models and images of social dynamism in accord.
13. Trend toward materialism, consumption, expense, to a material orientation.

*Source:* Cathelat and Matricon (1976).

somewhat different from those that COFREMCA found in a similar context. If one ignores a sometimes esoteric vocabulary, we see that certain sociocultural trends are complementary, others contradictory. This idea led to the second quantitative phase now presented, whose aim is to establish a typology of individuals according to the similarities in their views.

Each of the cultural trends can be tied to key issues and streams of thought. Surveys and questions are designed to reveal the behavior, interests, and opinions common to a group. Specifically, types can be distinguished based on themes, trends, and the level of an individual's personal involvement as evidenced by their answers. Table 4.7, borrowed from Christian Lhermie (see his 1984 dissertation), illustrates the different levels of these issues. Typically, individuals are shown pictures or drawings and asked to project the attitude of the person depicted in the image (see Cathelat, 1990, pp. 269–275, for current designs).

The statistical treatment used to interpret the results involves correspondence analysis, graph visualization on two main factors, and the projection of the initial variables to characterize the areas and define them. Cathelat (1977) notes that we obtain a graph or image that illustrates clustering of values, attitudes, opinions, and other leanings from the survey results. Trends in lifestyles from year to year can be noted in observable changes in the

Table 4.7

**Questions Revealing Level of Involvement, Derived from Work on Typologies by Christian Lhermie** (1984)

|  | Current Status | Future Trend |
| --- | --- | --- |
| Personal Involvement | Currently, for you . . . *(followed by the proposal to be assessed)* | According to you, it will become more . . . *(follow-up proposals to be evaluated)* |
| Social Involvement | Currently, everyone . . . *(followed by the proposal to be assessed)* | For the world, it will be more . . . *(follow-up proposals to be evaluated)* |

*Source:* Lhermie, C. (1984), The Lifestyles Matter in Marketing, PhD Thesis, State of Science Management, University of Paris-I, Pantheon-Sorbonne, p. 92.

data. Shifts in psychological geography, according to Cathelat, provide a clear sign of "the evolution of civilization." The screening of individuals in this way allows researchers to distinguish characteristic groups within French lifestyles.

Initially, the 1977 study of 4,500 people helped to highlight differences along the following two lines:

- the horizontal axis between the values of order, discipline, passivity, and individualism, and the values of movement, progress, originality, and liberalism; and
- the vertical axis between the values of positivism, realism, hierarchy, and individualism, and the values of sensualism, cooperation, symbolism, hedonism, and nature.

Three groups were identified:

- "Utilitarian" (20 percent)
- "Adventurous" (38 percent)
- "Centrist" (42 percent)

Figure 4.3 represents the mapping of these axes and groups.

After more precisely segmenting the French population, which the preceding three sociostructures did not permit, the CCA defined eleven exterior sociostyles or lifestyles from an analysis of attitudes, opinions, pastimes, and behaviors. Between May and June of 1975, they conducted a multiregional study on 1,300 men and women.

Figure 4.3  **Map of CCA Lifestyles**

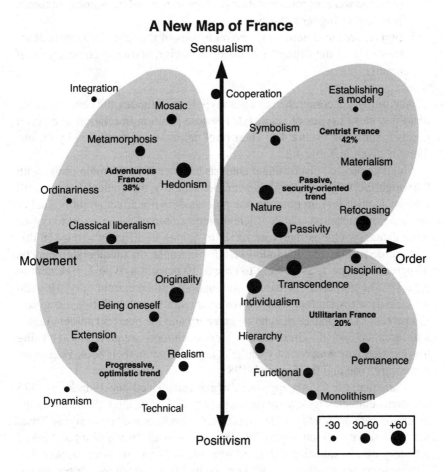

## A New Map of France

Source: Cathelat (1977).

The self-administered questionnaire was composed of:

- 250 items of the AIO type on the thirteen sociocultural fluxes;
- 200 other factors, such as frequency of use and preference for certain media, types of household equipment used, and sociodemographic characteristics of various behaviors (leisure, savings, family).

Responses to attitude items were obtained on a five-point scale, and the results were subjected to two types of analysis:

- *factor analysis* on 250 items of attitude, which verified that many factors obtained were regrouped within thirteen trends and the number of trends was neither higher nor lower;
- two *typological analyses*, one on modes of thought (250 items of attitude), and the other on items of behavior, showing consistency of results.

Accordingly, a comprehensive third typology (attitudes and behaviors) has identified eleven types of sociostyles, whose position in relation to cultural trends is shown in Figure 4.4. Their brief definition, as furnished by the authors, is given in Table 4.8.

Finally, note that discriminant analysis has identified the main issues with the weighting, to be reconstituted with a minimum of typological items overall (eleven sociostyles). In practice, the process does not affect an individual of one type. It determines the coefficient membership of each person to one or more category. One is therefore likely to belong to different groups in different proportions. For one individual, for example, the membership may be 65 percent to type 1, 24 percent to type 3, 10 percent to type 7, 1 percent to type 11. The numerous possible combinations produce ambiguity: How do we classify a respondent whose answers are consistent with two categories (50 percent of responses match one category and the other 50 percent match a different category)? These results occur even more frequently when using the questionnaire proposed by Cathelat and Mermet in their book *Vous et les Français* ("You and the French," 1985).

In practice, the CCA's approach, which established benchmarks in 1975 and then conducted follow-up surveys every two years after 1980, shows the evolution (or appearance) of these different mindsets and social styles. Thus, the 1984 survey, which covered 3,500 persons over fifteen years and asked a battery of 150 questions, defined five mindsets and fourteen sociostyles. The same survey repeated in 1986 helped highlight a third axis opposing the values of elitism, liberalism, and technocratic interventionism with values of mass, support and cooperation. Yet, reports in 1985 by Cathelat state: "The factor analysis usually defines a multidimensional space that has three main components." (Cathelat, 1985a, p. 21).

This axis reconstructs 18 percent of the variance, while the horizontal axis (adventure to conservatism or movement to order) reconstructs 44 percent in return, and the vertical axis (asceticism to sensualisn) reconstructs 22 percent (Cathelat, 1990).

Thus, six sociostyles of the fourteen are attracted by the pole of elitism: copiers, show-offs, defensive people, vigilantes (all three of the mentality of egocentrisms), profiteers, and the enterprising. Overall, the evolution between

93

Figure 4.4 **The CCA Sociostyles and Their Relation to Cultural Trends**

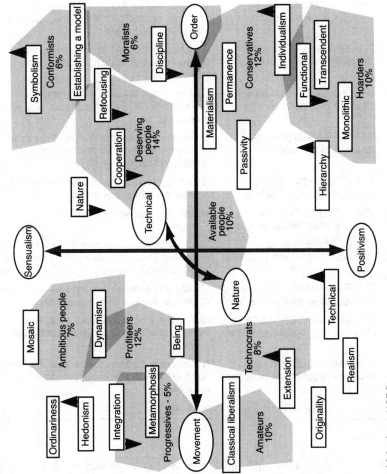

*Source:* Cathelat and Matricon (1976).

Table 4.8

**Presentation of Eleven Lifestyles Proposed in the Third Typology** (1976)

| | |
|---|---|
| A. THE AVAILABLE (undifferentiated mental structure) | Attitudes are heterogeneous and traditional; respects customs, defers to elders. |
| B. THE HOARDERS (mental structure of utilitarianism) | Looking for a utilitarian lifestyle; economic; practical, respectful of traditions, habits, and the established order. |
| C. CONSERVATIVES (mental structure of utilitarianism) | Attached to the past, order, saving and consumer accumulation, liabilities, and resignation. |
| D. THE MORALISTS (mental structure of passive safety) | Guards order; is puritanical, strict, authoritarian, tradition-conscious, and anti-innovative. |
| E. CONFORMISTS (mental structure of passive safety) | In search of safety, conscious of personal status, correctness, shuns innovation, relies on self and family. |
| F. THE DESERVING (mental structure of passive safety) | Seeks to integrate social and personal status; concerned with image and conformity. |
| G. THE AMBITIOUS (mental structure of optimistic progress) | Materialistic, active and dynamic. |
| H. PROFITEERS (mental structure of optimistic progress) | Values property, consumer image, standing in society. Successful example of pleasure-seeking modernist. |
| I. THE PROGRESSIVES (mental structure of optimistic progress) | Consumers of ideas; are innovative, cultured, curious activists with rich social life. |
| J. THE TECHNOCRATS (mental structure of optimistic progress) | Active, dynamic, aggressive, ambitious workers in search of social and personal success. |
| K. THE AMATEURS (mental structure of optimistic progress) | Nonactivists, hedonists, liberal and tolerant, open to innovation without personal involvement. |

*Source:* Cathelat and Matricon (1976), 47–48.

1985 and 1987 of different families remains low, as shown in Table 4.9. Thus, the most important amplitude stems from the examples passing from 10.6 percent to 9 percent of the total population. Figure 4.5 presents an illustrative map of lifestyles in 1988. For a complete description, see various works by Cathelat (1985 and 1990).

These quantitative analyses, leading to the achievement of sociostyles, are the centerpiece of the system advocated by the CCA. Conducted carefully,

Table 4.9

**Evolution of Different Sociostyles over a Two-Year Period** (in percent)

| Mentalities | 1985 | 1987 | Evolution (1987/1985) | 1985 | 1987 | Evolution (1987/1985) | Sociostyles |
|---|---|---|---|---|---|---|---|
| Activist | 13.3 | 14 | 0.7 | 3.2 | 3 | −0.2 | Political Activists |
| | | | | 10.1 | 11 | +0.9 | Enterprisers |
| Materialist | 26.8 | 24 | −2.8 | 7.9 | 7 | −0.9 | Utilitarians |
| | | | | 10.6 | 9 | −1.6 | Coipiers |
| | | | | 8.3 | 8 | −0.3 | Attentives |
| Rigoristic Centrist | 20.1 | 20 | −0.1 | 5.1 | 5 | −0.1 | Conservatives |
| | | | | 6.5 | 6 | −0.5 | Moralists |
| | | | | 8.5 | 9 | +0.5 | Responsible |
| Progressive | 17.3 | 20 | +2.7 | 5.8 | 6.5 | +0.7 | Libertarians |
| | | | | 5.7 | 6.5 | +0.8 | Progressives |
| | | | | 5.8 | 7 | +1.2 | Profiteers |
| Egocentric | 22.5 | 22 | −0.5 | 6.5 | 6.5 | — | Show-offs |
| | | | | 7.3 | 7 | −0.3 | Defensive People |
| | | | | 8.7 | 8.5 | −0.2 | Vigilantes |

*Sources:* Brochand and Lendrevie (1983); Dubois (1987); Mermet (1985).

their methodology continued to improve over the years. Valette-Florence (1989b, pp. 24–25) presented the methods in outline form, but Cathelat (1990, part 4, pp. 241–391) gave a more detailed analysis. The main steps involving the collection of data and various statistical analyses are summarized here.

The collection of information is done in two phases:

• Phase 1: The first stage, which aims to create tools for sociocultural reference, is called Scanner 1. It is very intense because it takes about two and a half hours to cover several thousand variables (around 3,000 questions and 1,500 to 4,000 people). The wealth of information collected then allows subsequent analysis that yields descriptive sociostyles. This first phase is very important because it reveals the means of discriminant analysis to reduce the questionnaire used in the second stage.

• Phase 2: The second stage, called Scanner Extension, then uses a shorter questionnaire (eighty to one hundred questions). Discriminant analyses are used to select the variables (questions) that most differentiated the groups in the first phase (the sociostyles). The corresponding classification functions can then directly affect the individual groups in their responses to these different

Figure 4.5    **Map of CCA Sociostyles**

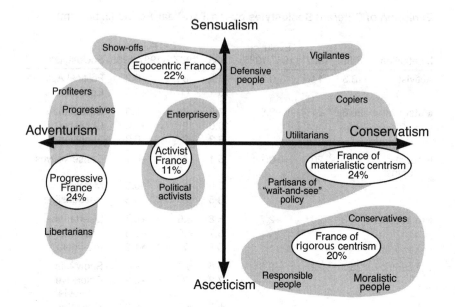

*Source:* Brochand and Lendrevie (1983).

questions asked outside of the second phase, which allows the assignment of individuals to statistical social styles found in the previous step. Given the lesser burden of the collection, additional issues concerning the media and various types of purchases and consumer markets can be added. The number of respondents is also higher (4,000 to 20,000 individuals).

Phase 1 is used because it allows calibration to define the social styles. Given its difficulty, it is carried out only every five years. In the meantime, approximately every two years, Phase 2 functions as a way to update information (thereby allowing for a revision of percentage terms) of the various groups highlighted in the initial study. The questions used are not identical. As a mere updating, they represent only a few questions (eighty to one hundred). In contrast, the study foundation (Phase 1) is supported by a comprehensive questionnaire, which is sufficient in seven main areas, spanning all sectors of life—private, social, and economic (Table 4.10).

Statistical analysis takes the mass of information that has been gathered and boils it down into data suitable for creating a typology of sociostyles. Table 4.11 presents the corresponding sequence of treatments and targets researched at each step. The number of dimensions generally obtained is included as well.

Table 4.10

**Private, Social, and Economic Areas for Investigation Addressed by the Founder** (CCA)

| 7 Principal Domains | Degree of Importance |
|---|---|
| 1. Private Life | |
| 2. Professional Life | 1/3 of questions |
| 3. Social Life | |
| 4. Political Life | |
| 5. Culture and Information | 1/3 of questions |
| 6. Trade and Economy of Household Consumption | 1/3 of questions |
| 7. Major Markets of Products and Services | |

*Source:* Adapted from Cathelat, B. (1990), *Socio-Styles systèmes*. Paris: Les Éditions d'Organisation, 288–289.

Table 4.11

**Sequential Structure of Statistical Analyses at CCA**

| Step Order | Nature of the Steps | Research Objectives | Number of Dimensions Obtained |
|---|---|---|---|
| 1. | A hundred analyses and principal elements, each one referring to an ensemble of about 60 to 100 variables. | • Reducing the number of variables to manipulate. <br>• Structuring the material of given data. | 300 to 400 psychological or behavioral factors. |
| 2. | Orthodox analysis studying the incidence of psychological factors compared with behavioral factors. | • Reducing the number of dimensions (factors) to manipulate. <br>• Structuring the nature of factors obtained during the previous step. <br>• Explaining the behavioral factors by psychological factors. | 20 to 40 orthodox axes or psychobehavioral meta-factors. |
| 3. | Mixed typological and hierarchical analysis (dynamic swarm, then ascending classification) referring to orthodox scores obtained during the second step. | • Obtaining groups of individuals who share the same beliefs with respect to the orthodox dimensions obtained in the second step. <br>• Progressive differentiation and refining at the level of the classification tree. | From 3 to 6 mentalities and from 10 to 20 sociostyles in the function at the desired level of perceptiveness. |
| 4. | Analysis of simple connections crossing sociostyles with sociocultural flux or the orthodox axes (variables that have become discrete). | • Visualization of the results in map form. <br>• Characterization and pedagogic presentation of the sensitivities unique to each sociostyle. <br>• Structuring of the space of the sociostyles. <br>• Utilization of illustrative variables. | From 2 to 3 principal factorial axes. |

*Source:* Adapted from Cathelat, B. (1990), Chapter 13, 299–362.

We have already noted the high quality standards and rigorous methodology followed by the researchers. This approach also has ties to methods used in other areas of application marketing (Frank and Strain, 1972; Fornell and Westbrook, 1979; Verhallen, Van Onzenoart, and Barzilay, 1989; Windal, 1990), but not yet implemented in lifestyles.

The various tests, which are described in the book already quoted (Cathelat 1990, pp. 299–362), will be developed emphasizing only a few methodological points. Different points of importance are proposed in Table 4.12. Let us look at them in turn:

• *Factor analysis* (principal component) has rightly established homogeneous sets of variables using a varimax rotation, leading to the orthogonality of the resulting factors. Such orthogonality provides mathematical proof for further treatment (potential problems of multicollinearity disappear) but is much less sophisticated on a theoretical level. Indeed, the dimensions (factors or factor axes) structuring a phenomenon are rarely independent. An oblique rotation compensates for this problem easily, while allowing us to better define the reality.

• *Canonical analysis* represents a judicious choice to capture the impact of psychological factors (motivation, sensitivity, attitudes, opinions, and so on) and behavioral factors (skills, habits, consumption, and so on). Its implementation reveals the following:

1. First, the statistical order is concerned only with how an analysis is being performed, making it truer to the tenets of canonical analysis than a canonical analysis itself. Indeed (Cathelat, 1990, p. 320), the process is to perform a principal component analysis on the matrix of partial correlations between all variables and explain them. In this regard, the method seems more applicable to that of the factorial analysis with inter-items (or between batteries of items, interbattery factorial analysis [Tucker, 1958]), which obtains factors representing the best intercorrelations between variables belonging to different sets. Note that the usual factorial analysis examines the intracorrelations that exist in a single set of variables. Although the traditional canonical analysis furnishes bipolar canonical axes (a linear combination of variables representing the effect we are testing) leading to the award of two canonical scores for each axis, the advantage of this method is to obtain a single factorial score for each axis. This score represents a meta-factor that brings psychological and behavioral orientations directly together. Nevertheless, the nature of the analysis becomes much more descriptive than explanatory (as is the case for a classical canonical analysis).

2. A second remark concerns the orthogonality of the factors obtained. It is unlikely that the different registration relations between psychological and

Table 4.12

**Remarks on Statistical Analyses at CCA**

| Phase | Nature of the Analysis | Methodological Notes | Eventual Oblique Suggestions |
|---|---|---|---|
| 1 | Factor analysis | • Orthogonal rotating factors (varimax rotation): in practice, the dimensions structuring a phenomenon are rarely independent.<br>• Exploratory analysis: the number and nature of the dimensions are not determined in advance. | • Oblique rotation of factors (oblimin or promax).<br>• Confirmatory factor analysis, using validated scales (particularly in an international context) whose structure is known. |
| 2 | Canonical analysis | • The analysis used is a factorial analysis of more descriptive inter-items rather than traditional canonical analysis.<br>• Orthogonality of axes obtained (see above).<br>• Not taking into account the respective weight (relative importance) of factors obtained in Phase 1.<br>• Limited analysis of two sets of variables. Extension of several variables seems to be more representative of reality. | • Use a genuine canonical analysis.<br>• Perform an oblique rotation (see above).<br>• Balance factor scores.<br>• Use a generalized canonical analysis (e.g., OVERALS program, SPSSX). |
| 3 | Cluster analysis | • Heuristic search of the number of groups (sociostyles) selected. | • Verify the stability of the classification using different algorithms (possibly using methods based on latent class). |

*(continued)*

Table 4.12 *(continued)*

| 4 | Correspondence analysis | • Impoverishment of initial information, rendering discrete (nominal) positioning of sociostyles on canonical factors or sociocultural fluxes.<br><br>• Strictly descriptive and none of the explicative cases of eventual associations.<br><br>• Only the distances within the same group of variables are comparable.<br><br>• The graphic superpositions of the sociocultural map with different markets of consumption remain descriptive. The recourse of the genuine explicative methods is necessary. | • Keep the continuing nature of variables (canonical factors and sociocultural fluxes); have recourse to appropriate explicative analyses; discriminant analyses (eventually hierarchical).<br><br>• Using genuine explicative methods (LOGIT, LOG-LINEAR models, etc.).<br><br>• Employing an appropriate norm, like canonical norms (e.g., ANACOR SPSSX program). Simplify, an analysis of multiple correspondences.<br><br>• Using genuine explicative methods: linear regressions, logistic regressions, multinomial LOGIT models, etc. |

*Source:* Adapted from Cathelat, B. (1990).

behavioral factors are independent. Under the methodologies followed by the CCA, an oblique rotation also seems preferable.

3. Factorial axes are of dwindling importance but could possibly reflect this hierarchy in the weighting of the canonical analysis. This solution is very simple to implement and would better reflect the priorities given various psychological and behavioral factors.

4. Finally, by its nature, the analysis is restricted to two sets of variables (explanatory and explained). On a theoretical level, it would be desirable to distinguish between each of the subsets of variables: They are either psychological in nature (motivations, attitudes, opinions, etc.) or behavioral (buying consumables, buying equipment, enacting habits, etc.). An improvement, based on generalized canonical analysis, seems quite desirable. It is also possible to conduct analyses with variables of different nature (quantitative and qualitative) using a generalized canonical nonlinear program that is available.

• *Cluster analysis* remains much more traditional. Given the enormity of available data, it is best implemented as a two-step process: first partitioning types into categories, then creating a hierarchical classification based on stable nuclei that has been obtained in the previous step. Note that a cutoff at a given level (i.e., breaking in the group of a fusion index) is then automatically assigned a sociostyle that corresponds to some aspect of the grouping (cf., Cathelat, 1990 p. 329, for an illustration). An automatic profile group is obtained thanks to an unfolding series of test results with these factors and initial variables.

• *Correspondence analysis* is the one that brought the most comments on methodology, at least in its presentation, its formulation, and its current use. The CCA's analysis presents educational reasons for all of its results in a sociomap, from the intersection of social styles with sociocultural trends and meta-canonical factors. The analytic type is a simple correspondence analysis, which operates only on a contingency table (sorting crosses between two variables). This methodological choice seems to us questionable for methodological, statistical, and practical reasons:

1. One must analyze correspondence dummy variables (simple group membership). The meta-canonical factors and real sociocultural trends are variables of a continuous nature. The dummy variable analysis should be used to reduce the information those variables contain either by cutting them into classes (categories or terms) or, what is likely given the choice of simple correspondence analysis, affecting an individual factor only for

which the corresponding score is higher (the analysis loses the information contained on other factors). An alternative methodology, discriminant analysis, would preserve the information contained in the factors. Such an approach provides a mapping for which three axes in general seem sufficient to describe more than 70 percent of the dispersion phenomenon. The representation of groups of people (sociostyles) and variables are also possible (Dillon and Goldstein, 1984). As the objective of the analysis is to explain the possible differences between the groups, the latter divisions are generally more clearly marked on the chart (unless the discriminatory power is low). Since the CCA uses this type of analysis to form the reduced questionnaire in Phase 2, an update would require the incorporation of data from sociocultural graphs. Finally, we note for purists that a hierarchical discriminant analysis (Tabachnick and Fidell, 1989) would simultaneously analyze the discriminating power of the respective trends and sociocultural meta-canonical factors, while they can be apprehended separately as part of a simple correspondence analysis.

2. Use of a correspondence analysis can be satisfied by the twofold aim of having, on one hand, a repository for all the same analyses (i.e., the axes defined the social structure), and, second, the possibility of using additional variables (or illustrations) of nominal passive nature. This choice, as limiting the number of tests available for selection of the method, is purely descriptive, as opposed to an explanatory discriminant optical analysis mentioned above. In the first case (correspondence analysis), we merely note the proximity between variables; in the second cases, there are research factors (discriminant axes) that better explain the differences between groups. Contrary to what Cathelat asserted (1990, p. 337), the analysis does not explain variables (columns in the sociostyles) and explanatory variables (lines in the sociocultural trends). It is simply the crossing of two variables (one row and one column) with exactly the same role. In this respect, identifying the proximity of a variable that is used to explain a variable called explanatory to detect a lifestyle is very questionable (Cathelat, 1990, p. 330).

From a statistical standpoint, the use of tools on explanatory dummy variables is necessary, such as log-linear models (Agresti, 1990; Evrard and Laurent, 1983), which makes for a more quantified associated force between the two variables of a different nature. We also know that the log-linear models are more efficient than the correspondence analysis for tracking and analyzing links between the two variables of normal nature, and they are therefore preferable (Daudin and Trécourt, 1980). Furthermore, the distances between variables of different nature (rows and columns) are not comparable when using simple correspondence analysis (Caroll, Green, and Schaffer, 1986, 1987, 1989; e.g., Cathelat, 1990, pp. 339, 354, 418).

Only distances within the same set of variables are comparable (Saporta, 1990). To compensate for this error, an appropriate norm should be utilized (Caroll, Green, and Schaffer, 1986, 1987). Controversy still exists about this issue (Greenacre, 1989; Caroll, Green, and Schaffer, 1989). because a canonical representation on dummy variables (De Leeuw, 1984) is preferable in that it allows simultaneous representation of two dummy variables (Saporta, 1990), or directly matching with a multiple factorial analysis. (One might even consider a multiple correspondence conditional analysis (Escofier, [1987]), making the analysis even more relevant.) This approach also directly compares the proximity between variables of a different nature In this case, unfortunately, many axes are observed, each representing a small percentage of total inertia. This issue is without doubt the practical reason why the CCA opts for a simple correspondence analysis.

3. From an operational and practical perspective, which is superimposed on a general sociocultural map (or a specific to a given market) with the outcome of a competitive analysis or graphical representation of one or several items, this course seems to be questionable. It should be stressed once more that correspondence analysis is a descriptive tool and not a narrative case. At most, it allows for the juxtaposition of certain behavioral sensitivities.

Consequently, the overall designs proposed by Cathelat in his book (e.g., pp. 418, 459, and 535) cannot elucidate the true predictive quality of studies of lifestyles. In fact, predictive statistical analysis (linear regression, logistic regression, multinomial probit or multinomial logit models) conducted from panel data show that sociodemographic and economic variables alone preformed better than the usual types of created lifestyles at the origin to replace them. (For more information, refer to Chapter 7 of this book on the criticisms of lifestyle approaches.) Some people believe that the classifications of current lifestyles are too general to have an impact on consumption. This view is probably the reason that the CCA offers sectoral typologies (food, drink, car, home, entertainment, banking, technology, etc.) that are better suited to the study of specific behaviors. Nevertheless, the CCA's approach does not clash with options that utilize explanatory tools for the operational validity to define typologies this specific (referred to as social targets by the CCA).

Beyond this critical analysis of methodologies followed by the CCA and some reservations against the current use of correspondence analysis, we accept the precision and seriousness of the proposed approach. In addition, the drawbacks noted are very minor and can be rectified easily. The only problem that remains concerns the use that is made of graphical results from simple correspondence analysis.

Overall, then, the approaches taken by COFREMCA and the CCA in identifying the characteristic values of society may be somewhat useful because they cover the entire population and, thus, the entire spectrum of marketing segments. On the other hand, although there is a difference in number and nature, they identify hypothetical types, which can leave us skeptical about the relevance, validity, and the practical results, if they are applied to the consumption of durable goods and general merchandise. Moreover, the lack of conceptualization and development of these empirical approaches suggests that they should have a value indicative of social behavior. (It was this connection that we noted the low predictive power of various classifications of lifestyles. This aspect is covered in more in detail in Chapter 7.) It should be noted that the use by these two organizations of questionnaire variables of the AIO type allows for the study of the concepts and attitudes of activities that have been developed in the previous chapter.

## SECTION 3: APPROACH OF CREDOC

Although CREDOC does not use AIO-type questionnaires, a brief analysis of the CREDOC proposal is included here for two reasons:

- first, to complete the panorama of the French approach to lifestyles
- second, because this last approach, although different in form, is similar in purpose to the earlier approaches in their study of social change and its evolution.

According to the director of CREDOC, Victor Scardigli (1976), the program of research called "prospective lifestyles" is intended to highlight the ongoing changes in the lifestyles of France and their development of potential future time horizons. Combining inputs from the macroeconomic analysis, econometrics, and sociological factors, this study aims to show the dynamic changes that can be seen over a long period of time (Lebart and Van Effenterre, 1980, 1981).

More precisely, the concept of living proposed by CREDOC covers three aspects:

- critical issues in space that take place in daily life (habitat, housing, commerce, transport, etc.)
- relations with the economic system (employment and financial resources, consumption and saving, etc.)

- the activities of human development (health, education, entertainment, communication)

Conducted since 1981 with quota samples of people eighteen years and older, the survey covers a series of thirteen subjects (Lebart et al., 1983). Initially, it was a rather mixed method: 734 persons were drawn at random from electoral municipalities with fewer than 10,000 inhabitants; 1,266 were defined through the classical method of quotas for other cities:

- The family
- Housing
- Lifestyle
- The environment
- Transportation
- Energy
- Employment and the quality of life at work
- Health
- The economic situation
- Social and familial environment
- Leisure
- Social participation
- Inequalities

This approach then gives rise to three types of operations and a breakdown according to conventional sociodemographic variables, a distribution of responses following major themes, and, finally, several analyses of multiple correspondences to more accurately identify the individual classes constituting French society.

These various tests are then used to identify the main lines of evolution of French society. As such, multiple scenarios are proposed: the nonproduction society, the society in disarray, and the productive and social society (Table 4.13). In an attempt to follow this evolution more closely, the CREDOC program also poses a series of indicators of lifestyles—statistics expressed as percentages of people who adhere to several socioeconomic principles (concerning work, leisure, health, etc.). The results point to the eight types shown in Table 4.14 (Lebart, 1986).

What characterizes the CREDOC approach is the aggregation of results from a socioeconomic standard in the format of simple tables. In fact, this approach, although it is called prospective, appears in its application to be more descriptive. (In this regard, Lebart and Houzel Van Effenterre [1980] state that the main objective of their approach lies in the establishment of an observation instrument willing to demonstrate "Modeling psycho-

Table 4.13

**Evolution of French Society** (CREDOC)

| Three Types of Societies for the Future | | |
|---|---|---|
| The nonproductive society | The society in disarray | The social and productive society |
| Regression of production. | Growth is weak and irregular. | Strong and regular growth. |
| Few social problems. | Multiplication of conflicts. | Development of lifelong learning and schooling. |
| Inequalities reduced by a leveling to the bottom. | Revolutionary action by minority groups. | Reducing social inequalities. |
| Increased leisure time. | Strong differentiation of incomes, lifestyles, and consumption between social groups. | Development of contractual procedures to contain the conflicts through social processes. |
| Development of artisan activities. | Significant pockets of poverty. | Markets for mass consumption. Social differentiation by recreation and culture. Development of public institutions. |

*Source:* Scardigli (1976).

Table 4.14

**Socioeconomic Indicators of Lifestyle** (CREDOC)

| I | Modernists (18%) | Modal Element: A young Parisian with no children, an advanced degree, but an average standard of living. |
|---|---|---|
| II | The Dissatisfied/Excluded (11%) | A worker or unemployed person without a diploma experiencing other serious difficulties (lodging, family, health) in an unpleasant life. |
| III | Pessimists/Moderates (16%) | A 50+ year-old married provincial, with children, low diploma, but with an average standard of living. |
| IV | The Traditionalists (15%) | A retired person with children, without a diploma, living in the equivalent of a house in rural areas. |
| V | The "I Don't Knows" (8%) | An elderly woman, without a diploma, living in a small town. |
| VI | Conservatives (13%) | A person close to 50, with a diploma, with a high level of income and property. |
| VII | Optimists/Moderates (12%) | A person around 30 years old, provincial, active with children, but with a low diploma. |
| VIII | Nonparticipants (5%) | A single male of varied age without a diploma and few resources. |

*Source:* Lebart (1986).

sociological or microeconomic models, while pretending they possess some operational value, fails from inaccessible neutrality.") The public nature and, thus, knowledge of the means of investigation and statistical processing make this method less attractive than other higher approaches to lifestyle.

Finally, CREDOC differentiates itself from other agencies in the sense that their concerns are less about the lives, behaviors, and attitudes of consumption than about living conditions and social attitudes. It incorporates a sociological sense into the social group. According to CREDOC, lifestyle represents (1) a coherent world of individuals and their relationships as part of a group; and (2) the ways in which changes in society overall are accompanied by change in individuals' lifestyles and vice versa (Scardigli, 1976).

## SECTION 4: OTHER SOCIOGRAPHICAL APPROACHES OF A FRENCH ORIGIN

Two other studies of lifestyles—namely, Agorametrics and the Belgium Socioscope—merit discussion, although more briefly, as they pursue the same objective: to study the evolution of the sociological landscape in France. In spite of the fact that the tools for gathering information are different, the methodologies are similar because both begin with sociological indicators (a battery of items tracking membership with different sociocultural currents, and so on). A factor analysis of principal components allows us to identify the factors of sociological interest; a typology performed on the factorial axes obtained in the previous step leads to the identification of relevant sociological groups; and, finally, in the context of Belgium, a multivariate analysis of proximity allows for the visualization of an affiliation with different sociological and sociocultural trends of various types. An introduction to this methodology is followed by a more detailed discussion of both studies.

### Analysis of Conflict of Agorametrics

The Association of Agorametrics (also known as AESOP, an acronym for the Association to Study the Structures of Public Opinion) aims to explore the changing patterns of public opinion through the annual identification of topical issues fueling French discussions. These themes are taken from a thorough analysis of the national press on diverse (more than 100) topics (see examples shown in Table 4.15).

---

Table 4.15

**Examples of Topical Issues Fueling French Discussions**

- Unemployment is very stressful.
- The liberalization of abortion is a good thing.
- Advertising is essential.
- We must continue to build nuclear plants.
- God exists.
- We can have confidence in justice.
- There are too many immigrant workers.
- They take us for idiots on television.
- We must sacrifice for the motherland.
- The reduction of military expenditures is required.
- Government lacks effectiveness.
- We're safer now than before.
- It is normal for the price of gas to increase.
- Homosexuals are people like everyone else.
- The defraud tax is not theft.
- Occupational accidents are rare.
- The Pope should intervene in the political world.
- We must institute a work week of 35 hours.
- Hashish should be legalized.
- The Communist ministers are doing a good job.
- We must save the free school area.
- It is right to give new rights to workers in businesses.
- Vacations are necessary.
- The Left will not last much longer.
- The Delors Plan (for European economic union) will succeed.

*Source:* Stemmelen (1984).

---

The Agorametrics approach is quite original because it focuses on conflict as a privileged place for observation of opinions. The themes become subjects of expression, whose corresponding questions are distributed over a five-point scale of disagreement. The area of social expression of time can then be visualized through the principal components of factor analysis (Figure 4.6). As indicated in Figure 4.7, the Agorametrics approach turns on two main axes: one of stability and movement, the other of compromise and dramatization. Four main regions are emerging between the values of a downward turn toward infringement, and the legitimacy of new challenges.

The collection of information, which features the usual sociodemographic as well as the elements of wealth or comfort (twelve entries), media (fifty-three items), and political views, also allows us to see the same space in the center of gravity of various social categories (Figure 4.8) on page 111. More instructive is the same representation of the temporal evolution of different

# Figure 4.6 Agorametrics—Social Expression of Time

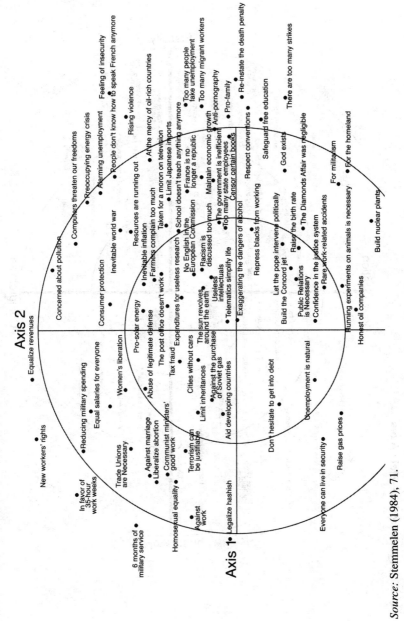

*Source:* Stemmelen (1984), 71.

110

Figure 4.7  **Agorametrics—Main Axes**

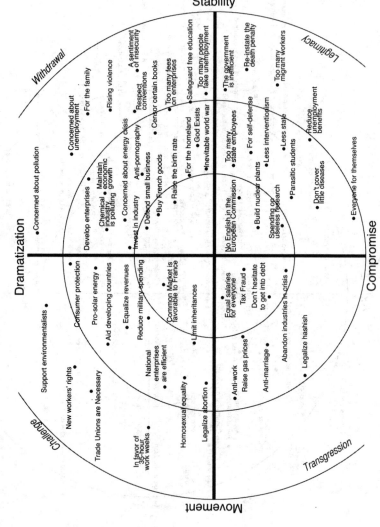

*Source:* Arnoux and Malet (1984).

Figure 4.8 **Agorametrics—World of Opinions**

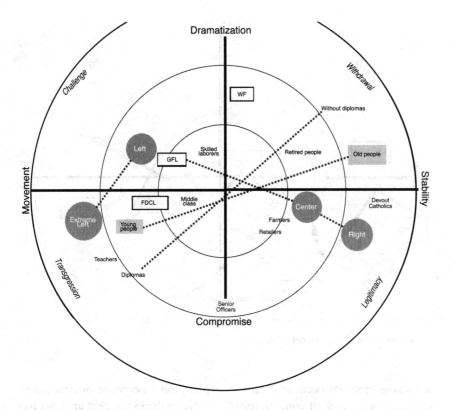

*Source:* Arnoux and Malet (1984), 27.

social groups on the same map (Figure 4.9). An analysis of four years of evolution is transcribed, although the mutation of the economic and political landscape of France (see Arnoux and du Malet [1984]) and the transition from a post-1981 "State of Grace" climate of rigor was established in 1984. By cluster analysis on the factor scores of individuals (i.e., their individual positions in the space of previous opinions), five portraits finally emerge—five schools of thought defined by shared beliefs (the conservative, 29 percent; the egalitarian, 17 percent; the helpless, 18 percent; the neo-liberal, 10 percent; and the impertinent, 26 percent).

In fact, the very characteristics that make the process of Agorametrics original and interesting also contribute to its weakness. It appeals to us because it permits us to follow the evolution of the French sociological landscape. Its

Figure 4.9    **Agorametrics—Temporal Evolution of Different Social Groups**

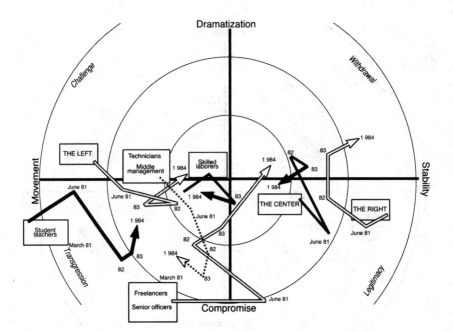

*Source:* Arnoux and Malet (1984), 28.

weakness emerges because it fails to explain the emergence of new issues or the growing lack of concern for others. Nevertheless, recent analysis has helped to show the relative stability of the temporal axis (Figure 4.10)—a theoretical opinion that is apparently on the rise (Pages et al., 1991; Durand et al., 1990). Through key words arranged in concentric circles (Figure 4.11), mechanisms of mental behavior can be interpreted as moving away from the center (for more details, see Pages et al., 1987).

### An Overview of the Belgian Socioscope

Conducted since 1977, the Belgian Socioscope is heavily inspired by the French approach, including that of COFREMCA, at least at its inception. Beginning in 1982, and repeated every two years thereafter, the survey consists of three main parts:

- the first measures adherence to current sociocultural trends (around 150 items);

Figure 4.10　**Agorametrics—Relative Stability of the Temporal Axes**

*Source:* Pages et al. (1979).

Figure 4.11    **Agorametrics—Structural Interpretation**

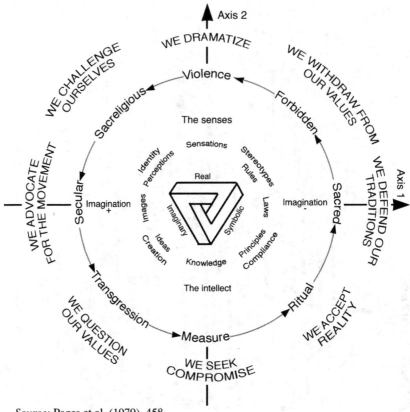

*Source:* Pages et al. (1979), 458.

- the second relates to consumption (more than seventy products) and usage of media (more than eighty media tests);
- the third is classical and measures the sociodemographic characteristics of the sample.

Statistical treatments by factor analysis are composed of successive principles, and can be established for each study, to structure the main trends of thought (twenty-four to twenty-six over the years) (Figures 4.12 and 4.13). The structure of trends evolved little, resulting in little change in the axes of interpretation in both cases.

A cluster analysis on the individual factorial coordinates in the system of lines yields eight specific sociotypes of Belgian society, evolving sensibly from

Figure 4.12 **Belgian Socioscope—Structure of Trends** (1987)

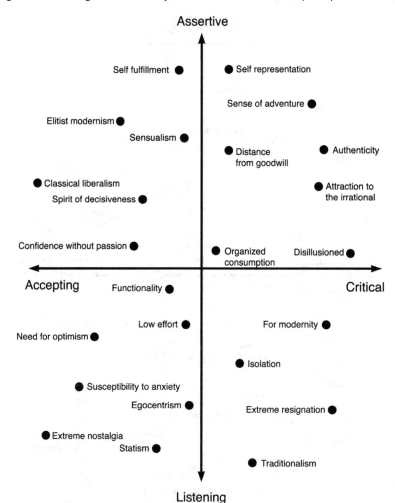

*Source:* Ronsse, J.M. (1991), *Media Marketing*. Paris/Brussels: De Boeck Université Presse, 208.

one study to another (Figures 4.14 and 4.15). Finally, projecting this initial space for variables contained in the database, it is possible to view diverse methods of expression in various fields and products—specific products, brands, communities, linguistics, and age. Thus, there are four main areas of products (portable products, exotic or emotional products, traditional products, peer-pressure products), with the significance varied in time (see Ronsse, 1991, 220–226, for a detailed presentation of the evolution of each

Figure 4.13   **Belgian Socioscope—Structure of Trends** (1989)

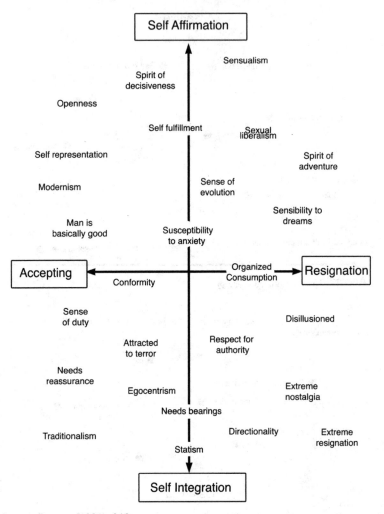

*Source:* Ronsse (1991), 212.

field). As an illustration, Figure 4.16 presents the expression field of running a jam-making business. It takes into account the production model (jam as a universal product) as well as the methods of distinguishing the brand from its prospective competitors.

While conducting research with care and rigor, the Belgian Socioscope suffers from the same criticisms as those leveled against Agorametrics. Indeed, the sociocultural universe deforms itself from changes in the instrument of

Figure 4.14    **Belgian Socioscope—Sociotypes** (1987)

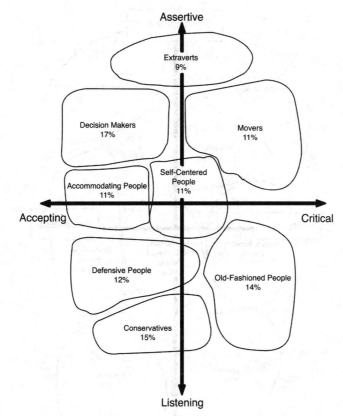

*Source:* Ronsse (1991), 207.

measurement and the evolution of the social landscape. This outcome is, in fact, from the time the instrument is almost defined (and then freezes) that comparisons become possible (for example, between 1987 and 1989). Ironically, it can only measure change when the measurement instrument is equally and perfectly applicable to both the earlier and the later time period.

## CONCLUSION AND SYNTHESIS

This chapter has identified the French approaches to lifestyle studies. Although different in their procedures and their results, all these approaches center on the identification of common values in each group. This method makes them more reliable under certain circumstances than the AIO studies of American origin.

The work of COFREMCA focused on the study of values under certain circumstances, while the CCA is concerned with preconscious values. This

Figure 4.15   **Belgian Socioscope—Sociotypes** (1989)

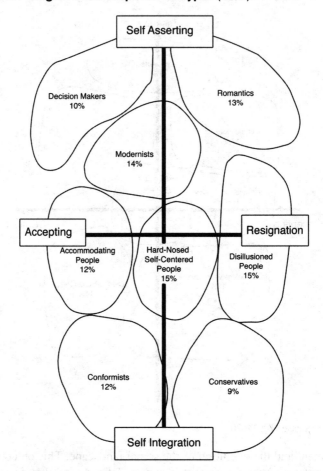

*Source:* Ronsse (1991), 211.

difference in orientation leads to different—sometimes even contradictory—results. The development of empirical approaches and dissimilar conclusions led to doubts about the precision of the methods and the value of the social behavior they observed.

The CREDOC approach differs from earlier work on the study of lifestyles, especially in relation to the methods of investigation and analysis used in earlier research. CREDOC focuses more on living conditions and social attitudes, and it presents its results in a far more descriptive than explanatory way; consequently, the results are considered much weaker.

Figure 4.16    **Belgian Socioscope—Expression Field of Running
a Brand of Jam**

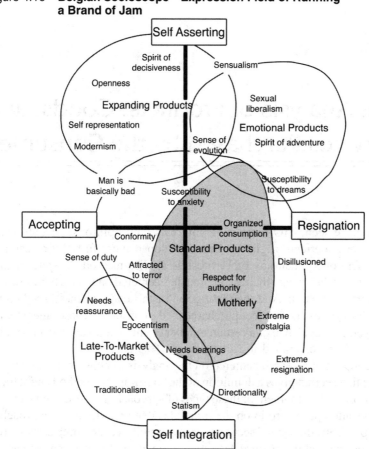

*Source:* Ronsse (1991), 217.

Finally, the sociocultural enterprises by Agorametrics in France and
Marketing Unit in Belgium each tried to trace the foundations of streams of
thought. Built out of an essentially empirical model, and thus a fairly faithful reflection of the spirit of the time, neither method attempts to explain the
observed changes over time. At best, they establish a record.

This chapter raises multiple problems of a methodological, conceptual, and
discretionary nature, which can also be applied to the previous chapter on approaches based on American attitudes and activities. It also closes the overview
of studies of lifestyles that we qualify as a priori, in the sense that they try to
define in advance the likely types of consumer behavior. It is now appropriate
to address the second orientation: a posteriori consumption patterns.

# 5

# The Analysis of Products, Goods, and Services Purchased by the Consumer

As we have seen, AIO (activities, interests, and opinions) inventories of French or American origin has been developed more fully by researchers and practitioners than any other lifestyle studies method. In spite of their primacy and theoretical interest, approaches centered on values have not seen widespread research. And the same goes for those approaches based on the analysis of goods and services purchased by the consumer. These latter studies, however, give evidence of a certain number of characteristics and advantages that should be examined in further detail. This chapter is dedicated to the consideration of research centered on the analysis of consumption methods.

The first section gives a definition of the consumption method and retraces the historical development of these types of approaches. The second and third sections attempt to zero in on the principles that underlie these approaches. More precisely, the second section focuses on studies concerning certain product categories, while the third deals with more general studies, encompassing a more vast range of currently used products. The fourth section involves more specific studies, carried out both in France and in the United States, regarding geographic segmentation and its impact on patterns of consumption. Finally, unique studies in Asia are briefly discussed.

## GENESIS AND DEFINITION

The study of consumable goods and services is tied directly to lifestyle. It is widely believed that a consumer's lifestyle is defined by the goods and services he or she buys, and also by the way he or she consumes them. This research method leads to the hypothesis that all the purchases made by any given consumer—in other words, the types of products he or she buys—are indicators of his or her lifestyle. Such an approach offers an a posteriori analysis (Wells, 1968a), which aims to determine individuals' behavioral norms by observing their purchases, their interests, and their goals.

This method derives its essence from the works of Levy, who, in 1963, demonstrated that products play an important symbolic or psychological role in humans. At the same time, Kelley (1963) noted that consumers seem to acquire the representative symbols of their lifestyles through their purchases. In the same sense, Moore (1963) suggests that consumption methods are an expression of an individual's lifestyle.

Thus, people buy products based not only on what purpose they will serve but also on their psychological significance. These products, therefore, define a certain image or lifestyle among the people who buy them. They are, at times, "the realization of a life plan and the expression of personal characteristics, of objectives, of social behavior, and of aspirations" (Douglas, 1976).

The two main studies linking lifestyle and consumption patterns focus on data collected between 1960 and 1975, and between 1976 and 1979. A third more general approach, has emerged more recently in Asia.

## INTEREST TOWARD SPECIFIC CATEGORIES OF PRODUCTS

The first studies were mainly interested in limited and specific product types. One example is that of Stoetzel (1960), which concerned French liquor consumers based on the specific types of products they bought. Several years later, Grubb and Grathwohl (1967) studied the symbolic value that purchased products held in the eyes of those who bought them. Such a study was later conducted by Alpert and Gatty in 1969.

Alpert and Gatty created a factor analysis of eighty different goods and services, using a sample of 5,480 men. They then determined sixteen fundamental profiles, three of which are shown in Table 5.1: *the heavy drinker, the automobile maniac,* and *the traveler.*

The researchers next examined the ways in which buyers of different brands of beer—and whether these buyers were occasional or habitual consumers of alcoholic beverages—conformed to these profiles. For example, certain brands have only a narrow connection with certain profiles.

Pernica (1974) conducted a similar study in a segmentation of stomach medications. Based on a factor analysis of eighty products, he identified four segments, characteristics, and personality traits; he described the segments as *extremely ill people, big medication consumers, hypochondriacs,* and *pragmatics.*

Apparently, these studies are the only ones of this type that have been published. In fact, these studies, due to their limited topics, do not allow us

Table 5.1

**Examples of Profiles Identified in Conjunction with Products Consumed**

| Profile | Strong consumer of: |
| --- | --- |
| The Heavy Drinker | Whiskey |
| | Canadian Whiskey |
| | Bourbon |
| | Scottish Whiskey |
| | Gin |
| | Vodka |
| | Cocktails |
| | Beer |
| The Automobile Maniac | Car Polish |
| | Motor Oil |
| | Antifreeze |
| | Distance Traveled by Car |
| | Gas |
| The Traveler | Airplane Flights |
| | Car Rental |
| | Gas Credit Cards |
| | Other Credit Cards |
| | Trips Abroad |

*Source:* Alpert, L., and Gatty, R. (1969), Product Positioning by Behavioral Lifestyles, *Journal of Marketing*, 33, 65–69.

to generalize about behavior types for different product categories. It also seems that since 1973–1974, just as much in France as in the United States, researchers have been constrained exclusively by the Activities, Interests, and Opinions approach, which has already been presented. Not until 1979 did a trend begin where studies were more generally centered on an analysis of a whole group of products purchased and consumed by individuals.

## GENERAL APPROACHES IN TERMS OF MEANS OF CONSUMPTION

Household consumption patterns are typically considered an economic phenomenon separate from other family activities. Any changes in consumption trends are usually explained purely by economic factors such as revenue and price variations, as in the majority of macroeconomic studies.

By contrast, the consumption-style approach defined by Uusitalo (1979a, 1979b) and by Arndt and Uusitalo (1980) is more of an explicative perspective of consumer behavior and of segmentation criteria research. Other recent contributions to the consumption-style methods are presented next.

## *Arndt and Uusitalo's Study of Consumption Style(s)*

During the 1970s, economic studies focused primarily on specific aspects of consumption (Prais and Houthakker, 1971); around the same time, however, other authors such as Goldberger and Gamaletsos (1970) and Lybeck (1976) began looking into functions of consumption by observing what products were consumed by households as a group. This relationship was simultaneously conceptualized by the theory of allocation of time (Jacoby, Seybilla, and Bering, 1976); yet, a majority of segmentation studies continued to be based upon specific brand preferences or upon the perception of proposed products' attributes (Arndt, 1976).

Since that time, a direction even more vast in its field of application has taken shape, developing from the work of Douglas and Le Maire (1973) and Evrard and Le Maire (1976), who found an interesting illustration in France regarding thirty-three contemporary products. This perspective, developed for the most part after 1979 around the works of Uusitalo, concerns consumption of popular goods by groups.

According to Veblen's (1899) old proposition, as restated by Mayer and Nicosia in 1977, consumption "is a part of people's way of life and . . . is dependent on . . . existing living conditions, social and physical environment, and culture." The definition proposed by Uusitalo draws on that proposition, "emphasiz[ing] consumption as a social phenomenon." Uusitalo states that the "consumption behavior of a household—when taken as a whole—is . . . dependent on social determinants other than income."

The author suggests that a collection of factors, both social and individual, influence consumption styles. On the social level, they are factors of organizational and institutional order, such as economic and social structure, the degree of modernism and technology available to consumers, the ideological climate, the cultural ambiance, and the geographic factors that predominate in their environment. On an individual level, they are factors such as household economic structure, personal resources, and personality traits. Globally, the ensemble of factors relates to the consumption styles presented in Figure 5.1.

With information on consumer expenditures in Finnish households in 1971 (furnished by the Central Bureau of Statistics), Uusitalo had access to a list of 220 products consumed by 1,908 households. The author isolated by factor analysis three principal consumption styles that accounted for 31 percent of the total variance. The results are as follows:

- modernism, 7 percent (modern consumption as opposed to traditional consumption);
- mobility, 13 percent (consumption implying displacement of people as opposed to consumption done in the home);

124

Figure 5.1  **Factors Influencing Consumption Style**

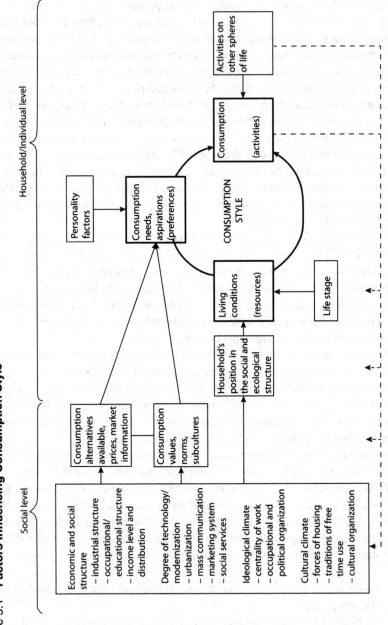

*Source:* Uusitalo (1979a), 34.

Table 5.2

**Typology of Consumers by Consumption Style** (Uusitalo)

| | | |
|---|---|---|
| 1. | "Youth, show-offs" | 9.3% |
| 2. | "The active family" | 17.7% |
| 3. | "The alienated loner" | 7.6% |
| 4. | "The repressed, the inhibited" | 12.0% |
| 5. | "The materialist" | 9.4% |
| 6. | "The private character" | 16.7% |
| 7. | "The marginal" | 8.8% |
| 8. | "The traditional repressed" | 18.5% |
| | Total | 100.0% |

*Source:* Arndt, J., and Uusitalo, L. (1980), Backward Segmentation by Consumption Style: A Sociological Approach. In R. Bagozzi et al. (eds.), *Combined Proceedings: Marketing in the 80s,* American Marketing Association, 128.

- diversity, 11 percent (varied consumption as opposed to consumption restricted only to products of primary necessity).

The weak percentage of variance stems from the fact that Uusitalo reduced the number of initial variables from 120 to 20 based on their importance, choosing only those variables of analysis having the highest correlation coefficients. This strategy led to a loss of information that significantly damaged the homogeneity of the answers for the remaining variables. The classification of the resulting eight styles of consumption was based solely on the comparison between the individuals' factor score on each axis and the average factor score by factor. In spite of its shortcomings, though, this study did provide new insights into consumer profiles, as shown in Table 5.2.

The interest in Uusitalo's approach is significant. Uusitalo defines the notion of consumer styles by giving them a precise conceptual framework and by extending them out over a vast group of consumer products in current use. This effort opened the way to other similar studies.

## *Contributions in the Domain of Consumption Styles*

One very interesting and innovative study was conducted in 1982 by Cosmas. He interviewed 1,797 women by means of an AIO questionnaire containing 250 items about 179 currently used products. Then, using two types of Q factor analysis, he identified seven types of consumption and seven lifestyles, classifying the individuals according to their highest factor score among those scores obtained (see Table 5.3).

Some observers questioned the applicability of Cosmas's methodology. What in a type Q factor analysis could represent an axis formed by the linear

Table 5.3

**Lifestyles and Types of Consumption as Proposed by Cosmas**

| Lifestyles | Types of consumption |
|---|---|
| 1. Traditional | 1. Personal care |
| 2. Frustrated | 2. "Stocker" |
| 3. Extraverted | 3. Cooking |
| 4. Mobile | 4. "Who refuses nothing" |
| 5. Sophisticated | 5. Social |
| 6. Active | 6. Purchases for their children |
| 7. Hedonist | 7. Personal aspect |

*Source:* Cosmas (1982), Life-Styles and Consumption Patterns, *Journal of Consumer Research,* 8, 453–455.

combination of individuals? In this sense, the critiques formulated by Evrard and Le Maire (1976) on the subject of type Q factor analysis appear to be completely legitimate. In addition, why classify the individuals while not taking into account the highest factor score?

Cosmas also analyzed the link between lifestyles and modes of consumption. The deceiving results indicate an effect of very weak interaction between the two groups.

In spite of the absence of conceptual and theoretical support and, seemingly, the inadequacy of the methodology used, it is nonetheless interesting to note that Cosmas's work represents the first attempt to relate two different lifestyle approaches: one measured by an AIO inventory, the other by the type of products consumed.

In a French context, this means of investigation was taken up again by the work of Valette-Florence (1985). He demonstrated the links, equally as weak, between (1) the types of consumption from an inventory of products currently in use, and (2) the lifestyles identified from an inventory of French origin (the COFREMCA type).

The methodology followed for identifying the different practices of consumption is, in principle, as follows:

- the first stage uses factor analysis to reduce the number of initial variables and more effectively target those dimensions most representative of the studied consumption (in this case, factor analysis identifies clusters or groups of related items [factors] that influence consumer attitudes and preferences);
- the second stage consists of the creation, by means of a typological analysis depending on the factor scores of the preceding factors, of homogeneous groups having similar modes of consumption;
- the last procedure characterizes the groups defined at the previous stage by discriminant analysis and validates the group of effected analyses.

Figure 5.2    **Analytic Scheme Clarifying Consumption Methods**

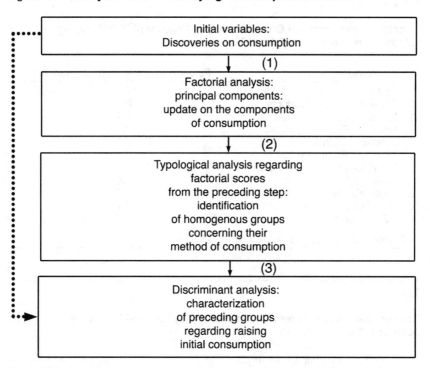

The proposed sequence is schematized in Figure 5.2. As an illustration, the results of the first and third stages are given respectively in Tables 5.4 and 5.5 according to the research of Valette-Florence and Jolibert (1985 and 1987a). Although the smaller size of the sample (300 people) alters the character of their work, we present it here in order to illustrate a connection. The categories listed are different from those presented in the previous research (Uusitalo, 1979b; Cosmas, 1982). This change is due not only to the different methodology, which here is more rigorous, but also to the nature of the consumer products used in the example (140 products, as shown in Table 5.6).

Studies by Valette-Florence and Jolibert (1988 and 1990) were designed to better target and explain consumption practices. Their conclusions show how different approaches to the study of lifestyles (values-based or AIO items) characterize the types of consumption. Furthermore, the findings indicate that the usual typologies are overly reductionistic in nature and lacking in explicative power. In addition, their results show the nonredundance of sociodemographic and classic, economic variables with the

Table 5.4

**Principal Dimensions of Consumption as Presented in a Study by Valette-Florence and Jolibert** (1985)

| Consumption factors | Percentage of the explained variable |
|---|---|
| 1.  Children's Clothing | 17.5 |
| 2.  Feminine Beauty Products | 8.3 |
| 3.  Men's Clothing | 6.7 |
| 4.  Breakfast Products/Snacks | 4.9 |
| 5.  Women's Clothing | 4.0 |
| 6.  Starches, Eggs, and Meats | 3.5 |
| 7.  Bath/Pharmaceutical Products | 3.2 |
| 8.  Alcohol | 3.0 |
| 9.  Women's Leisure Clothing | 2.7 |
| 10. High Quality Fresh Products | 3.6 |
| Total Percentage | 56.4 |

*Source:* Valette-Florence and Jolibert, 1985.

Table 5.5

**Consumption Modes Identified in a Study by Valette-Florence and Jolibert** (1987)

| Group | Profile: Consumption methods | Group size by percentage |
|---|---|---|
| 1. | Purchases for (the) Children | 8.3 |
| 2. | Groceries (flour, eggs, bread) | 10.7 |
| 3. | Modern Women (athletic clothing, makeup, etc.) | 2.9 |
| 4. | Natural (fresh natural products, organic bread) | 2.0 |
| 5. | Nonconsumer (reduced consumption in all domains) | 9.5 |
| 6. | Men's Clothing and Breakfast/Snack Products | 20.7 |
| 7. | Health and Hygiene | 10.4 |
| 8. | Women's Clothing and Breakfast/Snack Products | 11.6 |
| 9. | Low Consuming Men | 10.7 |
| 10. | Low Consuming Women | 13.2 |
|  | Total | 100.0 |

*Source:* Valette-Florence and Jolbert, 1987a.

values or lifestyles as an explanation of consumption. Each contributes to understanding unique variance. These last results seem pertinent in targeting a given practice of consumption and can help in defining the communication strategies of an advertising campaign and the corresponding positioning of a brand.

Practitioners classify individuals according to objective measures of their consumption. For example, data on the top-selling products can help identify

Table 5.6

**The Nature and Distribution of Currently Used Products in Valette-Florence and Jolibert's Study** (1985)

| | | | | |
|---|---|---|---|---|
| Food domain | 64 | | | |
| Hygiene domain | 25 | | | |
| Clothing domain | 51 | Broken down: | Men | 15 |
| | | | Women | 17 |
| | | | Children | 19 |
| Total | 140 | | | 51 |

*Source:* Valette-Florence and Jolibert, 1987a.

consumption patterns and potential sales of complementary goods. Over the course of a year, products that lead in sales offer insights on the evolutionary markers of consumption and variations in clientele. One knows, therefore, that mail-order sales organizations are actually able to define the profile of their clientele better by these means, according to the nature of and the increase in product demand. Kapferer (1985) highlighted the interest of this study by applying the results of cosmetics purchases to various typologies, showing the distinguishing sociodemographic profile of the typical consumer, as well as the effects of varying media choices.

## GEOSOCIAL APPROACHES

The most behaviorally oriented studies—developed first in the United States and then in France—have as their objective the identification of groups of homogeneous consumers by their consumption habits and their purchasing power. The same principle applies to combining information of a socioeconomic and demographic nature with geographic variables (where the consumer lives) and, of course, information on actual consumer behavior gleaned from surveys. The two most recognized geosocial market segmentation research tools are PRIZM and Cluster Plus. A similar method was proposed in France by COREF with the definition of *Ilotypes* and *Geotypes*. (These are both proper nouns created by COREF.)

### PRIZM and Cluster Plus

These two organizations propose, by typological analysis, forty groups for PRIZM and forty-seven for Cluster Plus. The active variables on which the regrouping is based are drawn from five principal categories:

1. external signs of wealth
2. indicators of (economic) standard of living
3. racial and ethnic "belonging"
4. mobility, location, and nature of habitat
5. the usual given sociodemographics

For efficiency reasons, groups were reclassified into twelve meta-categories for PRIZM and ten for Cluster Plus for more general actions such as mailings. The interest of this method resides in a refined description of the different behavioral types with respect to each segment, as well as in a more inclusive geographic location. Figure 5.3 illustrates our ideas concerning "the easily influenced youth," excessive consumers of yogurt and amateurs with beautiful cars!

Figure 5.3    **An Example of Automobile Geosocial Segmentation in the United States**

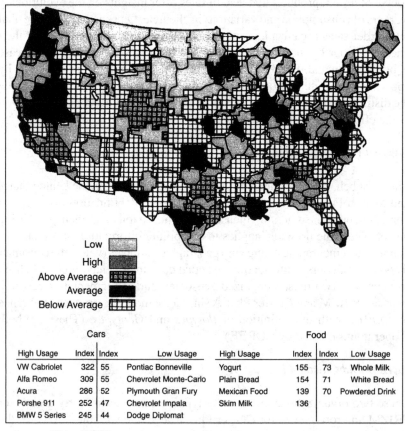

| | | | | Cars | | | Food | | |
|---|---|---|---|---|---|---|---|---|---|
| Low | | | | | | | | | |
| High | | | | | | | | | |
| Above Average | | | | | | | | | |
| Average | | | | | | | | | |
| Below Average | | | | | | | | | |

|  High Usage | Index | Index | Low Usage | High Usage | Index | Index | Low Usage |
|---|---|---|---|---|---|---|---|
| VW Cabriolet | 322 | 55 | Pontiac Bonneville | Yogurt | 155 | 73 | Whole Milk |
| Alfa Romeo | 309 | 55 | Chevrolet Monte-Carlo | Plain Bread | 154 | 71 | White Bread |
| Acura | 286 | 52 | Plymouth Gran Fury | Mexican Food | 139 | 70 | Powdered Drink |
| Porshe 911 | 252 | 47 | Chevrolet Impala | Skim Milk | 136 | | |
| BMW 5 Series | 245 | 44 | Dodge Diplomat | | | | |

*Source:* Weiss (1988).

## *COREF's Geotypes and Ilotypes*

In the same manner as the preceding American studies, the French organization COREF has been working on a project called Geodata since 1984. COREF followed the validated sociological hypothesis that choice of habitat is an act of reasoned consumption—consumption that (1) is linked to the network of households in a group, (2) is determined largely by financial and social constraints, and (3) typically leads to specific consumer tendencies. The organization's ambitious and result-seeking program of geosocial segmentation has two principal phases:

- First, the constitution of a *given communal base*: For each of 36,000 French communities, more than 6,000 socioeconomic indicators (based on community-wide questionnaires, National Institute for Statistics and Economic Studies [INSEE] data, general agricultural census results, indicators of rich communities by the general direction of taxes, etc.) were taken into account, thus going from individual revenue to the distribution of funds by age, type of habitat, and profession.
- Second, there is the creation of a basis of given *islets* (groups of people, communities) described by 600 census variables. According to the definition given by INSEE, these islets correspond to blocks of buildings containing anywhere from 20 to 100 households. Only the 894 cities with more than 10,000 inhabitants (54 percent of all French households) are studied communities (creating 182,209 islets). Two typologies, constituted by factor analysis of the correspondences and then by hierarchical classification, were developed:
  - The first corresponds to a typology of French communities, divided up into about forty smaller groups called Geotypes (rural areas).
  - The second, known as the Ilotype, consists of cities with a population greater than 10,000 inhabitants.

In order to ensure an exhaustive representation of French territory, communities of lower population are also included under the Ilotype heading. They are considered 31 homogeneous geographic units based on needs, able to be subdivided into fifty-two classes or to be reassembled into ten more general groups. Tables 5.7 and 5.8 present the headings as well as the percentages corresponding to the two classifications.

There are multiple uses for these two classifications. According to COREF, the most current ones concern:

Table 5.7

**Description of COREF Ilotypes in 1987**

| | | | Households | |
|---|---|---|---|---|
| Group | Ilotype | Description | Number | % |
| Posh | IA1 | Directors and executives | 479,308 | 2.4 |
| neighborhoods | IA2 | Success and prosperity | 270,972 | 1.4 |
| | IA3 | Old neighborhoods and city-center | 338,868 | 1.7 |
| | IA4 | Young and the up and coming | 424,440 | 2.2 |
| | IB1 | Stylish residential | 195,844 | 1.0 |
| | IB2 | Upper-middle class | 768,636 | 3.9 |
| | IB3 | Young and dynamic | 708,392 | 3.6 |
| | IB4 | Comfortable provinces | 524,608 | 2.7 |
| Middle class | IC1 | Flourishing villages | 2,092,340 | 10.7 |
| | IC2 | Mature age, few kids | 555,332 | 2.8 |
| City center and | ID1 | The heart of the city | 489,752 | 2.5 |
| commercial | ID2 | Secondary centers | 649,036 | 3.3 |
| quarters | ID3 | Students and lodgers | 140,996 | 0.7 |
| | ID4 | Local life in Paris | 337,136 | 1.7 |
| | ID5 | Historical districts | 560,372 | 2.9 |
| Working class | IE1 | Popular districts | 493,496 | 2.5 |
| | IE2 | Two income, small buildings | 451,160 | 2.3 |
| | IE3 | Working class aristocracy | 331,652 | 1.7 |
| | IE4 | Working class zone in recession | 1,560,400 | 8.0 |
| Unskilled working | IF1 | Council tower block and kids | 924,940 | 4.7 |
| class | IF2 | One salary and numerous families | 282,664 | 1.4 |
| Socially bleak areas | IG1 | Households of workers | 207,708 | 1.1 |
| | IG2 | Poverty crisis | 141,108 | 0.7 |
| Retired people | IH1 | White hair and old buildings | 414,816 | 2.1 |
| | IH2 | Grey hair and comfort | 258,344 | 1.3 |
| | IH3 | White hair and renting, 48 and older | 320,136 | 1.6 |
| | IH4 | White hair and serenity | 455,056 | 2.3 |
| The country | II1 | Only lively in season | 1,790,680 | 9.1 |
| | II2 | Industry in the country | 2,026,792 | 10.3 |
| Agricultural zones | IJ1 | Rural agriculture | 1,361,768 | 7.0 |
| | IJ2 | Urban agriculture | 32,420 | 0.2 |
| | | Total | 19,589,172 | 100.0 |

*Source:* COREF (used with permission).

- segmentation of clientele
- analysis of catchment zones (like U.S. zip codes)
- localization of sales spots
- direct marketing
- stating sales objectives
- merchandising
- media plans
- the study of social networks, etc.

Table 5.8

**Description of COREF Geotypes in 1990**

| | |
|---|---|
| P | PARIS |
| L | LYON |
| M | MARSEILLE |
| A | MAJOR REGIONAL CITIES (6.5%) |
| B | LARGE PROVINCIAL CITIES (11%) |
| | B1     Local centers (8.5%) (B11/B12/B13) |
| | B2     Large tourist cities (2.5%) |
| C | LOCAL CENTERS OF ATTRACTION (8%) (C11/C12/C13) |
| D | SUBURBS OF BIG CITIES (8.5%) |
| | D1     Wealthy suburb near Paris (1%) |
| | D2     Wealthy and working-class suburb of Paris (6%) (D21/D22/D23/D24) |
| | D3     Industrial suburb of Paris (1.5%) |
| E | RECENTLY EXPANDED SUBURBS (17.5%) |
| | E1     Suburb in transformation (5%) (E11/E12/E13) |
| | E2     Small villages experiencing fast growth (7%) |
| | E3     Rural villages (5.5%) (E31/E32) |
| F | INDUSTRIAL VILLAGES |
| | F1     Industrial centers (F11/F12) |
| | F2     Industrial basins in decline |
| | F3     Industrial suburb (F31/F32) |
| G | ATTRACTIVE RURAL VILLAGES (9.5%) |
| | G1     Towns in rural zones (5%) |
| | G2     Very small rural villages in expansion, near industrial zone (1%) |
| | G3     Small tourist villages (3.5%) (G31/G32) |
| H | INDUSTRIAL COUNTRYSIDE (7.5%) |
| | H1     Agriculture and industry (5.5%) (H11/H12/H13) |
| | H2     Residential rural villages (2%) |
| I | AGRICULTURAL ZONES (8.5%) |
| | I1     Dynamic agriculture (5%) (I11/I12/I13) |
| | I2     Rural areas in decline (3.5%) (I21/I22/I23/I24) |

*Source:* COREF (used with permission).

As illustrated by the following example, Geotypes are essential for gaining a better understanding of the clients because (1) they identify the most important geographic segments in an area, (2) they quantify the potential consumption of products, and (3) they help marketers communicate more efficiently with consumers due to a better knowledge of their exact residence. Table 5.9 compares the consumer profile of one product with that of the residents of a particular fixed zone. The relationship between the percentage of clients of one Geotype and that of households in the zone of this Geotype is measured by the consumption indicator (multiplied by 100). Therefore, the family from group D, with an index of 233, consumes the product in question two times as much as the average and 4.5 times as often as family A.

Table 5.9

**Consumer Profile of One Product with That of the Residents of a Particular Fixed Zone**

| Geotype | Clients | | Zone of Reference | | Consumption Index |
|---|---|---|---|---|---|
| | Absolute Value | % | Absolute Value | % | |
| A | 9,102 | 8.6 | 219,064 | 16.7 | 51 |
| B | 12,853 | 12.1 | 167,231 | 12.7 | 95 |
| C | 21,415 | 20.2 | 2,008,648 | 15.3 | 132 |
| D | 5,245 | 4.9 | 275,697 | 2.1 | 233 |
| E | 6,045 | 5.7 | 433,238 | 3.3 | 173 |
| F | 1,416 | 1.3 | 262,568 | 2.0 | 65 |
| G | 5,699 | 5.4 | 708,935 | 5.4 | 100 |
| H | 26,648 | 25.1 | 2,415,629 | 18.4 | 136 |
| I | 3,274 | 3.1 | 590,779 | 4.5 | 69 |
| J | 14,309 | 13.6 | 2,573,170 | 19.6 | 69 |
| Total | 106,006 | 100 | 13,128,420 | 100 | 100 |

*Source:* COREF (used with permission).

In addition, the discriminating capacities of Geotypes are increased by the crossover with other bases of information coming from societies, panels, or studies. Actually, many indications are available and come from:

- SECODIP, for products of great consumption;
- CREP, for banking products and insurance;
- Media metrics, for radio and television;
- CESP, for the press.

In order to better illustrate these ideas, Figures 5.4 and 5.5 show the indicator for fine wines and that for the number of *L'Equipe* (a French news magazine) readers.

The analysis according to the Ilotypes is just as revealing. In a small city like Rouen (Figure 5.6), the diversity of urban zones is taken into account, despite their being very close to one another. As with the Geotypes, the uses are quite diverse (for example, analysis and optimization of canvassing for advertisement by mail, analysis in the banking environment). Figure 5.7, as an illustration, visualizes the different rates of penetration for two sales catalogs. Thus, catalog A, geared toward the upper class, is much better received by group IA ("the fashionable district," index 300), but is also well received by group ID ("downtowners and commercial quarters," index 200), where the competition for other canvassing is considerably strong. Likewise, catalog B

Figure 5.4    **Differences in the Consumption Rate of Fine Wine by Geotype**

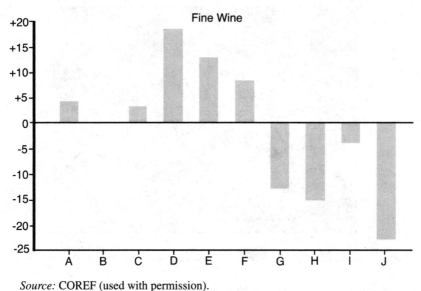

*Source:* COREF (used with permission).

Figure 5.5    **Number of *L'Equipe* Readers**

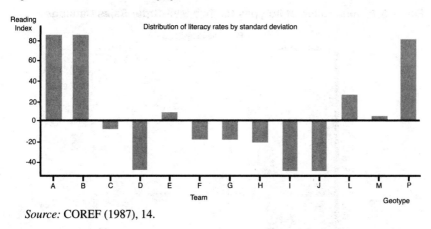

*Source:* COREF (1987), 14.

(for more traditional clientele) is well received by Ilotypes IC ("middle class") and by II ("country folk"), whereas Ilotypes IF ("nonqualified working class") and IG ("underprivileged sons") are clearly not targeted by these two catalogs.

Figure 5.6   **Magazine Subscription Rates by Geotype**

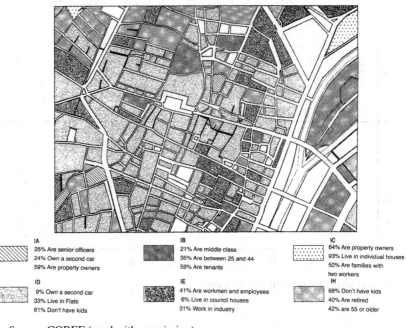

IA
25% Are senior officers
24% Own a second car
59% Are property owners

IB
21% Are middle class
35% Are between 25 and 44
59% Are tenants

IC
64% Are property owners
93% Live in individual houses
50% Are families with
two workers

ID
9% Own a second car
33% Live in Flats
61% Don't have kids

IE
41% Are workmen and employees
6% Live in council houses
31% Work in industry

IH
68% Don't have kids
40% Are retired
42% are 55 or older

*Source:* COREF (used with permission).

Figure 5.7   **Illustration of Ilotypes for Two Mail-Order Sales Catalogs**

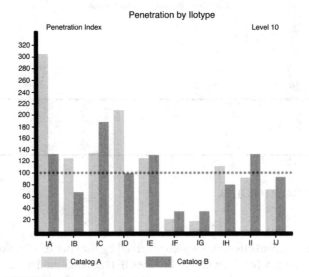

Penetration by Ilotype

Penetration Index                                        Level 10

☐ Catalog A      ■ Catalog B

*Source:* COREF (used with permission).

A growth in commercial impact on the better-targeted zones, linked to giving minimal attention to the less receptive zones, gives us these results.

COREF proposes otherwise diverse, complementary, high-performance services such as:

- a sophisticated mapping system, furnishing the representation of Ilotypes for a given area
- a database of addresses and their corresponding Ilotypes
- a minitel server, Geodatel (something roughly equivalent to a "Stone Age Internet" existing only in France) furnishing 800 socioeconomic indicators organized into 26 thematic tables for the entire French community

In France, the Ilotypes and Geotypes proposed by COREF represent the most elaborate and highly functioning system of geosocial characterization of consumption types. In addition, they offer the advantage of being based on directly measurable, objective criteria. This sense of objectivity differentiates the COREF approach from lifestyle approaches that use an AIO inventory of a much more subjective—and, therefore, less reliable—psychosocial origin. A real comparison with such studies would be strongly constructive in this sense because we think, contrary to Cathelat (1990, p. 205), that the system recommended by COREF is, in France and elsewhere, one of the best. Applied to other countries in Europe, it offers the advantage of being easy to implement, still taking into account the objective and indisputable character of the data used without running into problems with validity and linguistic equivalencies, which present themselves when one is focusing on the study of classic lifestyles in an international context (see Chapter 7).

## ASIAN RESEARCH

One of the most sophisticated programs of lifestyle research has emerged from a group of Asian marketing scholars at the National University of Singapore (e.g., Kau et al., 2004; Kau, Tan, and Wirtz, 1998; Tambyah, Tan, and Kau, 2010). They developed state-of-the-art sample profiles of Singaporeans in the social monitor tradition, considering marketing and lifestyle from the perspectives of quality of life and personal satisfaction. Separating and reporting their measurements in clear but distinct steps, these researchers have upheld the academic virtues of transparency and intellectual accessibility (cf. Kahle and Kahle, 2009). Their 2004 report included the "List of Values" and other well-developed measures central to understanding lifestyles, but they also gave detailed accounts of more specific behaviors, such as levels of media and internet usage, leisure activities, and life satisfaction, along with demographic perspectives. A growing movement that uses lifestyle and satisfaction measures as social indicators on a par with gross national product and employment rates (e.g., Ring et al., 2007) can point to this research as a model for effective social monitoring. Kau and his associates also developed Singaporean lifestyle categories based on their data.

The most recent report on lifestyles from Asia was released in 2010. It was based on the earlier AsiaBarometer Survey (Inoguchi and Fujii, 2008), a pan-Asian effort to look at social indicators across the continent. This particular instrument has less to do with specific product categories and brands than typical marketing lifestyle studies, but it does provide rich and useful data for social indicator researchers.

## CONCLUSION AND SYNTHESIS

In this fifth chapter, we examined developments in consumption-based studies of lifestyles. Beginning with Levy's groundbreaking work, this approach was then taken in different stages and directions.

The first orientation concerned only a small number of products and a specific marketing domain and offered few insights into lifestyle studies. However, a study concerning a much larger group of consumer products proved far more interesting. Arndt and Uusitalo's work demonstrates the connection between consumption styles and differing social or individual types or segments.

The study of Cosmas's work highlighted the importance of the links that exist between one study based on AIO inventory and another based on information taken from consumers' product choices. A similar conclusion was reached in a French context from the research of Valette-Florence and Jolibert.

Consumption practices offer pertinent information for lifestyle researchers and may even serve as a predictor of consumers' preferences of complementary goods. Already used by mail-order businesses, these methods may prove useful to other sales enterprises, as well.

The development of geosocial segmentation in the United States, Europe, and Asia fits into this tradition of identifying consumption practices objectively. In COREF's studies, we see the highest performance expression, with the advantage being that the data are easily interpreted in other contexts, European or international. It is unfortunate that, because of a lack of commercial aggressiveness on the part of COREF, such studies remain largely unrecognized. Likewise, the Singaporean studies are not as widely known as they deserve to be.

Thus, the preceding methods and propositions have seen very limited real-life application, contrary to those methods using classic AIO inventory. It is, essentially, these non-AIO methods of investigation that gave way to the diverse uses developed in the next chapter.

# 6

# Fields of Application of Lifestyles

The essentially empirical developments of lifestyle studies, in practice, have led to many diverse applications. Chapter 6 presents the different corresponding fields of application. It is useful nonetheless to ask oneself about the validity and reliability of the studies of lifestyles. In effect, they suffer from criticisms and problems that will be exposed in Chapter 7.

Before presenting the different fields of lifestyle application in more detail, it is important to note that they are mainly used to clear up hypotheses and generate creative ideas for diverse commercial strategies. Used as a decision-making technique in the field of management, they are often associated with other types of analysis, such as the creativity methods or strategic analysis of product-market concepts.

The general lifestyle typologies are often used in the advertising domain. They offer applications in commercial research, as well, and are classified into five categories, in ascending order of the degree of their use:

- decisions concerning distribution (section 1)
- conception and development of new products (section 2)
- strategies of segmentation in the market (section 3)
- identifying new marketing trends (section 4)
- advertising strategies (section 5)

Finally, we can add a sixth section, related more to management in general, sales forces, and how enterprises are run (section 6). Given their diversity, each one of these six uses requires its own description.

## DECISIONS CONCERNING DISTRIBUTION

Although rarely used in this domain, the analysis of lifestyles seems to lead to interesting results. Let us cite, for example, Reynolds and Darden (1972a) who, with the help of 148 general or specific characteristics, analyzed the lifestyles of American women who shopped in large stores situated on the periphery of the city. This study led to the formation of a very specific profile type: These women have a dynamic nature and are not concerned with the amount of time spent making their purchases; therefore, they are not loyal to any one specific store. Unsatisfied with the local stores, they prefer to frequent the suburban shopping malls.

Along the same lines, Bearden, Teel, and Durand (1978) conducted a study in the USA concerning sale shoppers, fast-food restaurant clientele, and "bazaar" shoppers. They showed that a link existed between the profile of the consumer (their tendency to be open-minded, modernists, traditionalists, etc.) and the places they chose to shop. For example, consumers only rarely patronizing stores in proximity to their homes appear to be traditional individuals, introverts, and very dependent on their social surroundings to make purchasing decisions.

Crask and Reynolds (1978), relying on one AIO study of large department store clientele in the United States, also released specific profiles of these shoppers. Large department store clientele appear to be very socially integrated individuals, very involved in group activities, particularly of an athletic and cultural nature. Sensitivity to style and the importance accorded to social image are two other traits of these individuals.

In France, however, there were few studies that attempted to analyze lifestyles according to shopping habits. Dizambourg's (1983) research thus constitutes an interesting contribution in this sense. He studied the links between individuals' lifestyles and their attitudes regarding the activity of buying during their trips to the shopping mall in the French city of Cretail. Three dimensions characterized the purchasing orientations of the consumer:

- The first refers to the interest in *shopping* as a leisure activity. It compares those consumers who actually like to go shopping with those who do not see going into a store as a recreational activity. If the *shoppers* seem preoccupied with the search for novelty and social differentiation, this does not hold true for the latter group of consumers.
- The second dimension compares and contrasts the loyal and traditional consumer with the modern and disloyal consumer. The traditionalists have a very conservative mentality, contrary to the modern consumers, who veer toward change and hedonistic values.
- Finally, the third dimension represents the degree of organization regarding purchasing activity. It demonstrates the contrast between price-conscious consumers (who are suspicious of merchants and plan their purchases carefully) and lax consumers (who do their purchasing in a

much more impulsive manner). The tendency to plan out one's purchases appears in consumers of a more traditional mindset, whereas impulsive buyers seem to be more open to pleasure-seeking values and change.

Finally, let us take note of the fact that the CCA also proposes a typology that describes different kinds of purchases and forms of business (see Chapter 4). In the early 1980s, for example, the "utilitarians" making the "functional" purchase, veered toward the large department stores, in contrast to choices when buying "nonfunctional" Items.

## CONCEPTION AND DEVELOPMENT OF NEW PRODUCTS

Although very rarely used until now, lifestyles can be employed beneficially for the creation of new products, by furnishing a more precise image of consumers' wants, needs, and uses.

Frye and Klein (1974) investigated the connection between psychographics and product purchases. A first profile is based on the psychographic elements (which use psychological traits to categorize consumers); a second is based on classic socioeconomic information. Frye and Klein's study provided evidence that, in general, the interviewees preferred products that most closely matched their given psychographics.

Another study conducted by Douglas and Le Maire (1976) furnished a second illustration of this application of lifestyles, this time testing the concept of a new dessert in the United States. First, the interviewed households were classified by their degree of interest in the idea; different segments of the market were more likely to purchase than others. At the same time, the researchers gathered information on 200 variables of lifestyles. Then, the lifestyle profiles for each group were constructed by a discriminant analysis. Table 6.1 shows two identified profiles and their corresponding characteristics.

The households most interested in trying the new dessert were innovative and laid back; however, they tended to view the kitchen and cuisine in general as "housework" and therefore avoided it. Many individuals in the sample perceived their principal role as that of mother. Purchasing ready-made desserts for their children was seen as a time-saving advantage. A practical application for these insights effects advertisement communication. The aspects of the product—easy to make, thereby decreasing preparation time and leaving more time for the mother to spend with her children—are important selling points.

Lifestyle studies, therefore, can help us better define new product profiles. They also allow us to target the consumers most receptive to a new concept. This interesting perspective opens up naturally to the use of lifestyles in strategies of market segmentation.

Table 6.1

**Profiles of Two Segments for a New Type of Dessert**

| | Segment 1 | | Segment 4 | |
| --- | --- | --- | --- | --- |
| | Woman with high probability to purchase (19%) | | Woman with low probability to purchase (16%) | |
| Socioeconomic characteristics | Married, young, 25–30 years old | | Older | |
| | Relatively high income | | Low income | |
| | Middle class | | Lower class | |
| Activities | Little interest in cooking from scratch | 2.1 | Interest in cooking | 4.0 |
| | Lots of socializing | 4.3 | Little socializing | 2.1 |
| | Concerned about the house | 2.9 | Concerned about the house | 4.5 |
| Attitude | Strong orientation toward their children | 4.5 | Orientation toward children | 2.3 |
| | Innovative | 4.9 | Not innovative | 2.5 |
| Opinion | Conservative perception of the role of women | 3.7 | Moderate perception of the role of women | 2.9 |
| | Optimism for the future | 4.3 | Little optimism for the future | 2.3 |
| Product performance | Frequently purchases desserts | 4.7 | Rarely purchases desserts | 2.3 |
| | Frequently purchases in supermarkets | 4.6 | Frequently purchases in small stores | 3.8 |
| | Always serves desserts to children | 3.9 | Does not always serve desserts to children | 3.0 |

*Source:* Douglas and Le Maire (1976).

## STRATEGIES OF SEGMENTATION IN THE MARKET

The analysis of lifestyles in market segmentation has been used to describe existing segments and to study potential segments.

### Description of the Existing Segments

In this case, the segments are initially described and identified by a priori criteria, such as users or nonusers and consumers who are faithful to a single brand or store. It is only then that the lifestyles of each segment are studied in order to better define the axes of marketing strategy.

In fact, according to Plummer (1974a, 1974b), segmentation based on lifestyles has several advantages:

- relevance and applicability often prove to be stronger than with the use of a single sociodemographic variable
- the operational character is likely raised, since lifestyle becomes an explanatory variable for diverse behaviors (media and retail store choices, etc.)
- segmentation would remain stable.

Plummer also studied lifestyles of credit card users. The author explained certain behaviors that could be analyzed only from the standpoint of social category (Plummer, 1971c). The analysis showed that credit cards users, contrary to nonusers, generally had a taste for risk, leaned toward advanced ideas, and rejected traditional orientations. Thus, male owners of credit cards were viewed as successful and led a very active life, considering themselves as having all the commodities of their credit cards and not their possibilities of deferred payment. Female users of credit cards seemed to lead a very similar life but were more worried about their outward appearance. They did not concern themselves with domestic work and perceived their role as women to be nontraditional. Plummer concluded from these facts that the principle obstacles to a widespread acceptance of the credit card were traditional and conservative attitudes toward money and life in general.

Another example of this method comes from a study of members of the leading French political parties (De Vulpian, 1976). A correlation was established between the affiliation with political parties and membership in certain sociocultural profile types in the French population. Figure 6.1 indicates the weight of each type in the realm of parties.

Profile types clearly differed along party lines. The profile type of PSU (the Unified Socialist Party of France) members differed significantly from the profile of those affiliated with all the other parties. Composed mainly of "pioneers" and "sociocenteric innovators," the PSU was characterized by strong ties to avant-garde sociocultural trends. This group shunned the media, which means mass communication methods often failed to reach them. Contrarily, the "old-fashioned" types, who represented a strong proportion of the UDR (Democratic Union for the Republic), watched television more frequently than the others and were therefore very receptive to this type of communication.

It should be noted that certain authors consider the explicit power of descriptive variables of lifestyles to be rather limited. Bearden, Woodside, and Ronkainen (1978) studied customers' purchasing behavior toward four brands of beer, measured by the frequency of consumption and by the brands they purchased. From this study, they came to the following conclusions:

**Figure 6.1    Distribution of Sociocultural Types in the Participant Audience: The Difference as Compared to the Entire Population of Salespeople** (Forces Vives/CCA)

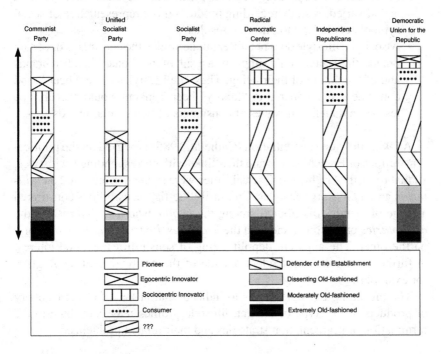

*Source:* De Vulpian (1976).

- The sociodemographic variables used (age, income, level of education, position in the family life cycle) did not seem to affect the frequency of purchase or the brands used.
- On the contrary, the variables of lifestyles did have an impact on the frequency of product consumption.
- The choice of brand, however, did not seem to be linked to lifestyle. The system of beliefs about products and the image of those products are more explicit criteria of the brand being consumed than the descriptive lifestyle values.

The authors therefore concluded that the analysis of a consumer's lifestyle can often furnish interesting information explaining the frequency of use or consumption of a product, but that same analysis cannot be used to predict the buyer's brand choice.

These results can, however, be moderate for the following two reasons:

- First, beer is not a product for which the function of social differentiation is that varied. A study regarding products more representative of social symbols could lead to different results.
- Also, if the lifestyle does not differentiate among the consumers of certain brands, this failure could simply be a result of the choice of studied brands and of the nature of their being. Thus, the lifestyles of new beer-brand consumers as compared to "luxury" beer drinkers would probably be less alike than the lifestyles of consumers of two similar brands.

A 1982 study on segmentation (Cathelat, 1985a) focused on the political sensibilities of French people and their links with corresponding sociostyles. At that time, the "right-wing" sensibilities were rather concentrated on *utilitarian* and *refocusing* lifestyles. Contrarily, "leftist" sensibilities constituted a range of profiles distributed among the *people who are vigilant* and the *exemplaries* on the one hand, and the *hedonists, libertarians*, and *amateurs* on the other. The apparent depoliticizing of sensibilities sparked interest in further research from leaders outside of the political field (ecologists, for example).

The preceding example seems to indicate that at least for one category of products or one type of market, lifestyle profiles may contribute to the formulation of segmentation strategies and their related problems.

### Study of Potential Segments

When studying potential segments, researchers look to preference variables and attitudes specific to the product. Then, the general lifestyle and related characteristics of these segments are studied.

This method was made famous by Haley's (1968) work on the toothpaste market in the United States. The six types of variables used were:

- consumer expectations
- personality
- behavior
- lifestyle
- sociodemographic characteristics
- opinions relative to the category of the studied product

These variables then allowed for the identification of four very specific segments:

- sensory-oriented people seeking pleasure in their lives;
- social people leading socially active lives;
- worriers with conservative tendencies and a pessimistic inclination; and
- independent people leading very autonomous lives.

Users who fall into each of these categories have different expectations from their brand of toothpaste: The first group is looking for a pleasant taste and scent; the second is focused on the whitening of teeth; the third wants cavity prevention; and the fourth seeks a low price. It is therefore easy to discern the advantages of segmentation in a strategy of marketing communication.

A similar approach is that of Segnit and Broadbent (1974), who studied the market of frozen entrees (referred to in the 1970s as "TV dinners") and ready-made desserts. Looking at the purchasing frequency of seventeen dishes, they divided the sample into three principal groups and six secondary groups. They then examined the socioeconomic characteristics and lifestyles of these nine groups. Table 6.2 illustrates the types of consumer behavior connected with each product. There are clear differences in the orientation(s) of the lifestyles.

Though similar in purpose, these two approaches vary in their methodologies. Assuming lifestyles are used in both cases to identify segments, Haley's study works around attitudes toward the product or the sought benefits, whereas the second study measures purchase frequency. These differences may affect the results of the segmentation: The first method places more importance on consumer expectations, while the second reflects their net consumption.

## IDENTIFYING NEW MARKET TRENDS

Lifestyle analysis has been used to discern market trends in two key ways:

1. through globalized studies of how trends in lifestyles evolve, and
2. in a more precise manner, based on studies of particular product choices.

### *Examining the Trends in the Evolution of Lifestyles*

Concerning the first point, lifestyle analysis can, in fact, make an important contribution to the understanding of the business environment. The breadth of the field of investigation (the group of social behaviors) allows for the dispersal of given information, which is based on the idea that consumer behavior is constantly evolving.

Thus, COFREMCA's inquiries revealed a tendency to adopt a simpler way of life, one closer to nature, as seen through the following examples:

Table 6.2

**Segmentation of the Market of Frozen Entrees and Prepared Desserts**

| Principal groups | Frequency of consumption | Socioeconomic characteristics | Lifestyle |
|---|---|---|---|
| 1. The reflective female | Average for packaged products. High for frozen products (particularly for peas, refrigerated fruit, and ice cream). | High income. Cultivated. Property owner. Owns a freezer. | I frequently try new recipes. I want my children to pursue higher education. My friends consider me successful. |
| 2. The over-protective mother | High for packaged products. Especially high for frozen mousse. | Raises kids. Property owner. | I don't always feed my children food they like. Our family is close. Unbranded products are just as good as branded products. |
| 3. The frivolous female | Average to high for packaged products. High for prepared meals. | Young. Raises kids. | I like romance novels. I like to look attractive to men. I dislike household work. |

*Source:* Segnit, S., and Broadbent, S. (1974), Clustering by Product Usage: A Case History, *Proceedings of the XXVth ESOMAR Congress,* Amsterdam, 118–124.

- the commercialization of natural foods (wheat and natural fruit juice);
- promotional campaigns favoring the use of natural fibers such as linen and cotton; and
- the promotion of rustic furniture and tools (a strategy adopted by Habitat, a British company specializing in household furnishings and home comfort).

Also, Jean Mauduit (1976) remarked that advertisements for toiletries are inspired not so much by sexual differentiation as by polysensualism and a certain sexual liberalism.

In an analogous manner, the CCA's proposal of a "refocusing" trend, characterized by an increased need for withdrawal to personal and familial life or cocooning, can explain the development of markets linked to home decorating, habitat, and all the products generally perceived as supportive of a new way of living. At the same time, individuals with a utilitarian mindset would be attracted to more useful products, cleaning equipment, and practical forms of packaging.

It is equally important to note that the evolution of lifestyles can suggest modifications in marketing strategy. Hodock (1974) felt that knowledge of lifestyles and psychographic types might help researchers follow the effects of lifestyle modifications on new forms of marketing and distribution techniques. For example, large department stores have the tendency to compartmentalize their floor space into rows or neatly individualized boutiques, each corresponding to a given lifestyle and specific clothing type.

A less global and less general use of lifestyles exists in the analysis of particular domains of human activity. This type of study can be very useful in the formulation of new products.

## *Examining Patterns of Consumption for Specific Products*

A product-specific analysis focuses on a particular aspect of lifestyle, such as a hobby or a pastime, which is incorporated into one's attitude toward and use of a given product. Apart from the specifics of a product, one identifies the market segments and then studies lifestyles in general.

The next example, borrowed from Douglas and Le Maire (1973), deals with a company wishing to establish itself as a seller of home improvement and repair products. A study was conducted on people's attitudes regarding the home and its role in the area of different lifestyles. The following points were emphasized in the study:

- the specific interest placed on home improvement and décor; the time, effort, and money involved; and the decision to hire a professional or pursue the "do it yourself" route
- certain aspects of lifestyle related indirectly to one's attitude toward housing, such as time spent at home versus away, the significance of the home in accordance with family life, the importance of "going out," and the role of social prestige in one's life

Three different segments were identified, and specific types of products were paired with each one according to the consumers' varied expectations. Table 6.3 sums up the characteristics of these three profiles.

Through this example, it is clear that the study of lifestyles allows us to better analyze the use of products in daily life according to varied consumer types. This example, among others, allows for the improvement of existing products and their appropriation to different segments of the market.

Table 6.3

**Lifestyle Profiles for Buyers of Home Improvement Products**

| Profiles | 1. The Enthusiast | 2. The Amateur | 3. The Nouveau Riche |
|---|---|---|---|
| Expectations | • devotes a lot of time to do-it-yourself projects on their home. | • frustrated by the lack of time for maintaining and decorating the house. | • want to spend the minimum amount of time on maintaining and decorating the house. |
| | • enjoy working on repairs themselves. | • apply themselves to work outside the home. | • appeals to professionals. |
| | • are concerned about price. | • not concerned about price. | • not concerned about price. |
| Activities | • staying at home. | • more introverted and concerned with aesthetics. | • extroverted and warm. |
| | • do not like sports. | • enjoy music and cultural activities. | • prefer active team sports. |
| | | • spend time on intellectual pursuits. | • go out frequently. |
| | | • sociable. | |
| Attitudes | • relatively attracted to innovation. | • relatively attracted to innovation. | • attracted to innovation. |
| | • place great importance on their home. | • place a great importance on their family. | • not interested in their homes or gardens. |
| | • conservative. | | |
| Opinions | • very concerned about pollution. | • relatively optimistic. | • optimistic. |
| | | • relatively concerned about pollution. | • are not concerned about pollution or environmental problems. |

*Source:* Douglas and Le Maire (1973).

## ADVERTISING STRATEGIES

Lifestyle analysis is widely employed in the field of advertising. It has been used to create and validate campaign themes and to identify and attract a precise target audience.

### Discovery and Validation of New Publicity Ideas

The use of data from lifestyle studies, particularly concerning segmentation, led to the creation of new communication strategies. In the United States, certain authors initially considered psychographics an essential tool for use in advertising (e.g., Dunn, 1971; Simmons, 1971; Young, 1971).

In practice, however, the advertising message is developed in conjuction with the lifestyle profiles of the targeted segments. This allows the advertiser to better analyze the characteristics of the audience with which he or she intends to communicate. Ziff (1971) estimated that one of the principal advantages of analyzing lifestyles is that it allows the designer of advertisements to suspend his or her personal system of values. Wells (1974) recognized three principal interests in the use of lifestyles in advertising material:

1. adapting the message, content, style, and structure of advertising campaigns to a determined segment;
2. realizing and renovating old themes; and
3. better understanding the different audiences by following their evolution.

Among the diverse uses of lifestyle analysis for the creation of advertisements, the example furnished by Plummer (1974a, 1974b) is particularly illustrative. One analysis allowed for the identification of beer consumers' psychographic profiles. These consumers were attracted to the ideals of virility, masculinity, competition, strength, heroism, and intense physical effort. They displayed a keen interest in sports. One campaign appealed to their manly inclinations by portraying the dangerous and adventurous lifestyle of a marine (and simultaneously, a consumer of beer). The targeted buyers could thus identify themselves with the proposed image, and the result was a strong increase in sales. In this example, the theme centered on an ideal "type" that emerged from the corresponding hidden aspirations of the target market.

An advertising message can sometimes develop from the lifestyle profile of target segments. The 1982 advertising campaign for Minolta cameras is a good example of this phenomenon. Realized apart from the current sociocultures, this campaign tried to target what COFREMCA would call *modernists*, in particular:

• pioneers with a "passion for conquering";
• innovators with a "passion for love"; and
• egocentric innovators with a "passion for life."

In spite of having a good general connotation for each of the segments, the campaign was abandoned a year later because the word "passion" provoked a negative reaction from the public. The company came back with a more classic campaign based on the technological value of their products.

In summary, if the two methods of passion and technology are similar in that they both drew good results from their targeted segments, they differ nonetheless in their approach. We still have not seen a study testing their effectiveness.

Another use of lifestyle analysis in the domain of advertising concerns the selection of media.

### Selection of Media

Lifestyle analysis in the domain of various media audiences, or the group of consumers reacting in different ways to one or another type of media, is systematically practiced in both France and the United States (Peterson, 1972). In fact, this study allows for the qualitative evaluation of media and the selection of these media in accordance with corresponding lifestyle profiles.

In the case of eleven types of magazines, Michaels (1973) examined the lifestyle profiles of American readers. He discovered different sensitivities, without specific relationships to the products being advertised. Thus, reading agricultural magazines is generally associated with a traditional lifestyle and receptiveness to ads concerning religion. At the same time, readers of the American magazine *National Geographic* are generally interested in artistic and ecological topics. It follows, then, that certain publications serve as better advertising vehicles than others for certain types of products. Particularly, agricultural magazines seem to be poorly adapted to technological innovations, but well suited to natural, wholesome, even spiritual types of products.

In France, numerous studies have focused on the relationship between the users of different media and various sociocultural values. Demuth and Neirac's study (1976) came up with nine groups of media habits, two of which form the two tiers of population: the anti-media group (34 percent of the population) and the group of people exposed solely to television (also making up 34 percent of the population). (Recall that in the 1970s, computers and handheld devices were not among the media being considered by Demuth and Neirac.) The correlation between these groups and eleven typologies identified in French society (based on shared values) was studied. It was also established that belonging to the anti-media group—those who did not watch television frequently—was closely correlated to belonging to the profile type considered "ahead" of sociocultural trends. Assuming this trend progressed in French society, advertising agencies would need to find new forms of communication or efficient means to surmount these negative attitudes toward the existing mass media.

The CCA also studied the links between media and sociostyles. Each sociocultural model has its own media, which defines its own values. *Le Chasseur français,* a magazine whose title means "The French Hunter," stresses the virtues of order, positivism, work, effort, economy, and production, all corresponding to utilitarian lifestyles. An opposing example would be the magazine *Actuel*, which is more escapist in nature and focuses on the appeal of wealth, fame, and beauty.

The CCA thus links each lifestyle to certain types of media; some examples follow:

- Moralist media attracts French utilitarian sociotypes by offering them the certainty of intangible values and great eternal principles. Some examples from the written press include *Le Chasseur français*, *L'Action automobile*, and *Historia*.
- Informational media attracts French adventure sociotypes with their direct and rational take on today's world. Some examples include *Le Monde*, weekly news publications such as *Le Point*, and economic reviews such as *L'Expansion*.
- Know-how (self-help and do-it-yourself) media, which apply to a refocusing France. Going from the most classic to the most modern, they give individuals advice on how to integrate the complexity of the world into their daily lives. These include, for example, *Sélection du Reader's Digest, Confidences, Femmes d'Aujourd'hui,* and *Jours de France.*
- Imaginative media which represent the France of *discrepancy*. These media, such as *Actuel* and *L'Echo des savanes,* incorporate elements of skepticism and nonconformity in their views and often feature short stories of the fantasy genre.

The CCA thus proposed a whole series of brochures linking lifestyles to radio, television, and the press. It also refined its presentations in function with twenty sections such as current events, leisure, sports, home repair, nature, women, and youth, among others. This classification allowed (at least in theory) advertisers to choose the most appropriate media according to theme and target market. Among the weekly news magazines in France, *L'Evenement du jeudi* is considered centrist and *Le Nouvel Observateur* offers a leftist perspective, thereby distinguishing themselves from other news magazines such as *L'Express* and *Le Point*, which try to maintain a distance from politics.

The principal interest of these studies resides in the fact that lifestyles allow us to differentiate audiences with more precision than classical criteria of a socioeconomic nature. (Kahle and Homer, 1985; Kahle, Poulos, and Sukhdial, 1986) In the following example given by Grandjean (1978), the readership of two magazines—*Femmes d'Aujourd'hui* and *Modes de Paris*—are compared. Table 6.4 shows the results. One sees that, on the basis of classical socioeconomic criteria (age, social status, profession, etc.), it is impossible to differentiate among the two magazines, whereas an analysis by sociotypes allows one to see the following differences: 20 percent of the *Modes de Paris* readers

Table 6.4

**Comparison of the Readers of Two French Magazines\* in Terms of CSP and Lifestyles**

| | Similarities according to socioeconomics Study of 100 readers | | | | Differentiation by sociotype |  |
|---|---|---|---|---|---|---|
| | • According to age | | | | Conservative | |
| | 15–24 | 25–34 | 35–49 | 50+ | | |
| Femmes d'Aujourd'hui | 18.8% | 19.7% | 24.7% | 36.8% | Modes de Paris | 7% |
| Modes de Paris | 21.2% | 19.7% | 23.4% | 35.7% | Femmes d'Aujourd'hui | 23% |
| | • According to socioprofessional categories | | | | Hedonistic | |
| | Executives, shopkeepers, employees | Foremen, workmen | Nonworkers, farmers | | | |
| Femmes d'Aujourd'hui | 44.1% | 36.2% | 28% | | Modes de Paris | 20% |
| Modes de Paris | 39.1% | 39.2% | 29.7% | | Femmes d'Aujourd'hui | 6% |

*Source:* Grandjean (1978).
*Note:* The numbers represent 1978 audiences.
*\*Femmes d'Aujourd'hui* (title means "Women of Today"); *Modes de Paris* (title means "Paris Fashion").

are defined by the hedonistic sociotype, while only 6 percent of the *Femmes d'Aujourd'hui* are considered hedonistic. Seven percent of the *Modes de Paris* readers belong to the conservative sociotype, as compared to 23 percent of the *Femmes d'Aujourd'hui* readers. Let us note, however, that such differences are not always explicit. For example, *L'Evenement du jeudi* is "out of line," whereas *Paris Match* is "refocused." In this case how do we explain the fact that these two publications, according to the CESP, sell 200,000 copies every week, when the mentalities to which they appeal are so opposite? What is to be said about the sociocultural profiles of these two magazines' readers? Many questions, in fact, indicate the limit of descriptive analysis and once more put an emphasis on the *sociocultural plurality* of individuals. These patterns are far from representative of a single class of lifestyle.

Another study conducted in France on the connections between centers of interest and media habits also confirmed a number of significant relationships (Agostini and Boss, 1973). As Wells (1974) noted, there are several examples of how lifestyle analysis facilitates the evaluation of media:

- They support advertisement, in order to determine their adaptation to different products and types of promotional events;
- They support vehicle choice, at the level of necessary positioning or repositioning in response to what the targeted segments expect;
- They support the messages' environment, a reflection of the characteristics of their context.

It is important to note that in all of these domains, lifestyle methods are rarely used alone. For the most part, they are combined with the usual sociodemographic criteria. Also, as is underlined by Kapferer (1985), the methodological problems of research on lifestyles seem actually to constrain their use. Nevertheless, this approach was used in the work of Cathelat and Ebguy (1987), the result of the work and experience of EUROCOM agents. The system they proposed, *Co-système*, was supposed to render the world of communication in sixty different categories, divided into three modes of evaluation (functional, sociological, and psychological). According to them, this new advertising approach would allow for the adaptation of advertising messages to each lifestyle. Thus, for example, an *institutional social* message for *Europe 1* would be better adapted to *Figaro-Magazine*, a more serious and conservative journal, whereas a *psychological message of derision* for this same radio station would correspond better to the modernist character of *Le Nouvel Observateur*.

## LIFESTYLES AND MANAGEMENT

Due to the initiative of CCA, studies of lifestyles are no longer the domain of commercial research; instead, they seem to lean more toward general management research. In spite of other uses being possible, it seems interesting (to us) to present the three principal applications. Two of the three emanate from the CCA. The last one is more original:

- The first and most specific application, realized toward the end of 1984 by Forces Vives (in collaboration with CCA) focuses on *lifestyles of the sellers*. (Further discussion on this subject appears in a series of articles by Gabilliet, 1987.)
- The second and more ambitious application, developed by the CCA, tries to define the different *styles of enterprise* (Burke, 1987).
- The third and final application, better founded, concerns the identification of *organizational values* (Bales, Cohen, and Williamson, 1979) and distinguishes itself very clearly from the first two.

*Styles of Sales*

In the first example, the study of 500 salespeople yielded twelve types, regrouped into four different mindsets that are positioned in the following system of axes: "all for me–all for the company" and "materialistic elasticity–psychological elasticity." As indicated in Table 6.5, the results allow companies to find the best fit for their employees, as different functions and positions demand workers with diversified profiles and motivations. In addition, the results led to numerous applications, among them the recruitment and training of salespeople by style. As noted by Petry (1987), such a study allows hiring managers to find workers who fit the *lifestyle of the company.*

*Styles of Enterprise*

This remark joins the second orientation proposed by the CCA, in order to define different *enterprises' lifestyles,* often referred to in the United States as *corporate cultures.* Mike Burke (1987) of the CCA identified four cultural mindsets—narcissistic, visionary, adaptive, and defensive—that were further subdivided into eight specific cultural indentities (Table 6.6). These styles represent richly diverse aspirations, convictions, and attitudes. In an analogous manner, but a little bit less imaginative, the authors produced four principal attitudes toward work:

- Work-Motivation, for the ambitious;
- Work-Protection, for the worried;
- Work-Necessity, for the diligent;
- Work-Destiny, for the resigned.

These four mentalities split themselves up into the twelve sociotypes presented in Table 6.7.

This effort to link up (and better understand) corporate culture, efficiency, competitiveness, and performance is commendable, but it is by no means revolutionary (see, for example, Lemaitre, 1984). Because of its obscure and complicated nature, other approaches with a firmer conceptual foundation might prove more useful in the identification of organizational values.

*Systems of Organizational Values*

As noted by Poumadère (1985), each organization is unique. The individuals and groups of which it is composed, the type of activities and jobs it offers, its beliefs, norms, and values—all of these differ. Its history, its collective rituals, and its taboos differ as well. The style of its leaders contributes further

Table 6.5

## Description of Four Sales Mindsets (CCA)

No more than the "average Frenchman," the "typical" French salesperson does not exist. The long discussions by CCA compared with a sample of 503 vendors, representing their 700,000 French colleagues, permitted the creation of an archetype of their lifestyles as a function of two dimensions: their materialistic or psychological resilience and their centers of interest ("all for me" or "all for the enterprise").

Four major distinct groups and six subgroups are positioned on this map. More than literal descriptions, they are more like centers of gravity, sometimes caricatures. Each particular vendor can seem globally more like a mindset that can equally borrow traits from other sociotypes.

### The Unconditional Ones: 31.6%

The most numerous one. "This is the hard-line of the sales people, perceived as noble, that allows for them to be relaxed socially." Often self-taught, very attached and faithful to the business of the employer, they obey the rules for recognition.

Their traditionalism nevertheless allows them to innovate in the field of sales. They are partly menaced by the transfer of clients, the elitism of directors, who prefer them over their bosses, and who lack the perceptiveness of the heads of sales.

Condemned? No. These persistent workers could continue to be effective, as long as they are taught new techniques as necessary. But they do not want their children to work in the same field as they did. They are very common in sectors such as the auto industry and real estate.

### The Climbers: 30.8%

Having come voluntarily to a career in the sales field, often to gain a skill, they are quickly frustrated by their work and wish to switch. For them, sales is a rite of passage that allows them to climb the business ladder and achieve executive status. One will not be surprised at the high rate of turnover that characterizes this group, for which money is a symbol and a means of self-evaluation: the regular salary increases are more highly valued than inconsistent commissions. To recruit them and to motivate them, it is necessary therefore to speak to them about "career" and "progression," for they believe—truly or falsely—in the longevity of a career. They can be found in every sector.

### The Infantrymen: 21.9%

Predominantly opportunists and adventurers, these people are in sales by chance. They adapt easily to all landscapes because of their ability to negotiate, to convince (all of the arguments are good) and to sell . . . no matter what. In a sense, they are closer to their customers than to their employers. But sales for them is mostly a fight (a solitary one). They are individualists who are motivated by profits. They take a sort of "revenge" on society and do not share any of their know-how and even less of their data. They are very difficult to manage. Nevertheless, they will always have their place as "commandos" in the expanding markets where they currently flourish.

### The Uninvolved: 15.7%

The latter group of salespeople does not know why it sells and isn't bothered by it. These are the progressives: Their centers of interest are elsewhere—in private life, for example. These people know to hold a conversation, but they are bought more than they sell themselves. This is the case, for example, in sectors where the products are already presold by the advertisements or on very specific markets (automobile, luxury products, etc.). They often work sitting, in stores or in offices, but that does not stop the businesses from retaining them. . . .

*Source:* Nouzille, V. (1985). Qu'est-ce qui fait courir les vendeurs? *L'Usine Nouvelle*, 47, Nov. 21, 1985, p. 134.

Table 6.6

**Four Corporate Cultures and Eight Cultural Identities** (CCA)

| Cultures | Cultural Identities |
|---|---|
| Narcissistic (27%) | Crop (14%) |
| | Greenhouse (13%) |
| Visionary (10%) | Wild Orchid (2%) |
| | Farming (8%) |
| Adaptive (31%) | Creeper (15%) |
| | Large Garden (16%) |
| Defensive (32%) | Kitchen Garden (16%) |
| | Formal Garden (16%) |

*Source:* Adapted from Burke (1987).

Table 6.7

**Four Work-Related Mindsets and Twelve Corresponding Sociotypes** (CCA)

| Mindsets | Sociotypes |
|---|---|
| Work-Motivation (28.8%) | Partisans (10.5%) |
| | Scouts (2.9%) |
| | Malignant (5%) |
| | Navigators (10.4%) |
| Work-Protection (30.6%) | Sentries (3%) |
| | Defenders (9.8%) |
| | Inconsistent (7.3%) |
| | Consistent (10.5%) |
| Work-Destiny (17.1%) | Devoted (16.3%) |
| | Taciturn (10.8%) |
| Work-Duty (23.5%) | Councils (9.2%) |
| | Opinionated (14.3%) |

*Source:* Adapted from Burke (1987).

to the unique structure and culture of an organization. Taken together, this collection of shared values allows us to characterize the *visible identity* of an enterprise (Strategor, 1988).

From this perspective, the identification of *organizational values* becomes very important, and two principal points require explanation:

- The first point, which concerns the particularly important notion of *habits*, was brought out by Strategor (1988), was originaated by Mauss (1969), and elaborated by Bourdieu (1982) and Strategor (1988).

- The second point relates to the values-identification method in function with the social system, proposed by Bales, Cohen, and Williamson (1979).

The habits correspond to the underlying conventions and attitudes—some instinctive, some socially acquired—that inform an individual's thoughts, feelings, and actions. Habits are a product of different social and economic conditions. (Kahle and Beatty, 1987)A variety of business practices and their corresponding styles of management are closely related to different habits. Finally, habits are also a process of *consensus*. Sharing a *values system* or *ethos*, constructed by habits, the members of an enterprise share responsibility and achieve stability and coherence as a group. Identifying the value system of an organization's members is, therefore, essential to discerning its collective identity.

For this very reason, Bales, Cohen, and Williamson (1979) developed SYMLOG, a method of determining the function of values within a social system. Strongly validated by an empirical plan, more than 5,000 hours of observation, and numerous factor analyses on values, this approach was also legitimized from a conceptual point of view. It conveys the ideas of many theoretic fields in a complementary manner, among them:

- the social theory of interaction processes (Bales, 1950 and 1970);
- the theory of field (Lewin, 1951);
- the theory of symbolic interaction (Mead, 1934); and
- the psychoanalytic theory.

In a general manner, Bales, Cohen, and Williamson (1979) agreed to unveil situations' collective and individual significance to communication phenomena in manner and content, rather than to single physical appearances in behavior.

The SYMLOG approach led to the definition of three dimensions:

- values tending toward dominance/values tending toward submission
- values tending toward egalitarianism/values tending toward antisocial individualism
- values tending to oppose work orientation around established authority/ values tending to accept work orientation around established authority

As indicated in the cubic model, Figure 6.2, there are twenty-six equal parts (the very central block being omitted) for which an evaluation formula of individual and organizational values (Table 6.8) exists. This allows us to measure corresponding orientations and explore an individual's *system of organizational values*. The resulting cartographies provide several levels

Figure 6.2    **Organizational Value Functions Measured in Three Dimensions** (SYMLOG)

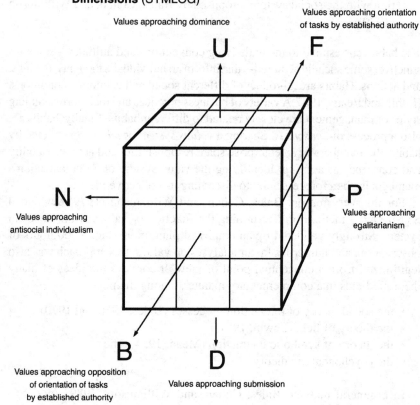

*Source:* Poumadère (1985).

of information concerning each person's perception of values as they are generally attributed to them by other people. In addition, the mapping allows for the analysis of typological relationships established within a field, or a global diagnostic of the group as a whole. This illustration depicts the SYMLOG method and its applicability to diverse managerial issues such as detecting work attitudes and identifying efficiency criteria for teamwork (see Poumadère, 1985, pp. 89–94 for corresponding illustrations).

In conclusion, we would like to summarize three principal thoughts:

* The studies on *enterprise styles* developed by the CCA appear to be studies made for specific analysis needs. Therefore, they should be considered only from a strictly theoretical perspective.

Table 6.8

**Description and Evaluation Formula of Organizational Values** (SYMLOG)

| Directions* | Values | Codification** | | |
|---|---|---|---|---|
| | | (0) | (1) | (2) |
| U | Individual material success, personal power | Rarely | Sometimes | Often |
| UP | Popularity and social success, acceptance and admiration | Rarely | Sometimes | Often |
| UPF | Unity and efforts toward common objectives | Rarely | Sometimes | Often |
| UF | Efficacy, a strong and impartial organization | Rarely | Sometimes | Often |
| UNF | Active reinforcement of authority, rules and procedures | Rarely | Sometimes | Often |
| UN | Reinforcement of self resolve and sharpness | Rarely | Sometimes | Often |
| UNB | Strong individualism, resistance to authority | Rarely | Sometimes | Often |
| UB | Amusement, relaxation, flexibility | Rarely | Sometimes | Often |
| UPB | Protect the weak, help them when necessary | Rarely | Sometimes | Often |
| P | Egalitarianism, democratic participation in decisions | Rarely | Sometimes | Often |
| PF | Responsible idealism, collaboration in tasks | Rarely | Sometimes | Often |
| F | "Correct" way of doing things, conformity and conventions | Rarely | Sometimes | Often |
| NF | Restrain personal desires to achieve goals | Rarely | Sometimes | Often |
| N | Self-satisfaction, personal interests first, self-sufficiency | Rarely | Sometimes | Often |
| NB | Reject established procedures, reject conformity | Rarely | Sometimes | Often |
| B | Change to new procedures and values, creativity | Rarely | Sometimes | Often |
| PB | Friendship, mutual satisfaction, relaxation | Rarely | Sometimes | Often |
| DP | Having confidence in the moral sense of others | Rarely | Sometimes | Often |
| DPF | Devotion, fidelity, loyalty to the business | Rarely | Sometimes | Often |
| DF | Obedience, respect of authority | Rarely | Sometimes | Often |
| DNF | Self-sacrifice is necessary for attaining objectives | Rarely | Sometimes | Often |
| DN | Passive rejection of popularity, staying home | Rarely | Sometimes | Often |
| DNB | Admit loss, abandon efforts | Rarely | Sometimes | Often |
| DB | Passive noncooperation with authority | Rarely | Sometimes | Often |
| DPB | Tranquil contentment, avoiding worry | Rarely | Sometimes | Often |
| D | Abandon personal needs and desires, passivity | Rarely | Sometimes | Often |

*Source:* Poumadère, M. (1985), op. cit., p. 83.

*Directions are used to locate values in the corresponding space (see Figure 6.1).

**The evaluation system with three choices (1 = Rarely, 2 = Sometimes, 3 = Often) was chosen because of its simplicity and speed; an evaluation system with five choices (0 = Never, 1 = Rarely, 2 = Sometimes, 3 = Often, 4 = Always) does not improve variance explained significantly (Bales, Cohen, and Williamson, 1979, p. 252).

- By their very nature, the studies concerning the identification of *organizational values systems* are aligned with approaches centered on values and presented in Chapter 2 of this book. This trend confirms the interest of values and their potential contribution, just as much for market analysis as for the resolution of managerial problems linked to conducting business.
- Finally, as was indicated by Strategor's team (1988), culture is reflected not only in *conscious* representations (values and beliefs), but also in *unconscious* representations of the individual. In this sense, the business takes equal part in the person's physical economy and mental economy. One better understands the contribution made by the study's psychoanalytic psychology of the unconscious. The first works in this domain are now considered classics, among them contributions by Zaleznik and Kets de Vries (1975) and Levinson (1981). Investigations that continue in this direction—and are complementary to the identification of organizational values that were just presented—therefore appear to be necessary, as little research in this domain has been conducted thus far. Research by Kets de Vries and Miller (1985) on the possible malfunctioning of an entire organization, Enriquez's analysis (1983) of the organizational image, and Pages's look at organizational power each deserve particular attention.

## CONCLUSION AND SYNTHESIS

This chapter allowed us to illustrate, by means of several examples, the principal domains of lifestyle-based studies. Thus, numerous applications were examined—some concerning decisions related to the conception, development, and distribution of new products, and others concerning the elaboration of market segmentation strategies, the identification of new market trends, the creation of advertising messages, and the choice of media.

In general, the results obtained were quite telling. The European study of "business managers' styles," proposed by Mike Burke of the CCA, is a revealing example (see Figure 6.3). Nevertheless, as we have already stressed, these uses are without veritable conceptual bases and are carried out in an empirical manner, thus serving best as a complement to more classic analyses using sociodemographic variables. On the other hand, the results are strongly linked to the types of variables used, these being far from identical in all of the studies. This diversity, linked to the different methodological problems evoked in all of the preceding chapters, poses a validity problem with respect to lifestyle studies. It is therefore appropriate, after this panorama of principal uses for lifestyles, to pinpoint the problems with this approach and attempt to solve them.

Figure 6.3    **Business Executives' Lifestyles** (CCA)

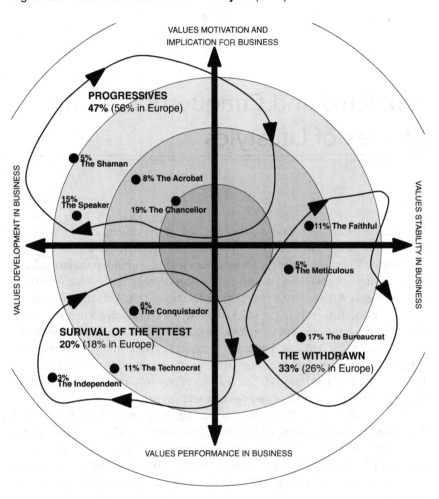

*Source:* Comment les Francais voient leur patron, *L'Expansion*, Sept. 8, 1988, p. 11.

# 7

# Problems and Critiques Raised by Studies of Lifestyles

The preceding chapters laid out the specifics of the principal approaches to lifestyle studies, as well as the theoretical fundamentals to which they are connected. The studies that center on values and consumption variables have the advantage of possessing a well-defined conceptual frame—the American example being AIO and the French examples those of CCA and COFREMCA. The works of Rokeach (e.g., 1973), which were introduced in the second chapter, define the concept of values quite clearly, along with their implications for behavior and one method of measuring them. In the same way, the foundations for approaches using variables of consumption are well defined by the works of Uusitalo (1979a, 1979b). They rely more on information gathered from panel studies and government statistics.

Some opposition to these methods exists among researchers. Critics find fault with the study of approaches centered on attitudes and activities (Chapter 3) due in large part to the essentially empirical development of their principal methods. Some of the criticism is methodological in nature, and some results from the transposition of cultural studies to an inappropriate foreign context.

## Problems Raised by Studies on Values and Variables of Consumption

The validity of the approach centered on values was tested in the United States by several authors (Rokeach, 1968a; Robinson and Shaver, 1973). Although the study was applied successfully in different cultural contexts (Rokeach, 1973), no definitive attempts were made to test a specific culture. In particular, one could ask about the stability of the two centers of values proposed by Rokeach in an environment culturally different from that of the

United States. In France, for example, Rokeach's research on values never gave proof of a structure developed around two dimensions that constitute terminal values and instrumental values (Arellano, 1983; Valette-Florence, 1985, 1988b).

Finally, we need to ask whether Rokeach's values truly reflect the actual values of our contemporaries. The answer is far from evident. In a little-known study, Jones, Sensenig, and Ashmore (1978) vigorously question Rokeach's values, stating that they barely present one-third of the values spontaneously mentioned by individuals. This reinforces the need to better adapt the values-based approach to reality. The criticism may not apply to methods that do not claim to study all values (e.g., Kahle, 1983).

The approaches centered on consumption variables appear reliable enough, because in general they precede the panel-given information. Note, however, that the risk of differences between real consumption and declared consumption persists. One study in particular focuses on food and drink preferences from one country to another. The comparison of consumption modes between different countries is challenging and explains the differences in research presented, for instance, by Cosmas (1982) in the United States and by Uusitalo (1979 a, b) in Finland. Finally, we can note one last point concerning accessibility to these studies: They were created by sales organizations for their own needs, and the results are generally unknown to the larger public.

These critiques are minor when compared to those of the objective approaches using American AIO inventories or the French approaches. Such problems are presented in the following sections.

## METHODOLOGICAL PROBLEMS POSED BY AIO INVENTORIES AND FRENCH APPROACHES

From a methodological point of view, certain problems arise that are due in part to the empirical development of the inventory-based approach to lifestyles. The main issues concern the conceptual framework and the pertinence of concepts used. Another problem, as noted by Le Maire (1981), resides principally in France, in the clandestine nature of lifestyle studies. Confidentiality hides problems common in all studies of lifestyles, among them the application of procedures, the validity and reliability of measuring instruments, and the formation of employed variables. Finally, one last critique deals with the lack of operational character in lifestyle studies, just as much on their level of predictive power as on the type of terminology used by researchers. Each of these points will be addressed, beginning with problems of a theoretical order.

## The Absence of Conceptualization and Justifying Those Concepts Used

In the United States, Wells (1975) was one of the first to point out the absence of conceptual bases characterizing the analysis of lifestyles. An apparent lack of consensus among researchers in the United States resulted in an ill-defined frame of reference for lifestyle approaches, with each team developing its own methods of analysis in a completely empirical manner. (See the works of Pessemier and Bruno [1971], Tigert and Arnold [1971], or Villani and Lehmann [1975] for examples.) Intuition and experience have dominated the composition of questionnaires and the choice of elements to take into account, more so than a clear conceptualization leaning on a solid theoretical foundation.

Thus, Table 7.1, adapted from Anderson and Golden (1983) and from Lastovicka (1982), indicates that in the United States, almost all of the studies unfolded without a theoretical frame of reference or any explicit definitions of lifestyles. These flaws called AIO-type studies into question and led to the rise of the VALS approach, which is more structured and built around the identification of values.

The French approaches tried to define a conceptual frame a priori, which allows for the building of a measuring tool. Thus, COFREMCA and CCA both used the complementary analysis of existing given information in order to determine *sociocultural* trends in lifestyle studies.

In spite of everything, the results obtained by the two approaches are not similar, notably because of the absence of theoretical references and concepts used. As noted by Le Maire (1981), the basis of most lifestyle studies remains very vague; it depends either on the method of collecting information, on the method of analyzing this information, or on both (which is the most likely case). This issue poses an immediate problem when it comes to validation. In his 1990 work *Socio-Styles systèmes,* Cathelat justifies his approach by the paradigm of complexity; however, the Socio-Styles System appears moreover to be a building block, certainly knowing but ad hoc, a clever juxtaposition but complex in methods. It is the fruit of the fertile imagination of the creators, of commendable desire but illusive of exhaustiveness and of never-ending requirements and of existing tool extension (for example, European *sociostyles* and *sociowaves*). It does not succeed as a scientific construction allowing for the explanation of a phenomenon.

Moreover, Le Maire (1981) emphasized that for the CESA, which carried out some research on lifestyles, the elaborated conceptual frame was based on three sources of information:

Table 7.1

## Synthesis of Lifestyle Studies in the United States

| Year | Author* | Definition | Explicit framework of theoretical reference | AIO Approaches |
|------|---------|------------|----------------------------------------------|----------------|
| 1963 | Kelley | | | |
| | Lazer | Yes | Yes | |
| | Levy | | Yes | |
| | Moore | Yes | Yes | |
| | Rathwell | | | |
| 1964 | King | | | |
| 1966 | Wilson | | | Yes |
| 1967 | Andreasen | Yes | | |
| 1969 | Alpert and Gatty | | | |
| | Tigert | | Yes | Yes |
| 1971 | Bernay | Yes | | |
| | Bushman | | | |
| | Demby | | | |
| | French and Glascher | | Yes | |
| | Garfinkle | | | |
| | Hasenjaeger | | Yes | |
| | Hustad and Pessemier | | | |
| | Nelson | | | |
| | Pessemier and Bruno | | | Yes |
| | Plummer | | | Yes |
| | Reynolds and Darden | | | Yes |
| | Simons | | | Yes |
| | Tigert | | | Yes |
| | Tigert and Arnold | | Yes | Yes |
| | Tigert and Lathorpe | | | Yes |
| | Wells and Tigert | | Yes | Yes |
| | Wind | Yes | | |
| | Young | | | |
| 1972 | Michaels | | | Yes |
| | Reynolds and Darden | | | Yes |
| 1973 | Wind, Green, and Jain | | | Yes |
| 1974 | Darden and Reynolds | | | Yes |
| | Demby | | | |
| | Hodock | | | |
| | Hustad and Pessemier | | | Yes |
| | Lovell | | | Yes |
| | Myers and Gutman | | Yes | |
| | Pernica | | | Yes |
| | Plummer | Yes | | Yes |
| | Reynolds and Darden | | Yes | Yes |
| | Reynolds, Darden, and Martin | | | Yes |
| | Tigert | | | Yes |
| | Wells | | | Yes |
| | Wind and Green | Yes | Yes | Yes |
| | Ziff | | | |

*(continued)*

Table 7.1 *(continued)*

| Year | Study | | | |
|------|-------|---|---|---|
| 1975 | Arnold | | | |
| | Bikert, Brunnet, and Simonetti | | | |
| | Cosmas | | | Yes |
| | Darden and Perreault | | | Yes |
| | Engel | | | Yes |
| | Felson | | Yes | Yes |
| | Greend, Haines, and Summers | | Yes | |
| | Hirarch | | | Yes |
| | Homan, Cecil Burnett, and Wells | | | Yes |
| | Lee | | Yes | |
| | Mehrotta | | | |
| | Villani | | | Yes |
| | Villani and Lehmann | | | Yes |
| | Wells | | | Yes |
| 1976 | Darden and Perreault | | | Yes |
| | Zins | | | Yes |
| 1977 | Becherer, Richard, and Wiley | | | Yes |
| | Crask | | | Yes |
| | Douglas and Urban | | | Yes |
| | Mehrotta and Wells | | | Yes |
| | Plummer | | | Yes |
| | Reynolds, Crask, and Wells | | | Yes |
| | Richard and Sturman | | | |
| | Satow | | | Yes |
| | Settle, Alreck, and Glasheen | | Yes | |
| | Venkatesan | | | |
| | Wells and Cosmas | | | Yes |
| 1978 | Bearden, Teel, and Durand | | | Yes |
| | Berkman and Gilson | Yes | | |
| | Burke, Conn, and Lutz | | | Yes |
| | Engel, Kollat, and Blackwell | Yes | | |
| 1979 | Ahmed and Jackson | | | Yes |
| | Burns and Harrison | | | Yes |
| | Laudon and Bitts | Yes | | |
| | Paksoy | | | Yes |
| | Roberts and Wortzel | | Yes | Yes |
| | Teel, Bearden, and Durand | | | Yes |
| 1980 | Hawkins, Coney, and Best | Yes | | |
| 1982 | Cosmas | | Yes | Yes |

**Synthesis**

| | |
|---|---|
| Percentage of definition | 12.8% |
| Percentage of reference to an explicit theoretical framework | 19.7% |
| Percentage of AIO approaches | |
| 1963–1982 | 58.1% |
| 1972–1982 | 71.4% |

*Sources:* Lastovicka (1982), On the Validation of Lifestyle Traits: A Review and Illustration, *Journal of Marketing Research,* 19, 126–138. Anderson and Golden (1983), Lifestyle and Psychographics: A Critical Review and Recommendation, *Advances in Consumer Research,* Association for Consumer Research, 405–411.

*See Lastovika (1982) for corresponding citations.

- the AIO approach, imported directly from the United States
- certain empirical works on *captive* populations (students)
- certain French sociological works, allowing for the transposition of American works to a different place

However, Le Maire notes that "the heterogeneity of sources, the difficulty of their integration, has led them (COFREMCA and CCA) to reject the notion of [a] general conceptual frame, without doubt, more because of their inability to define it in a satisfactory manner, than because of the theoretical impossibility of doing so."

### Problems with Confidentiality

The "professional secret" problem seems typically French but is, in fact, global in nature. It is possible in the United States to find relatively precise information regarding the methodologies used by researchers in existing literature, particularly those concerning statistical treatments; the problem, however, seems to be in questionnaires, which often remain the researchers' property and thereby remain confidential. One notable exception concerns the VALS program, whose corresponding questionnaire is available but whose algorithm is a mystery (Kahle and Kahle, 2009). As we will soon see, the problems relative to the validity and reliability of measuring scales, as well as the genesis of variables composing the different inventories used, are rarely taken into account.

In France, confidentiality is observed in the works achieved by both the CCA and by COFREMCA. No doubt, this approach stems from the fact that these organizations are private enterprises with financial concerns, providing services in a very competitive world. Consequently, they are disinclined to unveil their know-how and their approaches—particularly when it is these approaches that establish their reputations, add to their prestige, and generate a significant amount of business. Though *professionally* justifiable, this secrecy becomes even more problematic from a scientific point of view because it casts a shadow on the validity of the studies' results.

### Problems with Validity

There are three distinct sets of problems: The first one relates to the nature of procedures implemented. The second concerns the predictive power of these procedures. The third problem, which is more general, deals with the comprehension of terms, their evolution, and how they relate to lifestyles versus psychology and sociology.

*Problems with Procedures*

A key concern regarding the procedures used by the researchers is their reliance on *sample characteristics*. These characteristics are derived, for the most part, from panels or samples constructed according to a quota method rather than the preferable probability method. The only operational quota variables are socioeconomic and demographic variables. One might question the validity of a study for which the proposed measures of lifestyles are skewed by a dependence on socioeconomic variables from censored samples (Le Maire, 1981). In this regard, if the lifestyles are not uniformly spread among the diverse sociodemographic criteria, researchers run the risk of overrepresenting or underrepresenting certain lifestyle classes in the final result.

On top of that, the enormous amount of available data has led to an increased reliance on self-administered questionnaires. As did Lhermie (1984), one can plausibly propose the hypothesis that only very social individuals who uphold traditional moral values (workers, the upright, honest type) will answer questions as honestly as possible. In addition, the relatively small compensation offered to partake in these studies may prove differentially attractive to different socioeconomic groups. Finally, the complex nature of some questions—they may be lengthy and difficult to understand—has a tendency to eliminate the elderly and the less-advantaged social classes from study.

As for French procedures, one can blame COFREMCA, as well as the CCA, for basing their studies of motivation or of realized creativity on the people most receptive to this genre of study—younger people (typically over twenty but under fifty years old) with open, sociable personalities, middle- to upper-class, and living in cities (usually with a population of at least 100,000). This leads to a bias in the extrapolations upon which sociocultural trends or lifestyles are determined.

Another issue is COFREMCA's use of previous studies (more than ten years old) to make forward projections. The underlying hypothesis was that future tendencies might be predicted from past data. As is noted by Lhermie, the problem posed deals with the validity of endogenous methods of forecasting, founded on information that is difficult to validate. A methodological incoherence occurs when using the knowledge of past structures to define future tendencies; therefore, the hypothesis of linear change must be viewed with caution.

The second point is related to *variables employed* and to *scales of measure*. Professional secrecy in France undoubtedly leads to wondering about the validity of item choice and the reliability of the scales of measure. In the United States, few authors appear to have verified the validity and reliability of scales of measure. Among the important studies of lifestyles conducted in the United States,

Lastovicka (1982) counted only fourteen in which these factors were partially investigated. These studies contribute to even more unsatisfactory and contradictory results. In a certain sense, it seems as if an AIO-type study fails to properly question the pertinence of measures that identify different lifestyle choices. This practice is the target of considerable criticism. The use of a typology is deceptive if one is not assured beforehand that the questions on which they rely truly measure what they were intended to measure. Without going into the technical details, the calculation of Cronbach's (1951) coefficient $a$ (alpha) can help to address this issue easily. Measuring the coherence of the responses to different questions is a standard of scholarly research. How many commercial studies make an effort to verify their measuring scales' coherence? Moreover, Lastovicka, Murry, and Joachinsthaler (1990) recently confirmed—thanks to the credibility accorded to the structural equation methods of the second generation (Valette-Florence, 1988c)—the weak operational validity of the VALS approach.

This remark is equally valid for the formulation of variables composing AIO surveys. The items and measuring instruments were developed on an experimental basis, taking experience into account, as well as "intuition or informal discussion" among researchers (Wind and Green, 1974). Consequently, the variables generated are different in nature and number, ranging on average from 100 to 300. In certain cases, it is possible to find up to 500 items (Wells and Tigert, 1971) and even more in certain European studies, where there can be several thousand! However, at the time of creating the groups, the number of useful variables (determined by discriminant analysis) is considerably reduced (sometimes by a factor greater than ten). Thus, the questionnaire has only sixteen attitudinal items (about 70 initial questions), whereas the CCA uses between 80 and 150 questions from several thousand collected in the initial phase. Such a reduction can leave one perplexed and poses the question of whether studies of such great volume are necessary, given the evident redundancy of information collected. It also calls into question the actual *sociological significance* of questions intended to separate the groups. For example, what kind of credit can one accord to a sociocultural classification if only one question on the simple possession of domestic animals or attitudes toward widely varying marijuana laws served to separate certain categories of lifestyles?

Finally, from an epistemological point of view, one remains perplexed about the *retained/omitted items* for measuring certain values. Thus, in order to measure pleasure-seeking behavior, a French survey used the following two statements:

- "It is important that our daily dish [in reference to meals] is beautiful."
- "In a garden, I prefer to grow flowers over vegetables."

Such questions pose a problem when it comes to *frame of reference*. For example, the second statement plays a more important role for an upper-class inhabitant of Neuilly than it does for a blue-collar worker in Barbès.

In addition, among the variables used, it is important to note the distinction between (1) the independent, or explicative, variables concerning attitudes (measured in the form of interests and opinions) and activities (which were presented in Chapter 3), and (2) the dependent variables representing consumer behavior (Hustad and Pessemier, 1974). In this perspective, the recourse to explicit methods—like the canonical analysis recommended by the CCA— proves to be the best way to make a clear distinction between explicative variables and explained variables.

Nevertheless, as was noted in the presentation and definition of lifestyles, these lifestyle variables make up an equal part of a person's lifestyle and therefore can be used as independent variables. There seems to be no specific ruling on this subject, and its use depends on the circumstances and specifics of the study being conducted. For the most part, the variables are considered instrumental behaviors, serving to describe other lifestyle aspects in the individuals. They are, therefore, often used as independent variables and, according to Reynolds and Darden (1972a, b), can be regrouped into four categories:

- purchasing variables, characterizing either the innovative character of first purchases, the fidelity related to repeat purchases, or the manner in which a purchase is conducted;
- communication variables, linked to the research and diffusion of information prior to purchase and to relational interaction and effects;
- consumption variables, related either to how the products are used or to the time dedicated to making the purchase; and
- other variables related to how the information is treated and how its use can effect behavior.

From each of the cases, a list of numerous and very diverse variables results that should function within diverse situations. Variables explaining attitudes and activities are generated one time, and the specific study situation and the corresponding dependant variables are determined (for example, vacation or leisure).

The study remains problematic, yielding unpredictable and sometimes contradictory results. Thus, in certain cases, one incorporates a large number of isolated items related to a wide range of situations. In other cases, one begins by researching the items in relation to specific products and situations and then retains those variables that apply to multiple situations (Lunn, 1966).

In both cases, it is necessary to note that the researchers often retain elements that have been revealed as interesting in previous studies. Consequently, the resulting variables are numerous and varied. The use of different variables by different researchers leads to lifestyle categories that are not similar from one study to another—making comparison very difficult, if not impossible.

One last point concerns the level of *typological analysis* and a *series of statistical analyses* prior to obtaining the variables (in particular, this last point concerns the CCA's sociostyles system, detailed in Cathelat's *Socio-Styles systèmes* [1990]). First of all, following the degree of resemblance among the individuals being classified, one can obtain a large number of sparsely populated categories, or just a few categories that include many more individuals (e.g., "the uneventful marsh" proposed by COFREMCA in 1976). What kind of results would be obtained by the use of many programs using different algorithms? And on an individual level, what represents one's belonging to a group? A consumer's specific behavior, which is of primary interest to the marketer, can only be perceived as a difference from the norm of the group to which he or she belongs (for example, the center of gravity in a cluster of points). Unfortunately, this variance is lost in the publishing of a nomenclature. It is, in part, this degeneration—adapted to essentially all typologies—that characterizes the weak explanatory power of these methods. In other respects, the succession of statistical analyses (factorial, canonical, and typological) pose at least two other problems:

- The first, adapted to method use, resides in terminology reduction and terminology simplification (often to a single word) used to qualify an axis or a group (Antoine, 1986). These represent only one small aspect of the entirety of variables having served to mathematically define this axis or group. In spite of being inevitable, this character of reducing interpretation appears to be very problematic as soon as the number of variables to be treated becomes important because of the simplification.
- The second problem concerns the residual loss of information at each step. Let us imagine that a first series of factor analyses retains 80 percent of its initial information; the initial information conserved becomes only 64 percent. As a general rule with lengthy questionnaires, the subsequent analysis reproduces, at best, only between 60 percent and 70 percent of the initial information. The final typology, then, typically reflects only 50 percent of the total collected information—a superficial treatment of data to say the least. It is, without doubt, this *successive degeneration* of treated information that causes one to obtain such reduced affectation structures (a significant reduction in the number of variables really used), as was mentioned in the previous section.

Table 7.2

**List of Products Used in the Kapferer and Laurent Study** (1981a)

| | |
|---|---|
| Groceries | Shampoo |
| Fruit Juice | Balm |
| Soda | Hair Gel |
| Tonic Water | Body Soap |
| Cola | Beauty Cream |
| Lemonade | Body Cream |
| Whiskey | Makeup Remover |
| Air Freshener | Foundation Cream |
| Fabric Softener | Hand Cream |
| Wax Polish | Eye Makeup |
| Cooking Oil | Fingernail Clippers |
| Butter | Lipstick |
| Margarine | Sunscreen |
| Cheese | Hair Removal Cream |
| Yogurt | Deodorant |
| Dessert | Shower Products |
| Beer | Bath Products |
| Potpourri | Cologne |
| Puree | Towels |
| Dog and Cat Food | Tampons |
| Beauty Products | Perfume |
| Hairspray | |

*Source:* Kapferer and Laurent (1981a).

## *The Predictive Power of Lifestyles*

It seems paradoxical that so few researchers are interested in the predictive power of lifestyles. Lifestyle studies have always been regarded as a superior, if not infallible, field of research, but recent information has called this assumption into question.

In their study incorporating 2,634 households, Kapferer and Laurent (1981a) compared the predictive power of the CCA classification to that of COFREMCA and to that of the sociodemographic variables on the use of forty-three nutritional, beauty, hygiene, and healthcare products (Table 7.2).

According to Kapferer and Laurent, the process of categorizing individuals into the CCA and COFREMCA typologies shows that these two approaches explain very little about the purchasing habits of consumers—and even less than the use of classic sociodemographic variables. Their conclusions are illustrated in Table 7.3:

- From a general standpoint, the predictive power of the methods used by the CCA and COFREMCA on consumption appears to be weak.

Table 7.3

**Predictive Power of CCA, COFREMCA, and Sociodemographic Variables**
(by percent)

What is the predictive power of the two classifications and the sociodemographic variables? (Measure: $R^2$)

| Beauty products | COFREMCA Classification | CCA Classification | Sociodemographic variables |
|---|---|---|---|
| Hair Spray | 0.82 | 0.00 | 4.16 |
| Shampoo | 2.24 | 0.47 | **24.16** |
| Balm | 0.86 | 0.13 | 3.66 |
| Hair Gel | 0.04 | 0.00 | 2.57 |
| Body Soap | 1.67 | 0.23 | 5.55 |
| Beauty Cream | 2.59 | 0.00 | 6.98 |
| Body Cream | 0.00 | 0.54 | 2.36 |
| Makeup Remover | 2.28 | 0.00 | 5.46 |
| Foundation Cream | 0.65 | 0.12 | 4.32 |
| Hand Cream | 0.31 | 0.00 | 1.20 |
| Eye Makeup | 2.23 | 0.00 | 7.94 |
| Fingernail Clippers | 1.86 | 0.50 | 6.35 |
| Lipstick | 0.66 | 0.11 | 4.72 |
| Sunscreen | **2.76** | 0.12 | 7.83 |
| Hair Removal Cream | 1.66 | 0.50 | 2.45 |
| Deodorant | 0.94 | 0.00 | 6.02 |
| Shower Products | 0.08 | 0.02 | 1.93 |
| Bath Products | 0.45 | 0.06 | 6.18 |
| Cologne | 0.42 | 0.19 | 1.81 |
| Towels | 0.92 | 0.65 | **24.05** |
| Tampons | 2.50 | 0.00 | 7.47 |
| Perfume | 1.10 | 0.00 | 6.67 |

*Source:* Kapferer, J.N., and Laurent, G. (1981a), op. cit., p. 221.

The adjusted $R^2$ attains at maximum 2.76 percent, indicating that 97.24 percent of the variance of purchases are not predicted by the lifestyle or sociocultural approach.
- In all the cases, the sociodemographic variables' predictive power proved to be superior to that of the lifestyle or sociocultural typologies.
- There is often a considerable difference in predictive power between the new approaches and the sociodemographic approach.

The authors recognize that the CCA and COFREMCA classifications differ from sociodemographic profiles. In twenty out of the forty-three cases, however, one or both of them had better predictive value compared to that information already furnished by sociodemographic variables. In this sense, the information contained in the sociocultural or lifestyle types is not redundant with the sociodemographic information. In some business cases, a small improvement in predictive power can have large consequences. Imagine, for example, the economic consequences of knowledge that would allow one to gain an extra percentage of the share of the world's automotive market.

In a study using public communication (1983), one of the authors spread an analysis, always using the same basis of given information, and created a group of eleven qualitative choices distributed into four types of new products (sanitary napkins, deodorant, eye makeup, and shower gel), three specific brands among the makeup products, and four types of hygiene or beauty products purchased in selective distribution (perfumery or pharmacy) or in a big-box type store. The obtained results of logistic regression confirm these conclusions about the study of quantitative choice:

- In all of the cases, the sociodemographic variables had a significant correspondence with behavior, whereas COFREMCA's typology had a significant effect in only seven out of the eleven cases, and CCA's typology had a significant effect in only three out of the eleven cases.
- For the group of eleven qualitative choices studied, the predictive power of the sociodemographic variables was considerably superior ($R^2$ max = 19 percent) to that of the lifestyles approaches ($R^2$ maxCCA = 1.7 percent, $R^2$ maxCOFREMCA = 6.4 percent).
- Adding information gleaned from a CCA typology did not improve the predictive behavior furnished by the sociodemographic variables in any significant way. However, adding data from the COFREMCA typology allowed for improvement in three out of eleven cases. Hence, the information contained in lifestyle typologies is very similar to the information furnished by the usual sociodemographic variables.

In the same sense, the results proposed by Valette-Florence (1988a, 1991) regarding 1,500 people confirm the weak predictive power of the CCA typology (1985) regarding the consumption of two different products: oil and fine wine. Thanks to a PLS model of structural equations capable of treating both continuous variables (values) and categorical variables (sociostyles), a sequential procedure allowed for testing the respective inflows and junctures of values, lifestyles, and the implication for the study of the two proposed consumption types (Figure 7.1 top). It appears that only the values and the implications exhibit a satisfactory predictive power (Figure 7.1 bottom); the eventual incorporation of lifestyles provided only marginal information, which was statistically insignificant. One notices here the central role played by the mediating variable of values, solely responsible for the largest part of the variance explained by the two consumer behaviors analyzed.

Figure 7.1    **Predictive Validity: Globally Tested Theoretical Model (Top) and Accepted Model (Bottom)**

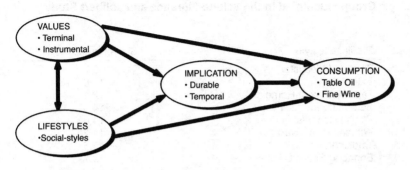

Note: All possible causal relations are shown.

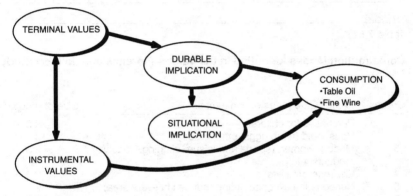

Note: Only statistically significant causal relations are shown.

In a series of articles, Valette-Florence and Jolibert (1985, 1990) confirmed the conclusions of the preceding studies (Valette-Florence,1988a, 1991). Their first work (1985), in spite of being based on a more limited number of households, underlined the lack of a link between the lifestyle typology resulting from an AIO-type inventory and the link resulting from the consumption of a series of 140 products (Tables 7.4 and 7.5). In fact, an extensive analysis of the effects of eventual interaction between these two typologies has proved, by the skewing of a log-linear model, that only the "household" means of consumption (focused mainly on nutrition) was related to the "hedonist, sensual" and "withdrawn, taciturn" lifestyles. These relationships, however, are not contradictory, though they seem to be at first glance. In reality, a means of consumption essentially oriented toward nourishment can very well be the

Table 7.4

**Lifestyle Groups Identified in the Valette-Florence and Jolibert Study (1985)**

| Groups | Profile: Lifestyle | Size of group (%) |
|---|---|---|
| 1. | Engaged Idealist | 3.7 |
| 2. | Extravert | 11.6 |
| 3. | Familial Stay at Home | 12.1 |
| 4. | Sedentary Moralist | 14.6 |
| 5. | Playful Hedonist | 14.6 |
| 6. | Withdrawn Introvert | 14.2 |
| 7. | Traditional | 9.5 |
| 8. | Engaged Social Climber | 19.7 |
| | Total | 100 |

*Source:* Valette-Florence and Jolibert (1985), op. cit.

Table 7.5

**Consumption Modes Identified in the Valette-Florence and Jolibert Study (1985)**

| Groups | Profile: Categories of consumption | Size of group (%) |
|---|---|---|
| 1. | Purchases for children | 8.3 |
| 2. | Household (flour, eggs, other foods) | 10.7 |
| 3. | Modern women (sports and leisure clothing, beauty products, etc.) | 2.9 |
| 4. | Environmentalists | 2.0 |
| 5. | Nonconsumer (consumption reduced in every area) | 9.5 |
| 6. | Male clothing and breakfast products | 20.7 |
| 7. | Maintenance and hygiene | 10.4 |
| 8. | Female clothing and breakfast products | 11.6 |
| 9. | Young nonconsumer men | 10.7 |
| 10. | Young nonconsumer women | 13.2 |
| | Total | 100 |

*Source:* Valette-Florence and Jolibert (1990), op. cit.

reflection of either pursuing a certain pleasure of life (hedonistic), or of being uncommunicative (taciturn).

In order to improve the preceding results, the authors took on a second research project (1990), the objective of which was to predict these same consumption modes. But this time, they used lifestyle components (factor axes), with which the values system components were associated (Tables 7.6 and 7.7).

Table 7.6

**Lifestyle Dimensions Used in the Valette-Florence and Jolibert Study** (1990)

| | Lifestyle factors | Percentage of variance explained |
|---|---|---|
| 1. | Traditionalism | 13.9 |
| 2. | Distraction | 6.2 |
| 3. | Joy and easy living | 5.4 |
| 4. | Professional development | 4.4 |
| 5. | Informative aspect of the media | 3.5 |
| 6. | Associative and involving life | 3.4 |
| 7. | Idealism | 3.2 |
| 8. | Cultural aspect | 2.9 |
| 9. | Distractive aspect of the media | 2.8 |
| 10. | Paternalism and a tranquil life | 2.5 |
| | Total percentage | 48.2 |

*Source:* Valette-Florence and Jolibert (1990), op. cit.

Table 7.7

**Values System Dimensions Used in the Valette-Florence and Jolibert Study** (1990)

| | Value system factors | Percentage of variance explained |
|---|---|---|
| 1. | Responsibility and self-control | 24.2 |
| 2. | Moral values and self-regulation | 9.2 |
| 3. | Intimate harmony and strength of character | 5.5 |
| 4. | Liberty and hedonism | 5.3 |
| 5. | Idealism | 3.8 |
| 6. | Wisdom and logic | 3.7 |
| 7. | Openness of spirit and efficiency of work | 3.4 |
| 8. | Personal harmony | 3.2 |
| 9. | Joviality and sociability | 3.0 |
| 10. | Accomplished and passionate life | 2.8 |
| | Total percentage | 64.1 |

*Source:* Valette-Florence and Jolibert (1990), op. cit.

A series of logistical regressions, adapted to the analysis of the dichotomous nature of the dependent variable (consumption modes), demonstrated the following points:

- Nine of the ten consumption modes studied are explained by lifestyles or values (the one exception being "young nonconsumer women").

- Lifestyle dimensions appear to explain consumption better than values do, except in the case of the "environmental consumer" group. Lifestyles, therefore, seem to be better at predicting commonplace consumption. The inverse would result for a more *ideological* consumption group ("environmentalist"), the values thus proving to be more significant.
- The explanatory power varies greatly from one consumption mode to another (from 3.4 percent to 14.6 percent for lifestyles; from 2.5 percent to 33 percent for values). Thus, an elaborate study of specific consumption modes best apprehended by lifestyles or values seems necessary.
- Lifestyles and values seem to be more complementary than redundant. Except for the "purchases for children" group, for which the same dimension (*idealism*) appears, they supply in each of the other cases supplementary information (see, for example, the "modern women" group). Such a result would find an immediate application in advertising.
- In spite of being able to predict nine out of the ten consumption modes studied ($R^2$ varies from 2 percent to 21 percent), the socioeconomic variables do not have a predictive power systematically superior to lifestyles or values (for example, "ecological" consumption is not explained by these variables). In addition, incorporating lifestyle or value dimensions leads to a systematic improvement in the predictive quality of the analysis: The information contained in the sociodemographic variables would not be (in this application) redundant in comparison to that contained in the lifestyle variables and values. (See Table 7.8.)

When compared with the conclusions of the previous studies (Kapferer and Laurent, 1981a, 1985; Valette-Florence and Jolibert, 1985; Valette-Florence, 1988a, 1991), these results are interesting because they put an emphasis on two points that have elemental importance in studying lifestyles:

- *Results based on typologies are deceiving, but those based on dimensions (factorial or canonical axes) are not.* Instead of operating at a typological level, one would do better to concentrate on identifying large trends (for example, sociocultural trends) that modulate a given society. Such information would prove useful in defining corresponding strategies of communication and positioning.
- *Lifestyle studies would allow for the enrichment of information brought by classic sociodemographic variables.* More specific studies might also lead the way in identifying further links to targeting and segmentation variables.

Table 7.8

**The Compared Predictive Power of Sociodemographic Variables and of Lifestyle Dimensions and Value System Dimensions**

| Methods of consumption (Explained variables) | Sociodemographic variables | Lifestyle dimensions | Value system dimensions | Dimensions of lifestyles and value systems plus sociodemographic variables |
|---|---|---|---|---|
| 1. Purchases for children | 1. Age (20–39 years old) **$R^2$ = 21%** | 1. Idealism 2. Paternalism and a tranquil life **$R^2$ = 6.5%** | 1.Idealism **$R^2$ = 2.5%** | 1. Age (20–39 years old) 2. Idealism 3. Paternalism and a tranquil life **$R^2$ = 28%** |
| 2. Household | 1. Sex (female) **$R^2$ = 2.6%** | 1. Distraction (−) 2. Paternalism and a tranquil life **$R^2$ = 6.6%** | | 1. Distraction (−) 2. Paternalism and a tranquil life 3. Sex (female) **$R^2$ = 9.4%** |
| 3. Modern women | 1. Marital status (single) **$R^2$ = 16.4%** | 1. Distraction 2. Joy and easy living **$R^2$ = 14.6%** | 1. Liberty and hedonism **$R^2$ = 9.1%** | 1. Marital status (single) 2. Distraction 3. Joy and easy living **$R^2$ = 35.3%** |
| 4. Environmentalists | | 1. Associative and involving life **$R^2$ = 9.4%** | 1. Wisdom and logic 2. Accomplished and passionate life (−) **$R^2$ = 33%** | 1. Wisdom and logic 2. Associative and involving life 3. Accomplished and passionate life (−) **$R^2$ = 39.4%** |
| 5. Nonconsumers | 1. CSP (worker) 2. Sex (male) **$R^2$ = 17.9%** | 1. Distraction (−) **$R^2$ = 5.4%** | | 1. CSP (worker) 2. Distraction (−) 3. Sex (male) **$R^2$ = 23.2%** |

(continued)

Table 7.8 (continued)

| | | | | |
|---|---|---|---|---|
| 6. Men's clothing | 1. Sex (male)<br>R² = 2% | 1. Joy and easy living<br>R² = 4.6% | | 1. Joy and easy living<br>2. Sex (male)<br>R² = 6.4% |
| 7. Hygiene and maintenance products | 1. Sex (female)<br>R² = 2% | 1. Informative aspect of the media<br>2. Joy and easy living<br>3. Distraction (–)<br>R² = 9.3% | 1. Personal harmony<br>2. Moral values and self-regulation<br>R² = 6.6% | 1. Informative aspect of the media<br>2. Personal harmony (–)<br>3. Joy and easy living<br>4. Moral values and self-regulation<br>5. Sex (female)<br>R² = 13.5% |
| 8. Women's clothing | 1. Sex (female)<br>2. Income (> 1,500 F)<br>R² = 13.3% | 1. Traditionalism<br>2. Distractive aspect of the media<br>R² = 6.8% | 1. Openness of spirit and efficiency of work<br>2. Responsibility and self-control<br>3. Liberty and hedonism<br>R² = 7.8% | 1. Sex (female)<br>2. Income (> 1500F)<br>3. Traditionalism<br>4. Distractive aspect of the media<br>5. Responsibility and self-control<br>R² = 26.4% |
| 9. Young men who consume little | 1. Age (less than 29)<br>2. Sex (male)<br>R² = 7.2% | 1. Traditionalism<br>R² = 3.4% | | 1. Age (less than 29)<br>2. Sex (male)<br>3. Traditionalism<br>R² = 10.5% |
| 10. Young women who consume little | 1. Marital status (single)<br>2. Sex (female)<br>3. Age (less than 29)<br>R² = 10.9% | | | 1. Marital status (single)<br>2. Sex (female)<br>3. Age (less than 29)<br>R² = 10.9% |

182

*The General Contribution of Lifestyles*

In the different lifestyle studies, the segments identified vary in significance and in number, both in France and in the United States. In France, for example, the CCA sociotypes do not at all correspond with the COFREMCA sociocultural types.

The terms employed in France are rather blurry and esoteric. Certain authors (Faivre and Le Maire, 1982) therefore speak of "stacking terms." Lhermie (1984) pointed out that readers must juggle terms such as *pleasure seekers, utilitarians, the meritorious, respectful individuals,* and *moderate conservatives,* and distinguish between the trends of *intraception, automanipulation, modelization, extension,* and *transcendence,* just to name a few. The result is a proliferation of terms that makes cross-checking among the diverse studies extremely difficult.

Another concern is how rapidly the results are evolving—a factor that reduces their credibility. For COFREMCA, the sociocultural trends went successively from twenty-eight to twenty-six in the late 1970s, and then from twenty-nine to thirty-five in the 1980s, and then up to forty. Even when explained by the authors, this evolution brings up the topic of "trends of variable geometry" (Barthélémy, 1980).

As for the CCA, the mass of people *refocusing* went from 36 percent of the population in 1975, to 42 percent in 1977, and then to 49 percent in 1980. Also in 1980, a new group emerged rather quickly. Known as the discrepancy group, it represented 22 percent of the population and resulted from an outbreak of seemingly *adventurous* mentality and the appearance of socio-styles *show-offs, profiteers,* and *libertarians.* This group contained at least 8.5 million people in France over the age of forty. Its sudden appearance, as noted by Lhermie (1984), poses a measuring capacity problem because there did not seem to be such a stunning revolution in French society. As noted by Antoine (1986), such a change merely reflects a modification in the way we measure, in order to account for a shifting mentality; this shift appeared by chance in a study of youth lifestyle. An analogous phenomenon occurred in 1984 with the outbreak of a *mainstreamer*-type mindset, the appearance of an *egocentric* mindset, and the diverse sociostyle movements that included the *dilettantes,* who, between 1982 and 1984, went from an adventurous mentality to a shifting mentality, or the *managers,* who over the same period of time evolved from an adventurous mentality to that of rigorous people *refocusing.* Table 7.9 illustrates these evolutions (see Cathelat, 1985a, b, for a more explicit visualization).

In a more global manner, an equally important critique of lifestyle studies addressed in France deals with a failure to incorporate the sociological aspect of consumer behavior (that is, the predetermination of behavior according to

Table 7.9

**Evolution of the Typology of CCA Sociostyles Between 1977, 1980, and 1984**

MENTALITIES

| 1977 | 1980 | 1984 |
|---|---|---|
| Adventure 37.7% | Discrepancy 21.5% | Discrepancy 17.3% |
| | Adventure 14.5% | Egocentric 22.5% |
| | | Activist 13.3% |
| Refocusing 41.8% | Refocusing 49.5% | Refocusing materialist 26.8% |
| | | Refocusing rigorist 20.1% |
| Utilitarian 20.5% | Utilitarian 15% | |

SOCIO-STYLES

| 1984 | 1980 | 1977 |
|---|---|---|
| **Profiteers** (5.8%) **Dilettantes** (5.7%) **Libertarianism** (5.8%) | **Show-offs** (16.5%) **Profiteers** (7.5%) **Libertarianism** (7.5%) | *Ambitious* (5.1%) *Innovators* (4.4%) **Enterprising** (7.1%) **Sensualist** (10.2%) **Dilettantes** (7.1%) |
| **Show-offs** (6.5%) *Defensive* (7.3%) *Vigil* (8.7%) | **Sensualists** (6%) **Managers** (3%) **Dilettants** (5.5%) | |
| **Enterprising** (10.1%) *Militants* (3.2%) | | |
| *Attentive* (8.3%) **Utilitarian** (7.9%) **Exemplary** (10.6%) | **Vigils** (6.5%) **Exemplary** (11.1%) **Floating** (12%) **Conservatives** (6%) | **Exemplary** (17.0%) *Peaceful* (7.2%) **Moralistic** (7.6%) **Floating** (10%) |
| **Conservatives** (5.1%) **Managers** (8.5%) **Moralistic** (6.5%) | **Utilitarian** (15%) | **Conservatives** (12.7%) *Laborious* (7.8%) |

*Source:* Adapted from Cathelat (1985) and Mermet (1985).

*Note:* The arrows indicate some of the principle tendencies of psychological changes over the course of a year. The sociostyles present over multiple periods are represented in boldfaced text, whereas those present only in one are in italics.

social group membership). Numerous authors have concluded that the results from these studies amounted only to the description of certain psychological types and their evolution.

Krieff and Loiseau (1979) argued against *taxonomic will*, or the classification of individuals into homogeneous groups in terms of behavior, habits, and psychology. Bernard-Becharies (1980) declared that sociostyles, based solely on behavioral similarities, do not seek to distinguish opposites and are only "psychological aggregates, perfectly heterogeneous from a sociological point of view." In the same way, Swiners (1979) wrote that it is not about "sociotypes" but simply the description of "personality types" belonging to different social groups. Bernard-Becharies also indicated the types could be found at all levels of society.

Relying on the works of Bourdieu and Passeron (1964), Krieff and Loiseau (1979) also decried the absence of sociological notions; they maintained that studying a group would result in a better understanding of consumers. The member cohesion of a social group and its characteristic "of real unity, directly observable and founded on collective, continuous, active attitudes" would contradict the artificial character of lifestyle groups that are composed of juxtaposed individuals whose norms are not the same. This concern brings up the importance of the link between social class and consumer behavior, as was noted by Martineau in 1958. And according to Henault (1973), the "social group is one of the key factors in the purchase decision-making process, and represents [consumers'] norms and values." The remaining debate focuses on the link between lifestyles and social classes and how to measure the real contribution of lifestyles to consumer habits.

The key criticisms of lifestyle studies involve the obscure terminology used and the rapidly shifting trends that, together, are its hallmarks. Lifestyle studies confirm the occurrence of sociocultural changes without explaining the origin of those changes or the manner in which they are created among social groups (Krieff and Loiseau, 1979; Herpin, 1986b).

## THE ADEQUACY AND USE OF LIFESTYLE STUDIES IN THE EUROPEAN AND FRENCH CONTEXT

The debate over the methodology of lifestyle studies is global in nature. In France, it is important to distinguish the interest and contribution of lifestyles as compared to sociology. A more fundamental problem is quite simply how appropriate this study is in a European context, taking into account the fact that it grew out of methods initially used in the United States. Douglas (1978) noted that these three principal characteristics of the European market may influence lifestyle analysis:

- market fragmentation;
- cultural differences from one country to another; and
- the importance of social differences.

Before discussing these three points, it is important to address the problem of measurement inadequacies in an international context.

## The Inadequacy of Measuring Scales in an International Context

The extension of lifestyle studies in a European context occurred without the necessary adaptations in information collection among diverse cultural groups. This failure leads one to believe that the actual instruments, developed in one single country (principally the United States or France), were simply rolled into other national contexts. One such study, qualified as "pseudo-etic" by Triandis (1972, p. 39), considers the measures developed in the country of origin as quasi-universal standards applicable to other countries in an undifferentiated manner.

This problem is amplified by the use of dense and lengthy questionnaires (like that of the CCA). Beyond the challenges of linguistic equivalency—for which a translation followed by a back-translation is necessary—there is the issue of stability with regard to the measuring instruments. In other words, are the factorial (or canonical) structures the same regardless of place or inquiry? If they are, a trans-European or even truly global typology remains conceivable. If not, typologies specific to each country or even to each ethnic or cultural group are necessary, and this implies the need to modify the information-collection tool. Nevertheless, it remains rather improbable, notably for obvious cost reasons, that such validation procedures will be put into effect. Such shortcomings can and likely will cast doubt on the relevance and interest of the European or truly global lifestyle typologies actually proposed.

## Market Fragmentation

Lovell (1974) noted that the size of European markets, the lesser economic power of individual European societies, the market fragmentation that results from it, and the lack of interest in research have created an obstacle to the development of European lifestyle studies, which are already very costly. He added that, given the smaller size of markets, European companies feel closer to their consumers and do not estimate that the incorporation of lifestyle analyses could lead to any new or major revelations. Companies in the United States may conduct such studies in order to optimize their product-positioning decisions and segmentation strategies. In Europe, marketing and publicity organizations are more essential in this realm. Ironically, the growth in importance of the European Union has facilitated market homogenization to some extent.

Consequently, in Europe, marketers try to obtain a "snapshot" of sociocultural trends or lifestyles that seem to influence patterns of consumption for certain products. However, this snapshot does not provide a deep understanding of foundational trends, contrary to analyses done in the United States.

From a cultural point of view, the lifestyles approach (due to its generality) allows one to apprehend a large number of variables and comparisons of sociocultural order. The weaknesses in the method stem from the inability to verify the underlying hypothesis or hypotheses upon which the profile types are based—types that presumably have homogeneous behaviors toward product consumption. The lifestyle aspects linked to purchasing behavior of any product are far from being clear and apparently have not yet been demonstrated. It is therefore necessary to ask oneself whether the voluntarily general aspect of European methods detracts from their credibility and their use in the concrete application of consumer types.

### Cultural Differences

Given the differing characteristics and cultural disparities existing from one European country to another, businesses want to know whether the analysis of lifestyles constitutes an appropriate means for identifying homogeneous behaviors in several countries. They examine whether uniform strategies, notably in terms of communication, can be adopted for use in transnational segments, or even whether adaptations specific to each national and cultural context should be proposed (Wind and Douglas, 1972).

In the United States, women who work outside the home show little interest in products designed to save time while doing household chores. Conversely, in France, it is the working women who buy such labor-saving products, while those who spend a majority of their time in the home seem almost to "compensate" by demonstrating an interest for the more traditional methods of household work.

Apparently, the contradictory results from these studies pose a problem. One must consider the adaptation of lifestyle approach for a given cultural environment, along with the transposition of a conceptual frame from one study to another. Thus, in Douglas and Urban's (1977) study, the differences can quite simply stem from the inadequacy of the tool destined to measure the same behavioral differences. The few studies done in this domain (Douglas and Craig, 1983) tend to confirm the lack of reliability accorded to these intercultural lifestyle studies. In this sense, France (being rather diversified according to its regions) would be only modestly consistent in terms of customs. One could question whether the same type of general lifestyles questionnaire is applicable to French culture as a whole.

### Social Differences

The social differences in Europe are very strong. In the United States, the study of lifestyles allows us to explain differences in behavior otherwise not explainable in terms of social categories (Plummer, 1971b; Myers and Gutman, 1974). In Europe, and particularly in France, the social hierarchy translates into notable differences in behavior. Some even go so far as to say that lifestyle typologies are a substitute for measures used in social categories (Peninou, 1980). The study already cited by Kapferer and Laurent (1981a) allows us to assume that, in certain cases, the information contained in the lifestyle or sociocultural typologies would not be repetitive when compared to the sociodemographic information (see the similar results already mentioned from Valette-Florence and Jolibert, 1988, 1990).

Nevertheless, since the language and habits vary in France from one social category to another, it is quite probable that lifestyle questions may not be interpreted in the same manner at all levels of educational attainment and in all social contexts. The need for a more in-depth study of interrelationships among social categories and lifestyles is obvious, as is the need to examine the different lifestyles within one category.

In Asia, intracountry homogeneity tends to be stronger; thus, understanding lifestyle nuances may prove more useful to marketers there. But it is possible, and even likely, that the meaningful lifestyles of Asia differ from both the styles of Europe and the Americas.

### CONCLUSION AND SYNTHESIS

This chapter has allowed us to examine some problems associated with lifestyle approaches. First of all, the values-based approach may be less than adequate when Rokeach's test is used in a cultural environment different from that of the United States. In particular, there is a possible problem with stability between the two (opposing) value poles—instrumental and terminal—proposed by Rokeach.

The study using consumption variables seems weaker because it relies on information provided by the consumer. There may be disparities between real and declared consumption. One can also notice a difficulty in comparing consumption modes among different countries, given their different customs and cultures.

The majority of critiques concern American AIO inventories and French conception inventories. These appraisals can be regrouped into two large categories (as shown in Table 7.10), the first concerning problems of methodology

Table 7.10

**Recap of Problems Revealed in Lifestyle Studies That Use the AIO Inventory**

**Methodological Problems**
- Lack of conceptual framework and excessive justification of concepts used
- Excessive confidentiality
- Questionable validity:
  - Sample characteristics
  - Genesis of variables used
  - Reliability of measurement scales
  - Statistical sequences
  - Low predictive power
  - Rapidly changing typologies proposed
  - Sociological interest typologies

**Problems of Appropriateness in the European Context**
- Adjustment of scales of measurement has an international context
- Fragmentation of important steps
- Cultural differentiation between countries
- Importance of social differences

regardless of the lifestyle origin, and the second dealing with the applicability of a U.S. study in a European context, specifically French.

The problems of methodology concern the absence of conceptualization. Other criticisms focus on the confidential and operational characteristics of the methods employed, and, more particularly, anything related to (1) the data-collecting procedures used, (2) the reliability, validity, and structure of the measuring scales, and (3) the origin of the variables. Still other problems relate to the rapid evolution of the proposed typologies, and whether these typologies make a contribution superior to that of social groups used in sociology. Finally, several research studies indicate the weak predictive power of lifestyles when compared to classic sociodemographic variables.

Concerns exist about the utility and adequacy of applying lifestyle studies to European markets—an issue directly related to the difficulty of adapting the measuring scales to an international context. It is, in fact, possible to note three characteristics of these markets that may influence the analysis of lifestyles:

- fragmentation of the market;
- cultural differences from one country to another; and
- the importance of social differences.

More precisely, a study of the links existing between the social classes and the diverse typologies of lifestyles has yet to be performed. On top of that, it is necessary to take into account the risk of inadequate means for measuring different cultural milieus, principally due to difficulties in translation and linguistic equivalencies.

One could conclude, therefore, that the drawbacks inherent in lifestyle studies can greatly reduce the contribution of their diverse uses. It is thus appropriate to present new propositions, both methodological and conceptual, that allow us to improve the real contribution of lifestyle studies to social trends and purchasing patterns. Such is the objective of the next chapters of this book.

# 8

# New Methodological and Conceptual Proposals

The previous chapter looked at current problems faced by lifestyle studies—problems that call into question their practical significance. Significant improvements, both theoretical and methodological, appear possible.

Indeed, two external expert options are offered: research methodologist and the theoretician. While remaining within the same field of investigation, the first option focuses on improved procedures for the handling and collection of information. These are presented in the first part of this chapter. The second option, also discussed in this chapter, is more difficult to undertake, because it departs from the original paradigm. It attempts to broaden the analytical framework, while retaining the same perspective to other psychosociological concepts that are judged most relevant to the study of behavior.

## THE PROPOSED METHODOLOGY IMPROVEMENTS

In the following examples of money, mastery of technical analysis is often regarded as the key to the success of research or relevant study. We present three types of improvements we think deserve to be highlighted and, where possible, illustrated. The first improvement concerns the use of generalized canonical analysis or confirmatory methods. The second relates to the analysis of temporal evolution of various classes of lifestyles. The third group has proposed the use of unclear typologies for which the same individual may belong to different groups, and is thus more representative of the multiple and polymorphic nature of behavior.

### *Generalizations of the Canonical Analysis*

As we noted in the chapter on the French approach to lifestyle studies (Chapter 4), the CCA is now using a canonical analysis, considered more efficient in explaining the impact of opinions and perceptions on behavior. Our core values influence our beliefs, which in turn determine our interests and, as a result, our behavior and attitude toward the world we inhabit. The use of generalized canonical analysis provides an understanding of multiple sets of variables at a time. In addition, statistical developments allow us to consider variables of a different nature simultaneously (nominal membership to an ordinal group such as preference, for instance; continuous variables such as age, income, purchase amounts, and psychometric scales or scores of attitudes). More powerful still is the general confirmatory canonical analysis. It utilizes the strength of structural equation models, which are capable of modeling the relationship of cause and effect that structures and determines the nature of a chosen phenomenon. In spite of its advantages, this kind of study is possible only through a prior theoretical specification. We should never forget that this art must serve as a solid conceptualization, not precede it. Among the methods available (Valette-Florence, 1988c), the PLS model (partial least squares) is the more useful, because it allows for:

- processing volumes of data, which is very important, both in number of observations and number of variables;
- analyzing variables of different types (nominal, ordinal or interval); and
- calculating mostly latent factor scores, later used in a subsequent cluster analysis.

With a judicious choice, the concepts incorporated into the analysis under such an approach can shed light on relevant and innovative practices of specific consumption. The group profiles obtained are also richer than the traditional approaches of lifestyles regarding both the specific and complementary nature of the concepts on which they are built. We can examine them about meta-psychosociological style, rather than only lifestyles, a term too restrictive for same such studies. The analysis can also be adapted to studies of general lifestyles. All research to date indicates that the predictive power of older approaches was much lower than that of specific studies focusing on particular behavior.

The following example, borrowed from Roehrich, Valette-Florence and Repacchi (1989), illustrates this point. The conceptual structure presented in Figure 8.1 is in line with the model of Midgley and Dowling (1978) and based on the previous results of Roehrich and Valette-Florence (1986, 1987a). One of the authors collected data on the psychosociological views of 380 people in the French city of Grenoble. The topic of study was perfumes and colognes. A typology operating on factor score concepts in the model tests (except innovative behavior) yielded four different groups; the dominant features of those groups are presented in Table 8.1. The typology is relevant only if the model test is

Figure 8.1    **Model of Causal Analysis of Innovative Behavior**

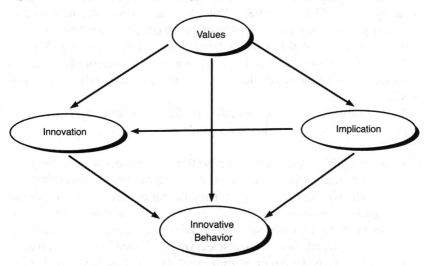

*Source:* Roehrich, Valette-Florence, and Repacchi (1989), p. 243.

Table 8.1

**Psychosociological Profile of Different Groups of Buyers of New Products**
(Perfumes)

|  | Group 1 Followers | Group 2 Hedonists | Group 3 Individualistic | Group 4 Innovators |
|---|---|---|---|---|
| Values |  |  |  |  |
| Security | −28 | 0 | +28 | −3 |
| Sociability | +65 | −1 | −32 | −27 |
| Development | +26 | +2 | −15 | −10 |
| Involvement |  |  |  |  |
| Fun and Interest | −133 | +107 | 0 | +35 |
| Importance and Risk | +41 | −32 | −9 | +10 |
| Brand Value | +30 | −39 | −5 | +8 |
| Probability of Error | +5 | +106 | −56 | −45 |
| Innovation |  |  |  |  |
| Social | +15 | +4 | −24 | +32 |
| Personal | −82 | +5 | +42 | +28 |
| Average age | 34.7 | 28.4 | 28.5 | 31.2 |
| Group size | 86 | 84 | 124 | 58 |

*Source:* Roehrich, Valette-Florence, and Repacchi (1989), p. 253.
    *The average values per group are all standardized, upgraded, and multiplied by 100
for ease of presentation.

valid. Multiple procedures that follow the same structure, are necessary to verify accuracy (Valette-Florence, 1988b). Note also that the consumption of specific brands of perfume may also be broken down into these different groups.

The procedure revealed a structural or dynamic typology (Valette-Florence and Rapacchi, 1990b). Each group or segment was characterized not only in terms of consumption in practice, but also in terms of psychosociological profiles.

Table 8.1 illustrates the corresponding profiles (standardized mean values). A more detailed description is then possible:

- Group 1, *the followers*, match a portion of the older sample. Very social and quite fulfilled, the followers want to purchase a functional and well-known brand of perfume. They do not ascribe to any significant hedonistic behavior, nor do they show individual innovation; rather, they exhibit a lax social innovation. Within this group, men are slightly overrepresented. They tend to select from a limited line of fragrances.
- Group 2, *the hedonists or pleasure seekers*, is a slightly younger population composed equally of men and women. These people essentially value pleasure and, therefore, seem very concerned about the risk of a purchase situation involving pleasurable fragrances. Having a low innovative sensitivity, they are only slightly more likely to buy new perfumes than the preceding group;
- Group 3, *the individuals*, attracts young women. Not very social, with more sensitivity toward individual innovation, these women exhibit low involvement when it comes to the purchase of perfume. They are naturally low consuming.
- Group 4 is composed of *the innovators*. This is the group whose consumption of new products is the most significant. Buying for pleasure rather than a following brand, they show a degree of innovation for social characteristics rather than individual brands. Of course, these consumers are the buyers of new products and are by far the most important to companies marketing new perfumes.

In our opinion, the approach that has been illustrated has at least three advantages, both methodological and theoretical, that should be explained.

• First, in contrast to traditional approaches (e.g., typology) that are limited by a purely descriptive approach, the innovative aspect of the methodology proposed here lies in the contribution it provides for the analysis of behavioral relationships that govern the phenomenon being studied. In addition, it is important to note that this analysis yields a pure explanation (i.e., without prior knowledge, what are the different consumer groups?); in addition, it opts for a much more combined approach (i.e., how are consumers distributed over multiple phenomena?). As noted by Valette-Florence and Rapacchi (1990b), it is precisely this approach that differentiates the structural segmentation, which we call *post-segmentation*, from what is usually used (what is known as data-driven segmentation vs. theory-driven segmentation).

• Second, this type of analysis better highlights the potential contribution of psychological traits such as involvement, innovation, and values in an understanding of consumption patterns. In particular, the proposed approach offers insights into the nature of structural relationships associated with segmentation and consumption.

• Finally, the typology constructed using this procedure allows us to refine de facto strategies for communicating with the different groups identified. It is also possible to describe the groups more accurately according to the initial variables or dimensions identified prior to the formation of the proposed model. Consider this example: group 4, the innovators, enjoys purchasing perfumes. Returning to the initial questions measuring this dimension, we can uncover the motivations that prompt an individual to purchase a particular fragrance.

## Analysis of the Temporal Evolution of the Innovative Group of Lifestyles

Lifestyles studies have focused primarily on describing the changing landscape of contemporary sociology. Thus far, the primary purpose of research in this area has been to propose typologies that, at a given time, reflect the major trends at work in the social mosaic. It is then easy to consider how the practical implications of such an approach may be improved or newly defined through positioning strategies and communication.

Unfortunately, lifestyle studies do not anticipate social changes that researchers or practitioners discover. Major changes may not follow the time-lags researchers choose. When a company chooses a specific location to launch one of its products, it is nevertheless important to consider two main points:

• What is the sociological stability of the target selected? In other words, to what degree might consumption patterns spread to other classes of related or different lifestyles? This issue is paramount. Indeed, what is the interest of focusing on a target whose brand loyalty is likely to waver?
• Might the future size of the selected target be approximated? It would be particularly useful, in fact, to focus on target increases or decreases in volume from year to year.

Obviously, the answers to these questions are relevant for only a limited time and typically have weak results. Thus, all social change notes should reflect the most up-to-date data available. As we have noted, the types of lifestyles have never consistently matched the number and nature of the groups identified. In addition, the typologies proposed by the CCA have increased successively from three groups in 1977, to four groups in 1980, to five groups since 1984, and so forth. Such fluctuations undoubtedly reflect changes and improvements to the tool as the social landscape evolves (Lhermie, 1984; Antoine, 1986). Note that it is not the number of classes of lifestyles that change but their respective weights (the types are updated every two years).

The algebraic method of spectral decomposition was used by sociologists of the 1960s to study the evolution of the population and the transitions between occupational categories (Matras, 1960; Duncan, 1966; McFarland, 1969). Grover and Dillon (1988), later extended the method to the field of marketing, and it can be adapted easily to lifestyle studies.

To avoid controversy, let us note already that the example that follows is a fictitious but illustrative practice of the method that in no way mirrors reality. If several companies are conducting studies of commercial lifestyles, CCA is undoubtedly one whose leadership, at least in terms of communication, is the most established. An advantage of the CCA leadership is to have fairly recent changes in classifying lifestyles that the company offers. That advantage is why the illustration we have chosen uses its typology.

We will first present the transition matrix T used, and also a reading of the spectral decomposition. A transition matrix can view the membership an individual has in a group at time $t + i$, knowing membership in a group time $t$. Traditionally, the terms correspond to the lines belonging to different groups at time $t$, while the terms in columns match those terms at the instant $t + i$. Because the data are expressed as percentages, the sum of lines in any condition is 100 (all persons belonging to one modality of time $t$ are distributed among all the possible ways at time $t + i$). Finally, we note that $i$ is a unit for some time (e.g., several months, a year or two).

*Constitution of the Transition Matrix T*

The study of lifestyles of the CCA is normally conducted every two years. It is reasonable to assume that such frequency is dependent on three imperatives:

- the practical aspect: the studies are difficult to conduct on a large scale and cannot be done quickly;
- the commercial aspect: a survey every two years is sufficiently regular, yet gives us timely access to new results;

Table 8.2

**Evolution of the Classes of Lifestyle**

| Mentalities | 1986 | 1988 | Tendencies 1986/1989 |
|---|---|---|---|
| Drivers (D) | 18% | 24% | |
| Rigorists (R) | 20% | 20% | |
| Egocentrics (E) | 23% | 22% | |
| Activists (A) | 13% | 11% | |
| Materialists (M) | 26% | 23% | |

*Source:* Adapted from Brochand, B., and Lendrevie, J. (1983).

- the theoretical aspect: it's probably the time deemed the most appropriate to measure the evolution of the typologies proposed.

The types identified by the CCA have been structured around five big groups: *Drivers* (D) or displacers, *Rigorists* (R), the *Egocentrics* (E) or selfish, the *Activists* (A) and the *Materialists* (M). These groups will be referred to for the remainder of this discussion by their initials (DREAM). Their evolution during these years and their representation are indicated in Table 8.2 and Figure 8.2, respectively. For simplicity's sake, the following analysis is for only the five major groups. A natural extension would be to perform the analysis directly on the fourteen sociostyles.

Before considering the formation of the transition matrix T, it is important to consider the application of the proposed method to the study of the temporal evolution of lifestyles. The proposed approach assumes that the process is stationary, that is to say that the transition matrices between $t$ and $t + 1$, $t + 1$ and $t + 2$, $t + 2$, $t + 3$, and so on, are similar, or the fluctuation rate between groups during a given period is identical. It is reasonable to consider that this case may be true for at least three reasons:

1. First, studies of lifestyles are supposed to represent distinct phases of sociological evolution, which shape the current sociocultural landscape. Migration between classes of lifestyles is a possibility, except where social upheaval is unpredictable, sudden, and anachronistic.

2. Since 1984, the measuring instruments for lifestyles did not seem to change, leading researchers to obtain the same number of groups from one study to another, such that we can then study their changes over time (especially size).

3. Finally, the application of the method of sociological phenomena evolving over the long term (such as transitions between socioprofessional categories) has always shown more than satisfactory a posteriori results

Figure 8.2    **The Mentality of Lifestyle 1986/1988** (CCA)

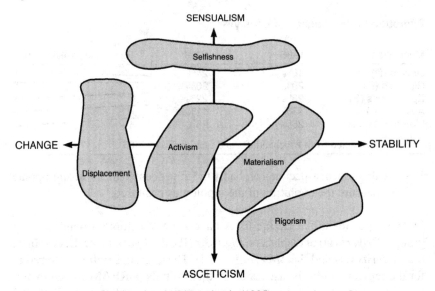

*Source:* Adapted by Brochand and Lendrevie (1985).

(McFarland, 1981). As already noted, changes in types of lifestyles in recent years are fairly stable, mostly reflecting slow sociological adjustments. By analogy with previous studies, the first approximation to use in this case is also the method of spectral decomposition.

Three findings then guide the construction of the transition matrix T, presented in Table 8.3:

- The trend in recent years is slow. We issued the first hypothesis that around 70 percent of individuals belonging to a class remained there in the next period (the corresponding values are shown in bold on the main diagonal of the matrix T in Table 8.3).
- The trade is mainly between the categories of lifestyles in the nearby area in Figure 8.2. For example, the staggered migrating occurs mainly due to the egocentrics and activists. For each category, we also noticed that there is little exchange with certain classes of lifestyles. These results are shown in gray in Table 8.3 (e.g., the offsets are unlikely to migrate to a rigorous area contrasted in Figure 8.2).
- A matrix proposed is a matrix T (fictional), for which the figures have been chosen to lead to an actual mathematical solution (all real, positive values), and also have a steady state in agreement with the current reality of typologies of existing lifestyles. It seems we need to ensure that

Table 8.3

**Transition Matrix T** (Notional)

| t* | t + 1 | | | | |
|---|---|---|---|---|---|
|  | D2 | R2 | E2 | A2 | M2 |
| D1 | **0.704** | 0.030 | 0.127 | 0.089 | 0.050 |
| R1 | 0.030 | **0.700** | 0.050 | 0.072 | 0.148 |
| E1 | 0.100 | 0.025 | **0.700** | 0.075 | 0.100 |
| A1 | 0.159 | 0.020 | 0.050 | **0.677** | 0.084 |
| M1 | 0.030 | 0.110 | 0.080 | 0.080 | **0.700** |

$t$ = *initial time*
*Source:* Valette-Florence and Rapacchi (1991c), Apport de la méthode de décomposition spectrale à l'analyse de l'évolution temporelle des styles de vie. *Actes du 7e colloque de l'association française du marketing*, 7, 165–182.

the proposed matrix can truly serve as an illustration for support of the proposed method.

*Grid Reading of the Spectral Composition*

The spectral decomposition occurs then on the matrix T. The spectral component $Z_1$, corresponding to the proper value unity, is easily interpreted, because it gives the steady state toward which the system changes after $n$ (as $n$ approaches infinity).

The following spectral components are equally enlightening, though more difficult to interpret. These four points may enhance the reader's understanding of the spectral composition:

• Each element $(i, j)$ of these matrices represents the propensity of an individual to go in the categories time $t + 1$ when he belonged to modality $i$ at the initial $t$. For interpretation, two characteristics of the element $(i, j)$ should be taken into account: its sign and its numerical value.
• The brand indicates the nature of the movement—positive if the tendency is favorable, and negative if it is unfavorable.
• The numerical value indicates the intensity of this migration. The higher the number, the more important the migration will be. Therefore, values near zero become negligible.
• Each element $(i, i)$ on the diagonal is a kind of index fidelity that has a modality. If an element $(i, i)$ is high and positive, it reflects a strong propensity to remain in the mode $i$. If it is negative, the opposite occurs, resulting in a strong propensity to change categories.

Furthermore, we insist that the elements $(i, j)$ or $(i, i)$ of various spectral components can be immediately interpreted as conditional (unlike the suggestions in the article by Grover and Dillon, 1988, p. 8). The elements actually represent the transient effects on the given generation, each element is weighted by its corresponding value $\lambda_k Z_k(i, j)$ for the first generation and $\lambda_k^n Z_k(i, j)$ for the generation of order $n$. We note therefore that when the values $\lambda_k$ are low, the more transient effects become negligible. This fact is why these effects are transitional, because they disappear quickly (significant values) and are usually the third generation and beyond (that is to say from $t + 3$). Apart from steady state, these effects can further be classified in a given generation, the nature and intensity of migration between modalities $(i, j)$. In general, these are arranged in a decreasing matching order of the values obtained $(\lambda_2 > \lambda_3 > \ldots > \lambda_k)$. In other words, they help to better identify the nature and intensity of the respective migration possible between different classes $(i, j)$ studied:

• Again, we note that the spectral components penetrate comparisons not directly observable on the transition matrix. Of course, they lead to detection of movements implicit in the original matrix T. But, besides obtaining the steady state, it is hardly discernible a priori, they're hiding explicitly the possibility of comparing the intensity of migration between terms; as we recall, all the lines $(i)$ and columns $(j)$ spectral components are proportional to each other. It is then easy to identify a method for online data $(i)$ (at time $t$), what its propensity is possibly the most significant upgrade to a modality $(j)$ in any column (at time $t + 1$).

• Finally, the spectral components bring computing at each step of the residual matrix corresponding to elements of the initial matrix not taken into account after extraction of first value precedents. Thus, for a spectral component $Z_e$, the matrix residual $T - \sum_{n=1} \lambda_n Z_n$ indicates what are the elements that remain to be analyzed with the remaining spectral components $Z_{e+1}, Z_{e+2}$, etc. This result therefore confines the decreasing interest in given spectral components, because the last cover residual matrices elements are rapidly becoming negligible (the residual matrix corresponding to the last spectral component was null).

*Comments on the Fictional Illustration*

Table 8.4 shows the resulting spectral decomposition, that is to say, the spectral components are $Z_1$ to $Z_5$ corresponding to value $\lambda_1$ to $\lambda_5$. In this example, all values are real positions. We recall that the trace of a matrix corresponds to the sum of elements on the main diagonal. As with any statistical analysis,

# Table 8.4

## Resulting Spectral Contribution

### Equilibrium $Z_1(\lambda_1 = 1)$

|   | D | R | E | A | M |
|---|---|---|---|---|---|
| D | .21545 | .14407 | .21018 | .19785 | .23244 |
| R | .21545 | .14407 | .21018 | .19785 | .23244 |
| E | .21545 | .14407 | .21018 | .19785 | .23244 |
| A | .21545 | .14407 | .21018 | .19785 | .23244 |
| M | .21545 | .14407 | .21018 | .19785 | .23244 |

### $Z_2 \lambda_2 = 0.73299$

|   | D | R | E | A | M |
|---|---|---|---|---|---|
| D | .27008 | .27174 | .17723 | .02734 | -.20290 |
| R | -.40709 | .40960 | -.26714 | -.04121 | .30584 |
| E | .12012 | -.12087 | .07883 | .01216 | -.09025 |
| A | .21789 | -.21923 | .14298 | .02206 | -.16369 |
| M | -.29208 | .29388 | -.19167 | -.02957 | .21943 |

### $Z_3 \lambda_3 = 0.61754$

|   | D | R | E | A | M |
|---|---|---|---|---|---|
| D | -.05330 | -.05009 | .09082 | -.02595 | .03852 |
| R | -.13146 | -.12356 | .22401 | -.06402 | .09503 |
| E | -.40908 | -.38449 | .69707 | -.19920 | .29570 |
| A | .76370 | .71778 | -1.30133 | .37188 | -.55204 |
| M | -.14927 | -.14030 | .25436 | -.07269 | .10790 |

### $Z_4 \lambda_4 = 0.58926$

|   | D | R | E | A | M |
|---|---|---|---|---|---|
| D | .33751 | .41288 | .21539 | -.10483 | -.43017 |
| R | .40091 | .49044 | -.25585 | -.12452 | -.51097 |
| E | .19441 | .23783 | -.12407 | -.06038 | -.24778 |
| A | -.83091 | -1.01648 | .53028 | .25808 | 1.05903 |
| M | -.02984 | -.03651 | .01905 | .00927 | .03804 |

### $Z_5 \lambda_5 = 0.54121$

|   | D | R | E | A | M |
|---|---|---|---|---|---|
| D | .23026 | -.23513 | -.26283 | -.09441 | .36210 |
| R | -.07780 | .07944 | .08880 | .03190 | -.12234 |
| E | -.12090 | .12345 | .13799 | .04957 | -.19012 |
| A | -.36612 | .37385 | .41790 | .15012 | -.57575 |
| M | .25575 | .26115 | -.29192 | -.10486 | .40218 |

$\lambda_1$ to $\lambda_2$ corresponds to proper values in the T matrix.

$Z_1$ to $Z_2$ represents the spectral components.

D, R, E, A, M symbolize the five mentalities of lifestyles proposed by the CCA:

D = Drivers; R = Rigorists; E = Egocentrics; A = Activists; M = Materialists.

two criteria for evaluation should be taken into account. The first concerns the overall quality of the analysis; the second the interpretation of results. Recall that the values correspond to the roots of the equation aside determined of the transition matrix T. If values are negative or complex, it will oscillate, that is to say, a phenomenon of clocklike alternating from one generation to another.

The interested reader will verify that the trail of T is equal to the sum of values: $tr(T) = \sum_k \lambda_k$ (here 3.48). Similarly, with the principal component analysis, the information returned by each spectral component is equal to $\dfrac{\lambda_k}{\sum \lambda_k}$. In our example, the three spectral first components re-create 67.51 percent of the information and thus appear sufficient to interpret the phenomenon studied. The second value $\lambda_2 = 0.73299$ also shows the rate of convergence to equilibrium represented by $Z_1$. In the absence of comparison with other research of this type, this rate is difficult to appreciate. It is still not very rapid because the transient effects induced on the second and third generations are respectively reduced by $(0.73299)^{2'} = 0.5372$ and $(0.73299)^3 = 0.3998$.

The matrix $Z_1^{'}$ indicates the equilibrium achieved. The values obtained are quite close to actual values, except for a decline in rigorists (14 percent) the gain seems to be for the activists (19.7 percent). Under these assumptions, this result is interesting in itself because it indicates the risk that a company would take exclusively on rigorists neglecting activists a priori is more promising. We recall that $Z_1$ is the steady state, which tends toward the system changes $(n \to \infty)$. Here, it would give respectively, 21.5 percent to drivers, 14.4 percent to rigorists, 21 percent to egocentrics, 19.7 percent to activists, and 23.2 percent to materialists.

As we noted above, the spectral components $Z_2$ to $Z_5$ allow us to understand better the movements between prospective class lifestyles. To define the nature of the migration potential better, we will comment after the results of Table 8.5 and elements have been reordered for convenience of interpretation according to their brand. Such rearrangement can detect in a single glance the nature of movements between classes that do not appear necessarily visible to demonstrate in the initial matrix T. The structures thus defined by the signs of elements in different spectral components somehow indicate borders of prohibiting migration between classes $(i, j)$ with opposite brands (see also McFarland, 1981, for an illustration). Such a phenomenon is to mark the spectral components $Z_2$ and $Z_5$.

$Z_2$ thus indicates that the exchanges are initially essentially between $D$, $E$, and $A$, on the one hand, and $M$ and $R$, on the other. This result, while logical and not surprising, had a connection to their respective positions in space defined in Figure 8.2. Note also that the terms are more stable (on

**Table 8.5**

## Symmetrical Changes

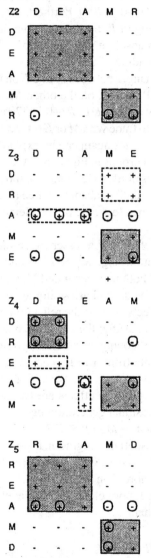

| $Z2$ | D | E | A | M | R |
|------|---|---|---|---|---|
| D | + | + | + | - | - |
| E | + | + | + | - | - |
| A | + | + | + | - | - |
| M | - | - | - | + | + |
| R | ⊖ | - | - | ⊕ | ⊕ |

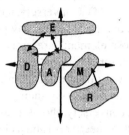

| $Z_3$ | D | R | A | M | E |
|------|---|---|---|---|---|
| D | - | - | - | + | + |
| R | - | - | - | + | + |
| A | ⊕ | ⊕ | ⊕ | ⊖ | ⊖ |
| M | - | - | - | + | + |
| E | ⊖ | ⊖ | - | + | ⊕ |

+

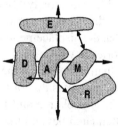

| $Z_4$ | D | R | E | A | M |
|------|---|---|---|---|---|
| D | ⊕ | ⊕ | - | - | - |
| R | ⊕ | ⊕ | - | - | ⊖ |
| E | + | + | - | - | - |
| A | ⊖ | ⊖ | ⊕ | + | ⊕ |
| M | - | - | + | + | + |

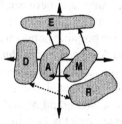

| $Z_5$ | R | E | A | M | D |
|------|---|---|---|---|---|
| R | + | + | + | - | - |
| E | + | + | + | - | - |
| A | ⊕ | ⊕ | + | ⊖ | ⊖ |
| M | - | - | - | ⊕ | + |
| D | - | - | - | ⊕ | + |

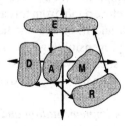

The parts in grey represent symmetrical changes.

The z elements (i, j,) in which the corresponding sign is surrounded have a numerical value > 0.30 in absolute value.

The arrows indicate the nature of the transitional effects on the corresponding graphics.

A, D, E, M, R refer to the families of lifestyles.

the diagonal), respectively $R$ (+0.40960), $D$ (+0.27008), and $M$ (+0.21943). Meanwhile, $E$ and $A$ are typically less stable, respectively $E$ (+0.07883) and $A$ (+0.02206). Finally, in case of migration, R has more of a tendency to migrate to $M$ (+0.30584). Conversely, it does not go to $D$ (–0.40709). Furthermore, $Z_2$ indicates that trade before any possible jamming of $R$, because it is the only class whose elements are greater than 0.30 in absolute value. We note also that this observation was not necessarily the reading of the matrix T.

$Z_3$ shows a different structure, allowing exchanges between $M$ and $E$ on the one hand and opposing their migration to D, R, and A, on the other. Meanwhile, A, conversely, shows a strong propensity to go to $D$ or $R$ (+0.76370 and +0.71778, respectively) and a clear opposition to trade with $M$ or $E$ (–0.55204 and –1.30133, respectively). Such observations once again can be explained according to the respective positions of different groups in Figure 8.2. We also observed that the displacements between classes of lifestyles jamming mostly only categories in which all elements are above 0.30 in absolute value and at least more than 3 times the other lines of evidence (e.g., the online elements of $A$ are worth 3 times that of line $E$).

$Z_4$ and $Z_5$ are relative and have transient effects of a lesser magnitude, strongly attenuated beyond the second generation (e.g., $\lambda_4^3 = 0.205$ and $\lambda_5^3 = 0.158$). $Z_4$ shows a structure allowed to trade both between A and M, which seems surprising, and between D and R (see the dashed arrow in the corresponding figure in Table 8.5). In fact, these effects are half the reflection of a low exchange possible between $D$ and $R$ of the data after the transition matrix T. They quickly become residual, beyond the second generation (negligible amplitudes). Note also the propensity to migrate from $A$ to $E$ (+0.53208) or $M$ (+1.05903). $Z_5$ stated, the nature of possible exchanges between $E$, $A$, and $R$, on the one hand, and $M$ and $D$, on the other. These effects are transient effects that are quickly becoming the second residual generation because of their low amplitude (i.e., $\left| \max Z_5 \right| = \left| Z_5(4,5) \right| = 1(A \to M) = 0.57575$.

We therefore retain from this analysis that essentially migration is possible between $M$ and $R$, on the one hand, and $D$, $E$, and $A$, on the other (matrix $Z_2$), and a propensity to go from $A$ to $D$ or $R$ more than $E$ or $M$ (matrix $Z_3$). Of course, such movements ask to be analyzed more closely at the level of sociostyles than the values corresponding to them.

*Problems of Implementation and Practical Implications*

In the preceding paragraphs, we offered a simple and easy way to study temporal-revolution lifestyles. The method of spectral decomposition we advocate is interesting because it allows, at a time, to predict the steady state toward the system studied, the convergence rate vets this condition, and the intensity and nature of possible exchanges between different classes of lifestyles studied. Observing the elements of the spectral components whose rows facilitate the prospective study of movements between the different terms and columns are all proportional to each other. Such a propriety can be detected and analyzed much more easily than on the transition matrix T initially.

This approach, quite common in sociology, is not typically applied to marketing. It could, however, be tested on the types or behavioral studies of image analysis that have led to phenomena developed via a continuous manner in the long term. It does require, however, obtaining the transition matrix T between the various terms of lifestyles. Note here that the spectral decomposition method applies only on square matrices $(n \times n)$. The study of the passage, for example, of a structure that has four main families in 2008 and has a structure of five families in 2010 is then more feasible. Recognize first that this problem is a limitation of the method just illustrated. A possible, but unsatisfactory, solution is to add an additional line $(i + 1)$ identical to the column $(j = i + 1)$ corresponding to a new class of lifestyles. But it should be noted, as was rightly pointed out by Antoine (1986), that at the time of social changes, these innovative approaches had not yet been developed. More-over, the number of families identified did tend to vary more. To illustrate the approach, we therefore propose a matrix whose fictional objects were by interpretations to comment on the method. Rather than focusing on results only, we would simply recall the conditions for the use and the application of the method:

• First, the interval during which the transition matrix T is made must be representative of the actual evolution of the phenomenon (cf., Kahle and Berman, 1979). If intervals are too short for a proper analysis, the fluctuations will not accurately represent the trends. Conversely, long intervals may not take into account the changes of a sociological modifier likely in the intervening term. Due to careful study of cultural trends identified annually by the Agora Metric Association, evidence indicates that significant changes occur about every two years, and that period is also the period used by the CCA to renew its investigations. Such intervals can be used in the first approach. It also apparently corresponds to what is used when updating other behavioral types (particularly in banking); however, much more research and theory needs to be done on time lapses.

• Next, such an approach is feasible only if the measuring instruments' correspondence to lifestyles is impeccable. In fact, any development of a sociological landscape ought to reflect a real change and not a distortion caused by an imperfection of the measuring instrument itself, even if the methods for forming groups are stringent (see Chapter 4).

• Finally, a more methodological approach that we propose is applicable only if the temporal evolution of lifestyles can be represented by a stationary Markov process of order (in other words, constants from one generation to another and depending only on the previous generation). If such an assumption seems unrealistic, it must be validated with actual data. Other methods, more complex, involving processes of generalized and/or latent Markov chains, are possible (see Poulsen, 1990, for an example, but in another context).

In any case, what approach should we adopt to address the aforementioned concerns? As we have indicated, only testing would validate the proposed method. The phenomenon of lifestyle changes is representative of sociological evolution. Therefore, it is likely that the technique applies well enough, by analogy, with its use for steps in the maturity phase, e.g., coffee (Grover and Dillon, 1988) or behavioral types in banking (Valette-Florence et al., 1992). Lifestyle studies are considered highly credible; still, conceptual and practical reservations remain, particularly regarding the predictive power of these approaches (cf. Chapter 7).

Researchers need to remain cautious with the method and use it only as a complementary addition to other studies. It requires more traditional methods to better identify its potential targets and strategies of communication. In this context, in the analysis of temporal changes in lifestyles, though neglected, it seems nearly everything is worthy of interest. For instance, if a company wants to focus on a specific lifestyle group, it is equally important for the company to know the fidelity or dispersal of the target in time as to know from year to year the gross percentage represented by this group. Such analysis makes it possible not only to know the evaporation time of a given target (i.e., trade with other lifestyles), but also to anticipate the target with the most important potential evolution.

A recent study (Gurel-Atay et al., 2010) looked at generational change in values in the United States starting in 1976. The study showed that self-respect and warm relations with others have become even more important in the United States, while the need to be well respected has declined. The newer generations place more emphasis on "excess" values, chosen by people who already have much of what that value implies (e.g., people who value warm relationships with others report having more friends than other groups). A corresponding decline of "deficit" values has been noted as well; deficit values are those selected by people who lack what the value implies (e.g., people who select security report a lack of security). Americans may be finding more value fulfillment than they did a generation ago, and the significance of various values for marketers to consider has changed greatly during that time.

On a more theoretical level, such an approach might shed light on socio-logical aging within different classes of lifestyles and could help define how individuals or classes of individuals change over time. Such a development would illuminate changes in consumption patterns from one generation to another and bring a fresh perspective to poorly understood factors such as fashion (Rose et al., 1994).

The biggest problem is the relevance of the method, that is to say its capac-ity for proposing a solution (state of equilibrium) that is in line with global trends measured every two years or at any appropriate lag. If a distortion simply reflected a shortcoming of the statistical method, other techniques do exist, but they tend to be more complex (e.g., the Markov chains of order greater than 1).

## The Use of Ambivalent Typologies

Human behavior is so complex that a person may very well possess multiple, and even different, sensibilities at the same time, depending on circumstances or simply on their mood. It is also interesting to note that profiles of lifestyles such as those developed in the work of Cathelat and Mermet (1985), some-times lead to ambivalent results, with individuals belonging to more than one group.

The use of statistical tools that can account for this inherently vague por-tion of human behavior seems necessary. Currently, three methodological approaches are possible:

1. The first and most traditional approach involves calculating probabilities for each person interviewed belonging to the different groups highlighted. This procedure is not often used, but is available with discriminant analysis, subject of course to having continuous variables (e.g., behavior, attitude scales, and views). It is easily incorporated into current studies and might lead to the design of questionnaires to reduce more categories (see Phase 2 of the CCA, Chapter 4). It is also possible to take into account the probability of a priori group membership, particularly in the context of a procedure of Bayesian categories. This approach has been successfully applied in bank-ing. It allows for a much better prediction of certain behaviors than the simple dichotomy of belonging to one specific group (Valette-Florence et al., 1992). When adapted to the field of lifestyles, it might help to improve predictive power.

2. The second direction allows for the incorporation of multiple assign-ment groups. Currently, three of the available methods are (1) the types with recovery (Arabie et al., 1981; ADCLUS—Shepard and Arabie, 1979; GENNCLUS—De Sarbo, 1982); (2) techniques from latent class models

based on mixtures of finite element data (Basford and McLachlan, 1985; De Sarbo and Cron, 1988); and (3) generalized typological regressions based on ambivalent set theory (Wedel and Steenkamp, 1989b and 1991). Although all methodologies are somewhat efficient, their use appears limited in the immediate future because of problems with program availability, complexity of implementation and evaluation of results, and the need to handle large volumes of data. From academic research, these developments probably will not be adopted by the agencies and research companies for several years.

3. The third type of investigation is sometimes called analysis of means-end chains. Easy to implement, it is based on the analysis of cognitive chaining (see Chapter 2). It also offers the advantage of not requiring a program of specific typological analysis. Presented in detail by Roehrich and Valette-Florence (1992), the analysis of means-end chains rests on the simple idea that information collected from respondents can be treated in different ways. Everyone—speaking in general multiple-chaining cognitions—can:

- make a typology on all channels mentioned. These typology channels allow observers to discover and recognize various styles of consumption. (This terminology is employed to differentiate consumption patterns presented here, and it is much more general in its wording.)
- also make a typology on the center of gravity of individual channels, so we can better classify interviewees. We obtain consumer segments grouped according to similar profile results. A single cross between two types leads to a description. Easy segments obtained according to various styles of consumption are then revealed. Each segment can also match several styles of different consumption. The practical implications come in terms of defining the position in which the strategies of communication are equally immediate (refer to Roehrich and Valette-Florence, 1992, for a more detailed illustration).

All references to methodological propositions thus far have been so explicit that it would be better to consider the theories underlying their use. These are discussed next.

## THE THEORETICAL PROPOSITIONS

To enrich and expand research on the studies of lifestyles, it seems appropriate to present briefly some theoretical developments in the field. Four propositions must be emphasized. The first is the issue of commercial research, which is undoubtedly the most original and most promising of the advancements. It is concerned with semiometrics (the notion that people's reactions to various

Table 8.6

**Semantic Fields Related to the Words "King" and "Marriage"**

| Semantic field of the word **King** | | Semantic field of the word **Marriage** | |
|---|---|---|---|
| Queen | 167* | Ceremony | 291* |
| Castle | 251 | Fidelity | 302 |
| Sovereign | 306 | Family | 308 |
| Glory | 343 | Birth | 314 |
| Power | 348 | God | 327 |
| Gold | 359 | Priest | 327 |
| Elite | 362 | Nursery | 332 |
| Wealth | 364 | Pray | 332 |
| Homeland | 369 | Faith | 334 |
| Praying | 377 | Politeness | 338 |
| God | 379 | Honest | 343 |
| Trinket | 389 | Honor | 347 |

Source: Steiner, J.F., and Auliard, O. (1991), La sémiométrie: un outil de validation des réponses. *La qualité de l'information dans les enquêtes.* Paris: École nationale supérieure des télécommunications, 225–240.
*Represents the distance from the word **King** or **Marriage**.

terms can reveal their values) and its applications in marketing and consumer behavior. The second issue relates to defining recent styles of time use and their application to the study of consumption. The third, highlighted in Chapter 2, deals with chained cognitive analysis. The fourth concerns the definition of new concepts of psychosocial origin, such as styles of persuasion or styles of homes.

*Semiometrics*

Introduced by SOFRES in 1989, semiometrics is based on the idea that human beings evolved through a universe charged by sensations. The places we live, the objects that surround us, and the events that occur in our lives all have a meaning. The word *meaning* spans three precise semantic fields (Deutsch, 1989):

• cognition: judgments, reason, wisdom, and ideas;
• sensuality: sensuous-affective experiences; and
• direction: orientation in space and time.

The central hypothesis of this approach implies that the meaning of words is contained in their emotional impact and that locating the sensuous value of a word can then control the other two values (cognition and direction). Jean-Francois Steiner (e.g., Steiner and Auliard, 1991), the inventor of this method, constructed a model of semantic space. As an illustration, Table 8.6 presents some details about the list of words and semantic fields associated with the differences between the words "king" and "marriage" (distance derivative of coefficient correlation).

In one study by Steiner and Auliard (1991), words were rated on a scale of + 3 to –3, depending on the pleasantness or unpleasantness of their character. This helped in visualizing the semantic space corresponding to three representative samples of the French population (1,089 adults older than 18, 970 home owners, and 955 heads of households). Up to five main themes were selected. The following is a description of the interpretations for the sample of heads of households:

- The first axis (horizontal) is very stable. It ranges between the instinctual life or liberty (sensuality, emotion, wildness, revolt) and the order or control of moral and social impulses (honor, God, discipline, virtue). It is Freudian (id versus superego) or, more concretely, "order" versus "chaos."
- The second axis (vertical) ranges between the world of pleasure, attachment, and harmony affiliation (poetry, tenderness, birth, gentleness, softness) and that of confrontation, conflict, and detachment (attack, power, gun, danger). In a Freudian sense, it symbolizes the opposition of the life drive and the death instinct, or simply aggression versus pacifism.
- The third axis represents the values of conquest and power (gold, silver, victory, glory, conquer). The values of wealth are internalized (soul, meditation, sacrifice, question). This axis corresponds to opposites such as power and poverty.
- The fourth axis runs between the values of progress and materials (dynamic production, utilitarian effort, equipment) and those of an imaginary, immaterial, and spiritual nature (God, prayer, faith, soul, consecration, meditation). It can therefore be classified as a representation of dualities—real/imaginary or rational/irrational.
- The fifth axis covers the values of expansion (audacity, imagination, evasion, growth) in opposition to that of stagnation or the ephemeral (mode, ceremonies, empty, fault, immobile). It represents the antagonism of approach/reply.

Note that the semantic vagueness obtained is the result of gender heterogeneity of the sample (Steiner and Auliard, 1991).

The practical implications are diverse. For example, the factors (Figure 8.3) contrast (by t test) different populations such as men and women (Figure 8.4) or supporters of fleecy "coats" compared to those of the thin-clothed "jacket" (Figure 8.5). Thus, men overinvest in power values and aggressiveness (gun, attack, danger) and women tend to affiliation and attachment (jewelry, slimness, perfume, fashion, mellowness). Similarly, fans of fleecy

# Figure 8.3 Semiometric Divisions

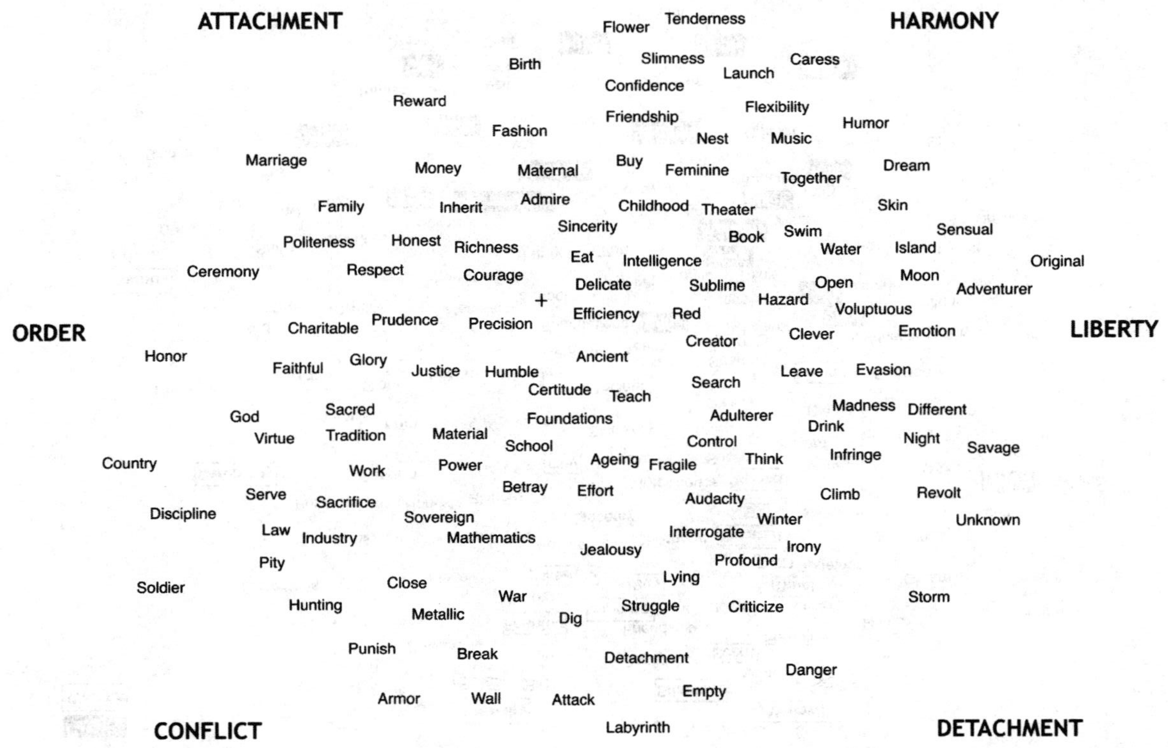

**ATTACHMENT**

**HARMONY**

**LIBERTY**

**ORDER**

**CONFLICT**

**DETACHMENT**

Marriage · Reward · Birth · Flower · Tenderness · Launch · Caress

Family · Money · Fashion · Confidence · Slimness · Flexibility · Humor

Ceremony · Politeness · Inherit · Maternal · Buy · Friendship · Nest · Music · Dream

Respect · Honest · Admire · Feminine · Childhood · Theater · Together · Skin

Charitable · Richness · Sincerity · Book · Swim · Water · Island · Sensual

Honor · Prudence · Courage · Delicate · Intelligence · Red · Open · Moon · Original

Faithful · Glory · Justice · Precision · Efficiency · Sublime · Hazard · Voluptuous · Adventurer

Sacred · Humble · Ancient · Creator · Clever · Emotion

God · Tradition · Certitude · Teach · Search · Leave · Evasion

Virtue · Work · Material · Foundations · Adulterer · Madness · Different

Country · Sacrifice · School · Control · Drink · Night · Savage

Serve · Power · Ageing · Fragile · Think · Infringe

Discipline · Industry · Betray · Effort · Audacity · Winter · Climb · Revolt

Law · Sovereign · Interrogate · Irony · Unknown

Pity · Mathematics · Jealousy · Profound

Close · Lying

Soldier · Hunting · Metallic · War · Dig · Struggle · Criticize · Storm

Punish · Break · Detachment · Danger

Armor · Wall · Attack · Empty

Labyrinth

+

*Source:* Deutsch (1989).

# Figure 8.4 Semiometric Divisions: Men vs. Women

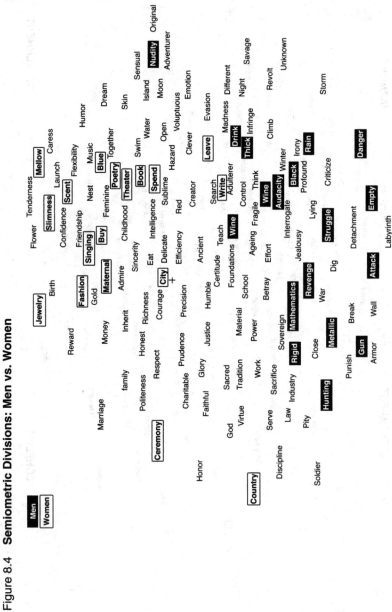

*Source:* Deutsch (1989), p. 9.

213

Figure 8.5   **Semiometric Divisions: Coat vs. Jacket**

*Source:* Deutsch (1989), p. 10.

"coats" are characterized by their sensibility values of tradition and the established order (moral, ceremony, discipline, virtue), while those who like the thin-clothed "jackets" favored values of seduction and sensuality (seduce, desire, together, nudity, sensual). We perceive therefore an interest in this approach to better define the sensibilities specific to a particular target or identity, depending on the age and the evolution of values espoused by the consumer toward a given product. We read in this context, the analysis strikingly suggested by Deutsch (1989), director of the SOFRES, on consuming mineral water. Although people under thirty-five are committed to the values of protection that provide law and the social order, people thirty-six to fifty years live with the hedonist orientation. Finally, women over sixty years over invest in tangible values.

Also used successfully in politics to characterize the different electorates (Deutsch, 1989, p. 11) or to separate voters from abstainers in a given population (Steiner and Auliard, 1991), the analysis can be extended to areas such as radio or television audiences or different media-press preferences. We perceive possible overlaps in the richness of this approach for the definition of publicity and advertising, including the choice of words (those words that are over-invested), which prove the most appropriate for targets.

Semiometrics is also used to define groups—called semiotypes—based on *overinvested* and *underinvested* words.

Thus, the typology for adults has eight groups:

1. the silent (15 percent)
2. the pragmatists (15 percent)
3. the authoritarians (16 percent)
4. the moralists (15 percent)
5. the narcissists (15 percent)
6. the rebels (6 percent)
7. the conquerors (10 percent)
8. the romantics (8 percent)

This typology should not be too strongly connected to the field of investigative studies of lifestyles (here, only the score or pleasant words are evaluated). Otherwise the risk persists of underrating the answers in accordance to their social value, while forgetting that a given group of words are overinvested and underinvested (cf. Table 8.7 for an illustration of the group of conquerors).

For studies of lifestyles, semiotics imports a conceptual basis (that is to say, it finds what field of theory is inserted, including consumer behavior) and compares (and shows) its predictive validation with conventional approaches, such as using sociodemographic variables.

Table 8.7

**Words Overinvested and Underinvested for the Conquerors Group**

| Conqueror | |
|---|---|
| Words overinvested in | Words underinvested in |
| Defeat | Faith |
| Irony | Pray |
| Command | Preach |
| Conquer | Charitable |
| Attacking | Ceremony |
| Power | God |
| Voluptuous | Sing |

*Source:* E. Deutsch (1989), p. 12.

## Styles of Time

Despite years of study (Jacoby, Szybillo, and Bering, 1976), the influence of time on consumption has generated only modest interest among theoretical and practical researchers (e.g., Bergadaa, 1989, 1990, 1991; Usunier, 1991). Since the late 1980s, two scales of time measurement have been presented and validated in a particular French context (Bergadaa, 1989, 1990, 1991; Usunier and Valette-Florence, 1991). Bergadaa stresses the measurement of temporal orientation (past, present, future) and the consideration of their cognitions and affective components. The approach proposed by Usunier incorporates psychosociological connotations and a variety of intercultural contexts.

To construct the scale proposed by Usunier and Valette-Florence (1991), emphasis has been placed particularly on the dimensions of time perception, which was described by both anthropologists and experimental psychologists (Kluckhohn and Strodtbeck, 1961; Calabresi and Cohen, 1968; Hall, 1959, 1976, 1983). Their combination in this scale can identify a multidimensional concept of time, a personal connotation, but also a societal impression of being concerning temporal patterns of a society and a specific environment.

These dimensions consist of:

• The economics of time and its perception by monochromic and polychromic reports (and anthropology). Monochromic people and societies have a rigid concept of time and value close adherence to schedules. Polychromic people and societies thrive on a looser concept of time; they are less concerned with *when* things happen and more confident that things will be discussed or acted upon when they should be, whether that coincides with a predetermined schedule or not. Economic linear time organization has been often described at an individual level by "structure" (Alreck, 1976) or "structured routines" (Feather and Bond, 1983).

• The temporal orientations are an important aspect of time studies. Individually, directions to the past, present, and future have been an important field of investigation for experimental psychologists. Broadly, their main purpose is to discover people's awareness of the spectrum of time; however, it is much easier to discover temporal orientations in society on an individual level.

• The psychological dimensions explain how each person manages his or her time (whether as an economic resource, a social process, or an expression of cultural synchronization). These psychological dimensions can be divided into two parts:

1. The motivational aspect—the capacity to undertake tasks or projects for which awards will not be obtained very quickly (the concept of tenacity and persistence). The idea of thinking about the future also shows motivational depth (Nuttin, 1979). Raynor and Entin (1983) believe, for example, that there is a sort of path to the future horizon, and recognizing the different stages involved in following that path increases the probability of success at each step. The rewards are more or less important: They are subject to impact and insignificant gratification; individuals tend to reduce their time horizon when rewards are obvious (Bouffard, Lens, and Nuttin, 1983). The orientation into the future includes a major component of imagination, which is linked to the individuals' cognitive attitude and a glimpse of what life could be—an imagination of the future (Holman, 1981).

2. Anxiety—notably, anxiety about time and the constraints it imposes on people. Faced with the problems of organizing their different activities (and the inescapable limits to their personal time), individuals may face problems of adjustment and feel varying degrees of anxiety. Calabresi and Cohen (1968) administered a questionnaire of forty-six items related to the experience of time. The questionnaire was answered by 508 participants, divided into two groups: students and individuals in psychiatric treatment. Among the four factors they found, one was the concept of discomfort and anxiety at the time and a need to control it (Calabresi and Cohen, 1968). Another factor, which the researchers termed "submission to time," corresponds to an attitude that is respectful and consistent with regard to time—one in which a person can focus on compliance with calendars and appointments. There is very clearly an emotional relation of the individual with time.

The full scale of Usunier and Valette-Florence (1991) incorporates eight current measurement precedents:

• the preference for economic time
• the preference for nonlinear and unorganized time

Table 8.8

**Examples of Items from Usunier and Valette-Florence** (1991)

| | |
|---|---|
| Economic times: | I plan my activities in a given way during the day. |
| Unstructured time: | I hate to follow a schedule. |
| Guidance to the past: | I am nostalgic. |
| Guidance to the future: | I spend time thinking about what my future might be. |
| Submission to time: | No matter how hard I try, I'm almost always late. |
| Anxiety in the face time: | I sometimes feel that the way I use time has little use or worth. |
| Instant gratification: | I preferred to do two or three things quickly rather than complete a large project over a long duration. |
| Toughness: | When I start an activity, I continue through completion. |

*Source:* Valette-Florence and Usunier (1991), Personal Value Systems and Temporal Patterns (Time-Styles): Exploratory Findings. In *Proceedings of the Workshop on Value and Lifestyle Research in Marketing.* Brussels, Belgium: EIASM.

- the orientation to the past
- the orientation to the future
- submission to time
- anxiety in the face of time
- immediate gratification (motivational aspect of short-term time)
- tenacity in the face of time

Examples of items are presented in Table 8.8.

Two studies analyze the impact of controls and values on various components of time and individual behavior. These are studies that incorporate the first six components that were just described. The first research (Valette-Florence and Usunier, 1991) has shown an effect of these two complementary concepts: the time structure (economic time and unorganized time) and social orientation explaining 34.9 percent of the attitude toward organized vacation. A second study (Usunier, Valette-Florence, and Faley, 1992) has extended the results by first specifying the nature of the relations at the global level between the value system of individuals and orientation toward time (Figure 8.6). Thus, the overall system of values of positive individuals affects both economic time and submission to time. We perceive a complementary nature in these two approaches to the study of behavior, which is why two typological analyses—one on values, the other on orientation toward time—have been undertaken (Table 8.9). Here again, a graphic display of their intersection (Figure 8.7) (factor analysis with multiple connections) illustrates their complementariness and similar behavior (the different groups circled on the diagram correspond to statistically significant associations confirmed

Figure 8.6    **Global System of Values Related to Time Orientations**

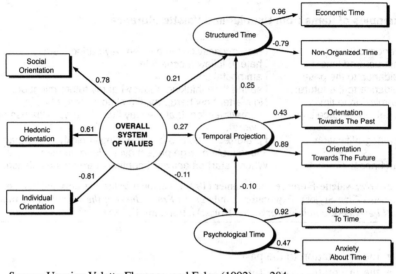

*Source:* Usunier, Valette-Florence, and Faley (1992), p. 284.

Table 8.9

**Analysis of Typologies**

**A. Definition of Values of Systems**

| Groups | Social orientation | Hedonic orientation | Individual orientation | Size |
|---|---|---|---|---|
| Individualistic | 0.131* | 0.112 | **1.158** | 47 |
| Withdrawn | **−0.655** | **−1.592** | **0.713** | 58 |
| Hedonists | 0.680 | **0.374** | −0.385 | 93 |
| Socially integrated | **1.011** | **0.556** | −0.638 | 94 |

**B. Definition of Styles of Time**

| Groups | Economic time | Non-organized time | Orientation toward the past | Orientation toward the future | Anxiety about time | Submission to time | Size |
|---|---|---|---|---|---|---|---|
| Nostalgic anxious | −0.363* | 0.38 | **0.554** | 0.14 | **0.517** | **1.443** | 63 |
| Unorganized anxious | **−0.889** | **1.03** | −0.017 | 0.137 | **0.721** | −0.468 | 48 |
| Rational futurists | **0.818** | **−0.726** | 0.266 | **0.475** | −0.185 | −0.479 | 108 |
| Playing in the present | −0.313 | 0.13 | **−0.86** | **−0.914** | −0.647 | −0.229 | 73 |

*Source:* Usunier, Valette-Florence, and Faley (1992), p. 285.
*Standardized factorial score.

Figure 8.7 **Lifestyles of Time and Values**

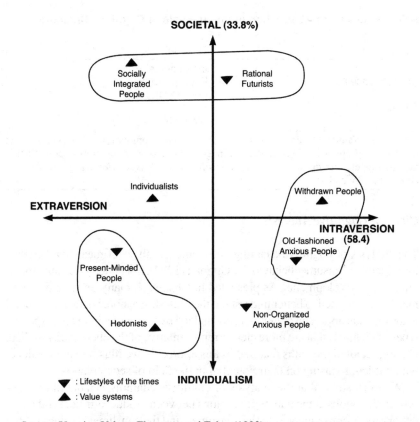

*Source:* Usunier, Valette-Florence, and Faley (1992).

by a linear log). Finally, a multinomial logistic model has demonstrated the impact of these two types of five attitudes ($R^2$ = 18.8 percent), confirming that the transition phenomenon is better explained when used as predictors of dimensions (factor scores, continuous variables) in lieu of a simple group membership (variable nominal) of too much reduction (cf. Valette-Florence and Jolibert, 1985, 1990, for results with similar values and lifestyles). Thus, styles of time alone (variable nominal) account for 11.1 percent of behavior studied against 16.9 percent when using factorial scores on time and not organized economics.

Of course, such an approach with a large application demonstrates other types of consumption for which the temporal aspect may be important, among them food consumption, banking, insurance, and travel.

Table 8.10

**Selected Levels of Abstraction in the Analysis of Cognitive Chaining**

| Values | Terminal |
| --- | --- |
| | Instrumental |
| Consequences | Psychosociological |
| | Functional |
| Attributes | Abstracts |
| | Concrete |

*Source:* Valette-Florence and Rapacchi (1990a), Application et extension de la théorie des graphes à l'analyse des chaînages cognitifs: une illustration pour l'achat de parfums et eaux de toilette. *Actes du colloque de l'association française du marketing,* 6, 485–511.

## Chained Cognitive Analysis

The analysis of cognitive chaining, also called analysis of means-end chains, introduced in consumer behavior by Gutman (1982), has undergone many methodological developments. As presented in Chapter 2, many of these developments are designed to better understand the multidimensional data not included in the original approach of Gutman, and to lead by various techniques to specific types of channels that are more clearly representative of the phenomena studied. Having recalled the paths featured in this approach, we illustrate the results to which it led, focusing on their potential in the field of segmentation.

We must stress that the analysis of cognitive chaining is a qualitative approach that looks at the nature of relations between product attributes (abstract or concrete), consequences to the consumer, and the consumer's values (Table 8.10). Note that Aurifeille (1991) has validated the inclusion of instrumental values. Once data collection is completed, an aggregate representation of the results in graphic form, called a hierarchical value map, is then proposed. This process of aggregation, critical in its current form (Grunert and Grunert, 1991), is highly instructive for the detection of the subjective reasonableness (the chaining) that a consumer gives a product.

As an illustration, consider the results furnished by the study of Valette-Florence and Rapacchi (1990a) on the purchase of perfumes (Table 8.11). The resulting graph (Figure 8.8) indicates the existence of three main functions, the largest (in a number of citations) being the "brand image to imaginary [a person's imagined perceptions of (or preconceived notions about) a product] to impact on personal incidence [personal experience using the product] to self-image to self-satisfaction " string. A representation in the form of a radius, which may be more appropriate to reflect the nature of hierarchical elements

Table 8.11

**Distribution of Different Levels with Their Corresponding Codes for the Purchase of Perfumes and Toilet Waters**

| | |
|---|---|
| Terminal values | Self-satisfaction (23) |
| | Hedonism (24) |
| | Personal development (25) |
| Instrumental values | Romanticism (20) |
| | Social deference (21) |
| | Social approval (22) |
| Psychosociological | Imaginary (11) |
| | Personal incidence (12) |
| | Femininity (13) |
| | Virility (14) |
| | Sensuality (15) |
| | Self-image (16) |
| | Distinguishing Feature (17) |
| | Comfort (18) |
| | Seduction (19) |
| Functional consequences | Prestige (8) |
| | Hygiene (9) |
| | Taking care of oneself (10) |
| Abstract attributes | Brand Image (4) |
| | Packaging (5) |
| | Smell (6) |
| | Shape (bottle) (7) |
| Concrete attributes | Price (1) |
| | Place of Distribution (2) |
| | Brand (name) (3) |

*Source:* See Table 8.10.

(from attributes to consequences to values), might also be proposed (Figure 8.9). In the last part of this scheme, the functions are named according to the attributes and consequences only. For example, the "brand image to imaginary to impact on personal incidence to self-image to self-satisfaction" string is qualified as a function of personal values explicitly by reference to the first five elements that compose it.

Based on a factor analysis of multiple matches, or what are preferable, a multivariate analysis (Aurifeille and Valette-Florence, 1992a) also helps in the visualization of the resulting semantic space (Figure 8.10). Notice the opposite junctions between personal and practical functions on the one hand, and imaginary and social functions on the other (horizontal axis). Similarly, the vertical axis opposes social visibility and self-expression. The variable illustration projections can then describe the sensibilities

## Figure 8.8   Means-End Chain for Perfume Consumption

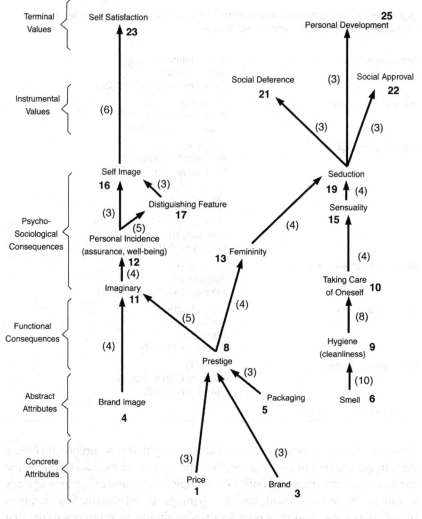

*The numbers in parentheses indicate the number of times or the connection evoked between
two successive elements (for example 4 direct connections between brand image and imagery).

*Source:* Valette-Florence and Rapacchi (1990a), p. 508.

toward consumption of a product. We also note that among the preferred
brands, Poison and Loulou are much closer to each other and more distant
from Opium, which, ironically, features traits that match it more closely
with masculine fragrances such as Anteus and Drakkar Noire. The same
approach can also be used to analyze different consumer groups (men/

Figure 8.9  **Cognitive Changes for Buying Perfume**

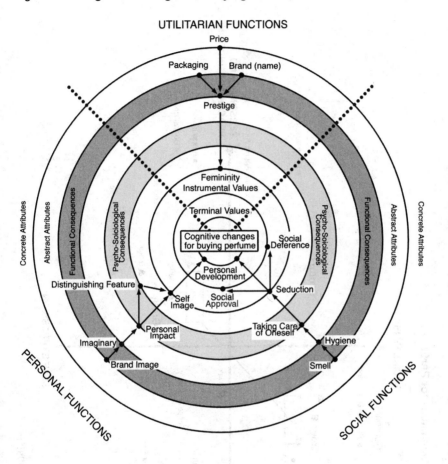

*The title of the three types of factors are defined by the attributes of the consequences only.

*Source:* Valette-Florence and Rapacchi (1990a), p. 209.

women) and especially specific segments (Groups A, B, and C) obtained by cluster analysis. We can then easily identify the specific sensibilities of the segment given. As an example, segment Group C is hedonistic, sensual, and seductive (smell/seduction/personal impact/hedonism); it is not on the graph of corresponding proximity linking it immediately to an existing fragrance. Such an absence may be indicative of an interesting niche for the launch of a new product if we perceive the Group C segment to be of sufficient size.

Figure 8.10 Gender and Preference Dimensions for Perfume

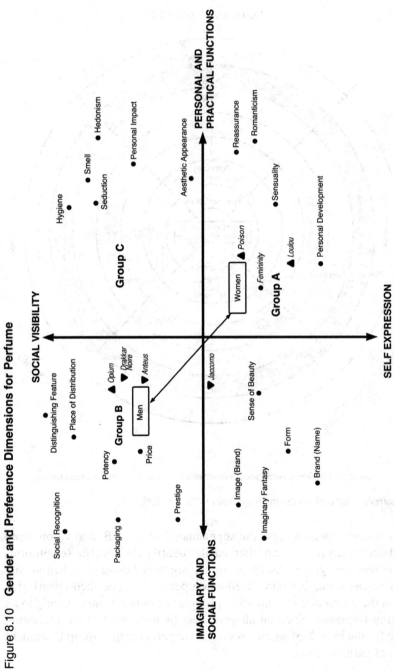

*Source:* Valette-Florence and Rapacchi (1990a).

Table 8.12

**Crossing the Cognitive Groups Chaining with Four European Countries**

| Country | Group | | | | Total |
|---|---|---|---|---|---|
| | A | B | C | D | |
| France | 5 | 9 | 15 | 80 | 109 |
| Italy | 26 | 25 | 20 | 39 | 110 |
| Germany | 65 | 21 | 5 | 49 | 140 |
| Switzerland | 69 | 16 | 15 | 15 | 115 |
| Total | 165 | 71 | 55 | 183 | 474 |

*Source:* Valette-Florence and Rapacchi (1991a), A Cross-Cultural Means-End Chain Analysis of Perfume Purchases, *Proceedings of the Third Symposium on Cross-Cultural Consumer and Business Studies*, p. 170.

This type of study yields results that are rich for teaching, including the eventual identification of cross targets. The previous study, extended by Valette-Florence and Rapacchi (1991a), identified four specific segments (Table 8.12) and projected variables illustrative in the resulting semantic space (Figure 8.11). We observe the existence of specific segments in a given country, such as Groups B and C for Italy, or segments for Groups A and D, in Switzerland and Germany. It is even possible, by isolating a particular segment, to draw the corresponding chain hierarchically (Figure 8.12 for Group D).

Through successive zoom effects, the analyst can examine a general population overall, or concentrate on a specific portion of a group based on specified variables and importance. In addition, a typical study (Aurifeille and Valette-Florence, 1992b) indicates that the analysis of chaining cognitions exhibits twice the predictive power of a conventional approach centered on only the values for the study of a specific type of consumption (cigarettes, in this case). Improvements that take into account issues of semantic coherence have been proposed (Roehrich and Valette-Florence, 1991, 1992; Aurifeille, 1991, 1992; Aurifeille and Valette-Florence, 1992a, 1992b, 1993). There is no doubt that this type of approach will continue to find a number of relevant applications in the future.

### *Means-End Theory Recent Developments*

Since the pioneering work of Gutman (1982) and Reynolds and Gutman (1988), empirical laddering studies have been widely used in academic as well as commercial settings. In a recent review, Reynolds and Phillips (2008)

226

Figure 8.11   Pan-European Lifestyle Segments for Perfume

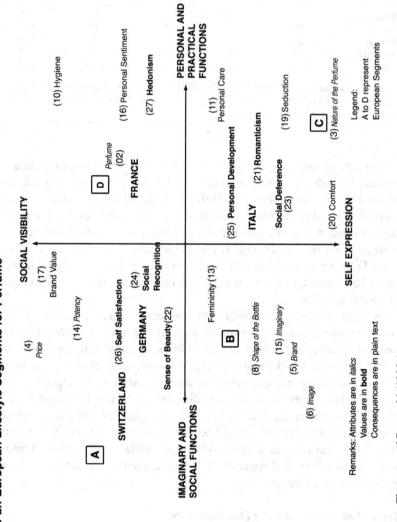

*Source:* Valette-Florence and Rapacchi (1990a).

Figure 8.12   **An Example of a Means-End Chain for Pan-European Segment D**

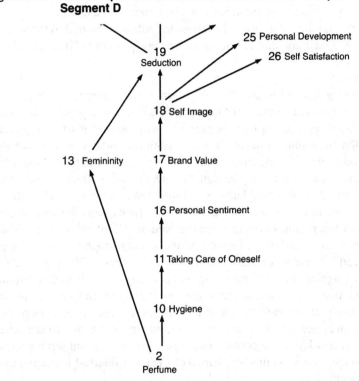

*Source:* Valette-Florence and Rapacchi (1990a).

listed more than sixty applications of laddering research among academics. All these applications outline the unique ability of the laddering research method to identify and define the drivers of consumer choice. In addition, Reynolds (2006; also Phillips, Reynolds, and Reynolds, 2010) has stressed the development of a segmentation approach, using choice-based means-end chains to offer marketers an added level of knowledge that is extremely valuable in the development of a promotional strategy. As stated by Reynolds (2006), the initial problem with implementing the means-end chain framework for segmentation is that the Customer Decision Maps (CDM) display only respondents' aggregate decision structure, which cannot be related to specific operational criteria.

Although some segmentation approaches have been proposed (Valette-Florence and Rapacchi, 1991a; Aurifeille and Valette-Florence, 1992a), Reynolds (2006) has proposed a methodology based on the actual means-end chain data. His deterministic segmentation analysis involves setting three values:

1. a minimum threshold value that defines the initial level for significant implication to be included in a given means-end chain;
2. the number of desired clusters in the solution (from 2 to 9); and
3. the maximum number of codes the may be included in a chain (4, 5, or 6).

Both Reynolds (2006) and Phillips, Reynolds, and Reynolds (2010) provide sound arguments in favor of the new segmentation approach. However, the methodology—at least in its present form—seems hard to replicate. In addition, it implies a deterministic assumption involving the fact that means-end chain segmentation should conform to the structure of the original ladders. By contrast, we postulate that the original collected ladders are nothing more than observed ladders belonging to diverse and differentiated *unobservable latent means-end dimensions*. To explain the interactions between different items contained in the ladders, Valette-Florence (1988c) originally recommended the use of optimal scaling properties of nonlinear generalized canonical correlation analyses. In his review, Reynolds (2006) did not recognize that different respondents may elicit distinct attributes while, for instance, evoking the same consequences and values. In that sense, it could be the case that, at the latent level, a means-end orientation might retain consequences and values without any connection to attributes. Ultimately, this latent conception corresponds to the causal structural approach to means-end chains, explained elsewhere (Valette-Florence, Falcy, and Rapacchi, 1993).

To sum up, we propose that—contrary to Reynolds's (2006) deterministic observed approach—a latent, unobservable, probabilistic means-end segmentation approach seems preferable. The following example illustrates our position (Valette-Florence, Ferrandi, and Roehrich, 2003). Data stem from a pilot study on two representative samples of 200 men and women on their perfume preferences. On average, respondents evoked 3.8 individual ladders. In order to gain a better understanding of the proposed approach, two parts deserve attention:

1. *Methodology*. There are three main steps, as described in Figure 8.13. The first one is based on a generalized canonical analysis of the collected data (coded 0, 1) that helps to get a multidimensional space displaying distance between stimuli (attribute/consequences/values). We stress the fact that the analysis is not limited to three sets of elements (i.e., attributes/consequences/values). In a second step, usual cluster analyses (or more sophisticated mixture models)—performed on the stimuli coordinates (A/C/V) within the aforementioned multidimensional space—give the resulting means-end solutions in a final step. A simple constrained alloca-

Figure 8.13  **Proposed Main Steps in a Means-End Segmentation Approach**

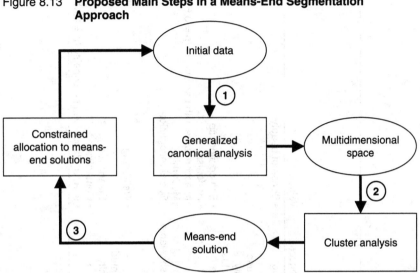

*Source:* Valette-Florence, Ferrandi, and Roehrich (2003).

tion of the collected ladders gives the percentage of these ladders matched by each means-end solution.

2. *Criteria for assessing segmentations reliability.* Four points deserve attention. As for many segmentation studies, the *chain's importance* relates to the number of original collected ladders matched by the means-end solution. The *semantic coherence* relates to how closely plotted (or connected) the elements (A/C/V) are for a given solution within the obtained multidimensional space. In spirit, this measure, defined as the mean of distances of all the elements within a means-end solution to the center of gravity of this solution, provides means to evaluate the overall coherence of the means-end solution (the lowest the distance, the best coherence). In addition, it is also possible to display the *semantic proximity* between the means-end solutions. This approach helps to identify which solutions are closely related to those that are more specific. Finally, the *chain's composition* (i.e., the number of elements) gives the overall means-end hierarchy. Moreover, it is possible to identify *prototypical* elements within the solution, that is to say, those elements that are the most representative for each level (A/C/V).

Tables 8.13 and 8.14 display the results for both men and women. For women, the most important chain ("Sensual Well-Being") matches 41.8 percent of the original ladders. In addition, it exhibits the best coherence index. Worth noticing is the fact that some elements may belong to differ-

Table 8.13

**Means-End Solutions for Men**

| Main orientation | Importance | Coherence | Attributes | Consequences | Values |
|---|---|---|---|---|---|
| Functional beauty | 21.5% | 0.92 | | • Collecting perfumes<br>• Ease of use<br>• Originality<br>• Signal value | • Sense of beauty |
| Self-expression | 25% | 0.59 | | • Elegance | • Self confidence<br>• Hedonism<br>• In accordance with personality (p = 0.6) |
| Social visibility | 10% | 1.34 | • Brand image<br>• Brand name<br>• Perfume name<br>• Price | • Having the choice<br>• Being fashionable | • Modernity<br>• Social recognition |
| Sensuality | 43.5% | 0.57 | • Fragrance | • Being complimented<br>• Masculinity<br>• Seduction | • Well-being<br>• Cleanness<br>• Romanticism<br>• In accordance with personality (p = 0.4) |

Table 8.14

**Means-End Solutions for Women**

| Main orientation | Importance | Coherence | Attributes | Consequences | Values |
|---|---|---|---|---|---|
| Social visibility | 16.8% | 1.56 | • Brand name<br>• Price | • Having the choice<br>• Ease of use<br>• Originality<br>• Distinctive signals<br>• Elegance (p = 0.25) | • Sense of belonging<br>• Social recognition<br>• Sense of beauty |
| Modernity | 7.8% | 1.28 | • Shape of bottle<br>• Novelty | • Collecting perfumes<br>• Being fashionable | • Modernity |
| Self-expression | 33.6% | 1.02 | • Long lasting (p = 0.54) | • Elegance (p = 0.75) | • Respect others (p = 0.55)<br>• In accordance with personality<br>• Hedonism |
| Sensual well-being | 41.8% | 0.59 | • Fragrance<br>• Smell<br>• Long lasting (p = 0.46) | • Being complimented<br>• Femininity<br>• Seduction | • Well-being<br>• Self-confidence<br>• Cleanness<br>• Romanticism<br>• Respecting others (p = 0.45) |

ent means-end solutions. For instance, the attribute "long lasting" is either related to chain solutions 3 or 4. For men, means-end solution number 4 is the most important and coherent. More important is the fact that two chains do not have any attributes at all. Although this result is at first glance rather surprising, it means that for these two means-end solutions, individual ladders only correspond to shared consequences and values, whatever the chosen attributes are. This finding is of prime importance because it shows that consumers may seek perfume that satisfies desired consequences or goals, independent of the intrinsic or extrinsic attributes of the product. Finally, Figure 8.14 displays which specific perfumes are related to specific means-end solutions. This piece of information marks an important advance in contrast to other proposed approaches. Briefly stated, some brands are related to only one specific means-end solution, as for instance XS for men with "Social Visibility."

On the other hand, other brands exhibit a polymorphous profile in the sense they are related to different means-end solutions. For instance, Opium for women is either connected to "Social Visibility" ($p = .7$) or "Self-Expression" ($p = .3$). This result could be very helpful for brand managers seeking to reposition their brands or launch new fragrances. Ultimately, no brand for women was related to the segment labeled "Modernity." Because this means-end solution represents 7.8 percent of the original ladders, it could be seen as a potential niche for the launching of a new fragrance geared to fulfill novelty, trendiness, and modernity. Ultimately, a look at the proximities between means-end solutions (Figure 8.15) shows that the "Modernity" segment is well apart from other means-end segments, hence reinforcing the viability of this potential niche. Also, on that chart, the two means-end segments "Sensual Well-Being" and "Self-Expression" are closely related, pointing to the fact that those two segments share more in common in terms of latent means-end hierarchies than the other two remaining means-end segments.

As a final point, we reiterate that our *latent means-end conceptualization* closely corresponds to the cognitive representations driving consumers' behaviors. In contrast to other available approaches, our proposed methodology already affords many advantages related, just to name a few, to diverse criteria developed to assess the overall quality of the means-end solutions, the polymorphous nature of items (A/C/V), and more precisely the probabilistic links with preferred or purchased brands or usage contexts. Hence, our approach gives brand managers the means to more precisely define advertising and positioning strategies. To date, prestigious companies such as Chanel or Firmenich and many others have already applied our proposed methodology in international settings.

Figure 8.14 **Specific Perfumes Related to Specific Means-End Solutions**

| | General Orientation | Brands | |
|---|---|---|---|
| **MEN** | Functional Beauty | **Hugo Boss** **Egoïste** | |
| | Self-expression | **Eau Sauvage** **Kouros** **Farenheit** | |
| | Social Visibility | **XS** | |
| | Sensual Well-being | **Kenzo** **Le Male** | |
| **WOMEN** | Social Visibility | **Angel** **Coco Mademoiselle** **Hugo Woman** Opium ($p = 0.70$) Trésor ($p = 0.46$) Flower de Kenzo ($p = 0.30$) | |
| | Modernity | | |
| | Self-expression | **Chanel n° 5** **Jean-Paul Garnier** Opium ($p = 0.30$) Trésor ($p = 0.46$) Flower de Kenzo ($p = 0.70$) Ô de Lancôme ($p = 0.45$) | |
| | Sensual Well-being | Ô de Lancôme | |

*Source:* Valette-Florence, Ferrandi, and Roehrich (2003).

Figure 8.15 **Proximities Between Means-End Solutions for Women**

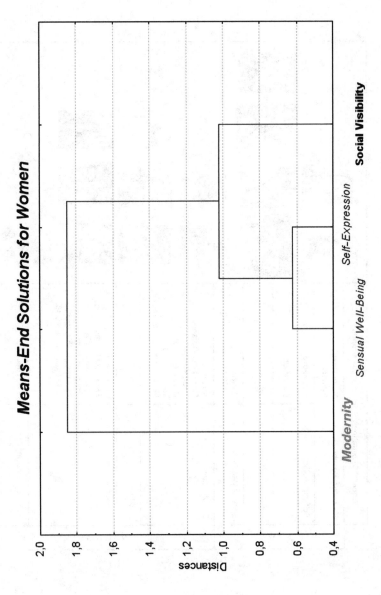

**Means-End Solutions for Women**

Modernity  *Sensual Well-Being*  *Self-Expression*  **Social Visibility**

Distances

2,0  1,8  1,6  1,4  1,2  1,0  0,8  0,6  0,4

*Source:* Valette-Florence, Ferrandi, and Roehrich (2003)

## New Conceptual Propositions of Psychosocial Origin

The realm of the study of lifestyles can be enhanced by the formalization of new conceptual tools such as home styles or styles of persuasion. Until now it has increased its focus to individual lifestyles. In fact, in a household, decisions are often made after a consultation between family members (Rigaux-Bricmont, 1986). In making decisions on the realm of households, we could describe various relational dyads. By incorporating these tests on inventories of traditional lifestyles (or values), we also define the styles of home best suited to identify current challenges in consumption practices. To our knowledge, such research has not yet been undertaken. Yet it would be quite interesting.

Alternative investigation resides in the field of advertising. By extending the usual paradigm of inclusion of the mechanisms of perception (emotion/attitudes/beliefs) and incorporation of psychosociological (values/needs/cognitive stimulation) and situational (mood/involvement) variables, it is possible to consider the definition of how styles of persuasion can be highlighted among individuals sensitized to different types of advertising. Some studies (Falcy, 1992) are very promising, enabling us to shed new light on the methods of persuasion, characterizing them based not only on the characteristics of the main advertising media used, but also and above all on individual traits. The extension of such research at a European or other international level, for example, would also characterize the specific nature and identify the useful approaches of implementing communication strategies, general and/or specific.

## CONCLUSION AND SUMMARY

This chapter has proposed several improvements or extensions of current lifestyle studies. The proposals of methodological incident were the first use of the generalized canonical analysis, if possible in a confirmatory approach to reflect better the number, diversity, and complexity of conceptual relationships that are being utilized in studies of lifestyles. In this context, the appeal of structural equation models (PLS) seems quite relevant (cf. Rogers, 2010). Other improvements are also possible, taking into account the temporal aspect of the changing types of lifestyles and the desire to discern between types of ambivalence, which are certainly more complex to handle, but alone they may reflect the intricate nature of human behavior.

On a more conceptual level, the semiometric approach undoubtedly has contributed a most promising method and some original results. The corresponding study, which is flexible, objective, and easy to implement, has already shown its potential for the characterization of specific consumption practices. It has ease of use of the results and proposes extensions to international trends to allow it to enhance approaches to lifestyle research as usual.

For a thorough study of consumption pattern particulars, the appeal of incorporating new concepts such as styles of time may also be judicious. They may find application in the areas of banking, insurance, and tourism, among other fields. Similarly, analysis of cognitive chaining is very qualitative in nature and can renew the traditional world of market research. The versatility, predicative quality, compatibility with international research, and especially the graphical display of results, are promising elements worthy of further application.

Finally, new research on the identification of styles of homes and styles of persuasion has been introduced. We view them as potential substitutes for standard lifestyle methodologies. We also hope to see an increase in cooperation between the academic world and that of business and research companies. It is now time to conclude this overview of the realm of lifestyles studies, and to consider the current and future trends in this area.

# 9

# Social Media and a Theory and Method for Future Research

## SOCIAL MEDIA STATUS

The emergence of social media in recent years has been a fascinating phenomenon, encompassing the growth of the Internet and new technologies that few people could imagine just decades ago. Kaplan and Haenlein (2010) define social media as "a group of Internet-based applications that build on the ideological and technological foundations of Web 2.0, and that allow the creation and exchange of user-generated content." Social media encompass many thousands of websites, including Facebook, YouTube, Wikipedia, Twitter, Second Life (cf., Wood and Solomon, 2009), FriendFeed, LinkedIn, eHarmony, Yelp, HuffingtonPost.com, and Amazon.com. Numerous social media formats exist, among them blogs, forums, wikis, podcasts, RSS feeds, widgets, comments, ratings, and instant messaging. Social media share key characteristics that lend themselves to advertising, marketing, and lifestyle studies; these include interactivity, the potential for widespread distribution (but conversely the potential to be highly targeted), democracy of content (often without editors), an experimental format, relatively low cost, and alterability. New social media can spring up overnight, while others transform their functions, forms, social norms, and content quite rapidly, rendering any catalogs or descriptions of the new media outdated nearly as quickly as they are produced. Several books have provided good advice on effective social media marketing (e.g., Buss and Strauss, 2009; Comm, 2009; Evans, 2008; Gillin, 2007, 2009; Holtz and Havens, 2009; Holzner, 2009; Li and Bernoff, 2008; Silver, 2009; Weber, 2009), but in this ever-changing world, bet on the fleet-footed to win the race.

Social media have transformed business, making it easier to provide the right information to the right people. For example, podcasts offer customer information on demand, whether that information is entertainment, updates on company marketing efforts, how-to guides, or even sermons (Scott, 2009). Business can engage in mass personalization, by means of, say, sending a birthday greeting to every customer on the appropriate day. Most important, social media provide opportunities for aggressive interaction with customers in various lifestyle groups, for purposes ranging from resolving complaints to extending brands, to creating product cocreation.

One reason social media have such tremendous importance for lifestyle marketing is that they have completely changed the lifestyle landscape. Before social media, marketers developed lifestyle groups based primarily on statistical aggregation. A questionnaire's responses would be submitted to a statistical procedure; those calculations would then serve as the basis for generating clusters of like-minded people. These lifestyle groups sometimes shared a reality apart from their artificial statistical aggregation; other times, however, the fictional groups had no reality apart from the computer-generated clusters. Either way, mass media outlets may have found it difficult or impossible to reach the right lifestyle group in any meaningful way. Publishers and broadcasters have created such outlets, hoping to reach the statistical aggregations. For instance, *Monday Night Football,* a prime-time television staple, seeks to attract young American males with an interest in sports. Soap operas originally targeted stay-at-home women who seemed likely to buy consumer packaged goods. The lifestyle target market for *Tennis* magazine is rather self-explanatory. But the marketer stereotype based on data-reduction computer programs may have sometimes been incomplete, misleading, or inaccurate. Not every person who purchases consumer packaged goods loves soap operas, for example, and vice versa. When a lifestyle classification is constructed primarily by correlational relationships among demographic variables (such as with VALS), the cohesion of the group is not based on the substantive motivations that will necessarily influence consumer action.

Social media, on the other hand, aggregate real lifestyle groups. The social media group members have opted in to a category that embraces a cluster of motivations they possess. Those social media groups may not always have an immediately obvious theme, but the groups are not statistical abstractions. Real people have expended a real effort to associate with certain other real people for some purpose. Looking at places people choose to go is generally more informative than looking at where statisticians have pigeonholed them (Kahle, 1980). Because of these aggregations, the importance of understanding lifestyles is, today, infinitely more valuable and more important for effective marketing than it was in previous generations. This is why now is such a pivotal time to review and revive lifestyle marketing, and *why this book is necessary as we progress into the twenty-teens.* Marketers need to understand how lifestyles matter to consumers, because twenty-first century target markets construct and/or choose their own categories and exist in genuine lifestyle clusters in cyberspace.

The reality of the "real" people on social media does have its limits. Consumers can assume virtual identities, in which they pretend to be something they are not. Second Life participants or gamers playing World of Warcraft provide good examples of this trend. Virtual identities can be idealized or fictionalized, but in some cases the line between reality and fiction becomes blurry. Many people participate in a number of social media groups; thus, lifestyle and identity have a fluidity and a multiplicity. Likewise, so-called lurkers may eavesdrop on social media discussions without participating themselves, implying a shadow constituency may be attaching itself to a specific social agenda. Therefore, the interaction patterns between reality and fiction can provide some interesting challenges for untangling real identity.

Social media mean different things to different people. Novak and Hoffman (2010) described the roles and goals of social media consumers: People use social media to create, to connect, to consume, and to control. Their goals include sharing, socializing, seeking knowledge, and making sense of the world. Often, the role-goal coordination involves the pairing of "create and share," "connect and socialize," "consume and seek," and "control and sense." Understanding the roles and goals of consumers will increase interaction efficiency.

In an earlier age, maybe 150 years ago, people marketed products mostly to friends and neighbors whom they knew well and understood thoroughly. One of our grandfathers ran a country general store, and his customers were mostly friends who lived a lifestyle very similar to his own. He did not need multivariate statistics to appreciate his customers' lifestyles. As selling moved to mass markets based on mass production in an industrial age, marketers no longer knew their customers as well; hence, they needed to conduct marketing research to determine what customers wanted and needed, as well as how to reach them. Social media have enabled community-based marketing to reemerge.

The theory of marketing as interaction with customers has been articulated for some time (cf. Kotler and Keller, 2009; Tull and Kahle, 1990). The *selling orientation*, based on marketers doing something *to* consumers, has theoretically given way to the *marketing orientation*, based on marketers doing something *with* consumers. But the promise has not been fully realized because interactions with consumers and understanding of consumers are too often either superficial or difficult to achieve. In a social media environment, however, it is possible—even necessary—to engage consumers as major partners in developing and improving products and services. This partnership flourishes with an understanding of the lifestyles of consumers. Because we know that lifestyles often drive purchases, marketers need to have a thorough grasp of the relevant lifestyles; such information can often be obtained through social media.

Consider issues that might confront a marketer working on Facebook (Holzner, 2009). Nearly every Facebook group, large or small, is composed of members who share lifestyle characteristics that actually motivate their actions. Effective marketers must deal with these new realities by profiling a "presence" for a business, making effective use of groups by locating or even creating targets, organizing events to market the business, and adopting applications appropriately.

Perhaps the most profound aspect of social media, in contrast to conventional media, is interactivity. Businesses generally can and must enter into a dialogue with their customers in order to understand their lifestyles (Boush and Kahle, 2001, 2005). Honest blog and forum discussions can provide valuable information about what customers want and need to serve their lifestyles. Nike famously developed a brand around the concept of the lifestyle of the performing athlete. It talked to and listened to athletes in order to serve their needs, and athletes and aspiring athletes responded favorably to the brand. New brands that serve lifestyles will have a much easier time today if they embrace social media.

Every step of the way, the marketer needs to understand the consumer and treat the consumer with respect. Customers are like friends, and they need to be treated with the same common courtesy one would extend to a friend. Keep in mind that consumers can "unfriend" a rude or fraudulent huckster with the click of a mouse. The marketer who truly understands the lifestyle of a target group and integrates products and services with that lifestyle in a mutually beneficial way will reap rewards in the form of increased traffic and sales, but the marketer who is disrespectful of the indigenous norms and manners or has ulterior motives will eventually run into trouble (Holtz and Havens, 2009). Spam is old-school; Google search ads are in style. Deception is out; spontaneous, user-generated validation and positive word of mouth are in. Appropriate privacy is always fashionable.

Lifestyles are dynamic. Social media provide instant information, thus matching communication with dynamic social contexts. When trends, fashions, and lifestyles shift, the evidence pops up on social media quickly. Marketers who can experiment and readjust their focus appropriately will prosper in this environment. Just following social media can help marketers learn what customers are saying and thinking.

In recent years, *customer relationship management* (CRM) software has flourished. This positive development has allowed computer-assisted marketing to proceed more effectively. Much of the CRM software, however, has emphasized demographic data over the lifestyle-based understanding necessary for effectively dealing with consumers' core motives. Data mining can provide many valuable insights, but if a miner wants to find gold, it helps to dig where the gold is. Data mining from social media groups often provides valuable insights into customers and potential customers.

Because social media aggregate like-minded people, target marketing can be performed quite effectively. A timely product modification, sale, coupon, or contest can quickly attract a high percentage of people from a particular social media group if properly targeted. Social media can be useful for subtle brand building and reputation management. Providing easy access to appropriate applications can be quite helpful. Target markets—even specialized ones—tend to come prepackaged and easy to reach in the era of social media.

Democracy of content implies that social media allow free discussion, or at least very inexpensive discussion: You do not need to invest millions of dollars to launch and maintain a Facebook page. However, as in any democratic institution, irresponsible and unfair claims can, at times, permeate social media and "go viral." Damaged reputations are hard to repair, so marketers need to be ready for such occasions and deal with negative publicity in a straightforward manner. Marketers thrive on popularity, but peer-group influence is harder to deal with in an environment with the two-way communication that exists on the Internet. Understanding the theory of these motivations has important implications for approaching lifestyle groups.

## FUNCTIONS OF SOCIAL INTERACTION AND CHANGE

Many critics of applied lifestyle research criticize it because it lacks sufficient theory and emphasizes quantitative analysis of items gathered for insufficient theoretical purposes. Conversely, applied lifestyle researchers often criticize academic theories as too simplistic, as covering only a few situations and not guiding more sophisticated practice in any meaningful way. Functional theories of attitudes have approached social influence from a more complex perspective that offers specific, practical advice to applied researchers. The key is to understand that different attitudes serve different functions. Shavitt (1990), for example, showed that products matched to attitude functions are more attractive than mismatched products. We believe that the realm of social media provides an opportunity to explore functional theory in a way that could be beneficial to both practitioner and academic by allowing its full complexity to be observed (cf. Kelman and Eagly, 1965).

Social media consumers may have different levels of association with Internet lifestyle groups. Kelman (1958, 1961, 1974) proposed a theory about the functions that attitudes serve in social interaction. He identified three major functions: compliance, identification, and internalization.

## Compliance

The first and lowest level of attitudes formulated in response to social influence is compliance, which Kelman described at its most superficial level in this way:

> Compliance can be said to occur when an individual accepts influence because he hopes to achieve a favorable reaction from another person or group. He hopes to perform the induced behavior—not because he believes its content—but because he expects to gain specific rewards or approval and avoid specific punishments or disapproval by conforming. Thus, the satisfaction derived from compliance is due to the social effect of accepting influence" (Kelman, 1958, p. 53).

People develop compliance attitudes when social influence governs reinforcements and punishments. Someone might modify a behavior based on concern over the social consequences of that behavior. One might ask, Will someone important to me like me more if I express this attitude?

## Identification

The middle level of attitudes formulated in response to social influence is identification. According to Kelman,

> "Identification can be said to occur when an individual accepts influence because he wants to establish or maintain a satisfying self-defining relationship with another person or a group. This relationship may take the form of classical identification in which the individual takes over the role of the other, or it may take the form of a reciprocal role relationship. The individual actually believes the responses, which he adopts through identification, but their specific content is more or less irrelevant. He adopts the induced behavior because it is associated with the desired relationship. Thus, the satisfaction derived from identification is due to the *act* of conforming as such (Kelman, 1958, p. 13).

Identification attitudes are driven more by the anchoring of behavior. Attractive, imitation-worthy people provide the most important social influence here. Understanding role requirements is critical in bringing forth identification attitudes and social influence.

## Internalization

The third and highest level of attitudes formulated in response to social influence is internalization. Kelman notes that (1958 p. 53):

Internalization, can be said to occur when an individual accepts influence because the content of the induced behavior—the ideas and actions of which it is composed—is intrinsically rewarding. He adopts the induced behavior because it is congruent with his value system. He may consider it useful for the solution of a problem or find it congenial to his needs. Behavior adopted in this fashion tends to be integrated with the individual's existing values. Thus, the satisfaction derived from internalization is due to the content of the behavior.

Internalization attitudes are the most private and the most deeply rooted of all attitudes. They tend to be salient when one is concerned with explicit value-behavior consistency, with credibility, or with means-end networks.

### Activation and Change

What activates an attitude depends upon the function it serves for an individual (Eagly and Chaiken, 1993). An attitude based on compliance will be activated depending on power relationships and the ability to influence important outcomes. To change such an attitude, the external demands of a situation or the perceptions of rewards and punishments must change as well. Reinforcement and punishment dominate behavior, much as one of the three major philosophies of psychology—behaviorism—predicts (Skinner, 1974; Watson, 1913, 1925).

An attitude that is based on identification will follow more classic neo-psychoanalytic influences (e.g., Erikson, 1968), the second of the three major philosophies of psychology. When the attractiveness of an agent changes, the influence of that agent to model responses will also change. Likewise, if one's self-defining expectations change, an identification attitude will also be likely to change.

To change an internalized attitude, something needs to change about one's core values and how they are perceived. The relevance and maximization of values drives change in this function, much as one might expect behavior to be driven in the third major philosophy of psychology, humanism (e.g., Rogers, 1961).

Thus, we see that the conditions to activate and change attitudes related to social influence depend very much upon the functions those attitudes serve in a person's life. To change those attitudes, a practitioner of social influence must determine (1) what type of power relationship dictates or motivates a particular attitude; and (2) which major approach to psychology will be most helpful in that situation. A clear understanding of the first point will reveal the nature of the second. The social influence that drives people to use one type of social media or another must be determined before it is possible to understand how to work with one attitude or another.

## INFLUENCE IN SPORTS AND SOCIAL MEDIA

In many respects, managing communications in an era of social media is much more like running a franchise for sports fans than like traditional marketing communications. The marketer has only a limited degree of control over events and messages, and the manager must work with each day's developments. Fans have long memories and deep opinions. With this in mind, it is worth taking a look at research on the functional role of attitudes and how social influence works in sports.

Kahle, Kambara, and Rose (1996) studied the functions that "being a fan" serve for individuals, much as one might study the functions served by membership in a social media group. After a number of focus groups and pilot studies, the questionnaire in Table 9.1 was administered to a group of people with varying levels of commitment as fans. The goal was to understand what motivates fans to buy tickets and attend a game. Table 9.1 presents the questions used, and Figure 9.1 graphically represents the results. Every arrow in Figure 9.1 represents a statistically significant path, and every lack of an arrow represents a lack of a statistically significant path. The first thing that becomes obvious is that three clusters of social influence hypothesized by Kelman show up very clearly. It is also evident that the two lower-level functions, compliance and identification, broke into two parts, one public and one private. (Note that we called "private" compliance "obligation," and we referred to the combination of the two aspects of compliance as "camaraderie." Likewise, we found a public dimension of identification in the concept of "identification with winning," and a private dimension, which we labeled "self-definition." The two elements of identification combined to form a dimension of "self-expression." For "internalization," the views are so strongly held that there is no public versus private dimension.

The lesson from these data for managing something such as a sports franchise is that different consumers have different social relationships with the team. You must approach them differently and communicate with them differently if you want to tap into their social influence network. For example, a fan whose attendance is dependent on gaining praise from friends may skip a game if his or her friends do not want to go on one particular night, whereas a loyal fan who has internalized the values of the team may go regardless of what friends do. A good deal of research supports the use of functional theory in this context (Bee and Kahle, 2006; Jones et al., 2004; Kahle and Close, 2011).

The sports motives are reminiscent of the roles and goals discussed by Novak and Hoffman (2010). You will recall that they found in social media that often the "role-goal" coordination involved the pairing of "create and share," "connect

Table 9.1

## Description of Scales for College Sports Fan Attitude Functions

How would you rate your agreement to the following items:

| Construct / • Items | Mean (sigma) | alpha |
| --- | --- | --- |
| Compliance | 3.25 (1.98) | 0.53 |
| • I only go to football games when my friends go. | 3.57 (2.57) | |
| • I'd be more likely to attend a game if my friends and relatives were allowed to sit with me in the student section. | 2.92 (2.20) | |
| Obligation | 3.49 (2.45) | 0.64 |
| • People have an obligation to support their local football team. | 3.03 (2.44) | |
| • The football team represents me and the university. | 3.95 (2.60) | |
| Camaraderie | 4.63 (1.87) | 0.72 |
| • I'd be more likely to attend if there were a pep rally a day before the game. | 5.39 (2.49) | |
| • I'd be more likely to attend if there were more activities to make students feel integrated and contributory to the spirit of the game. | 4.60 (2.53) | |
| • I'd be more likely to attend if there were more fun things to do while sitting in the stands. | 3.89 (2.00) | |
| Identification with winning | 4.24 (2.05) | 0.59 |
| • I'd be more likely to attend if the team consistently had a better win-loss record. | 5.45 (2.65) | |
| • I'd be more likely to attend if the team's style of play were more exciting. | 3.03 (2.44) | |
| Self-defining experience | 5.27 (1.92) | 0.61 |
| • When I watch football games, I imagine myself competing in sporting events. | 6.88 (2.50) | |
| • I feel a sense of accomplishment when [our team] wins a football game. | 4.80 (2.55) | |
| • Watching football teams of [NCAA Division I conference] caliber appeals to me. | 4.12 (2.65) | |
| Unique, self-expressive experience | 3.18 (1.89) | 0.56 |
| • Football allows me to spend a few hours on a Saturday in a different atmosphere than where I spend my time on weekdays. | 3.36 (2.33) | |
| • Attending a football game live is more exciting than watching it on television. | 2.99 (2.20) | |
| Internalization | 4.11 (2.09) | 0.80 |
| • I enjoy watching "the game" at football games. | 3.67 (2.40) | |
| • I consider myself more knowledgeable about football than most students. | 5.47 (2.794) | |
| • Football is good entertainment. | 3.184 (2.272) | |
| Mean reliability score: | 0.635 | |
| Dependent variable: Number of games attended | 2.57 (2.08) | |

*Source:* Kahle, Kambara, and Rose (1996).

Figure 9.1   **Model of Attitude Functions for Sports Fans**

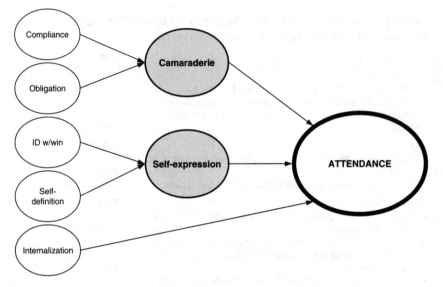

*Source:* Kahle, Kambara, and Rose (1996).

and socialize," "consume and seek," or "control and sense." Connecting and sharing are reminiscent of compliance and camaraderie. Consuming and seeking echo the process of identification. Control and sense point to self-expression. Internalization fits with creating and sharing. Thus, Kelman's theories of motivations work as well for sports fans as they do for social media consumption.

## SOCIAL MEDIA RESEARCH

The questions in Table 9.2 expand the logic of Table 9.1 to social media. Administering this questionnaire—asking participants to rate their agreement with each item on a scale of 1 (strongly agree) to 9 (strongly disagree)—could help reveal people's level of social connection to a site or an activity. It might also prove to be an important step in understanding consumers.

## CONCLUSION

Social media have opened new realms and reasons for lifestyle research. Progress will depend on understanding social media through quality research. We believe that understanding social phenomena is difficult but well worth the cost. Researchers should use the techniques we have discussed in Chapter 2 (especially the List

Table 9.2

**Scales to Study Social Media Functions**
How would you rate your agreement to the following items:

| Construct | Items |
| --- | --- |
| Compliance | • I only go to [this social media site] when my friends go.<br>• I'd be more likely to visit [this social media site] if friends and relatives were to interact with me there. |
| Obligation | • People have an obligation to support [this social media site].<br>• [This social media site] represents me and my friends. |
| Camaraderie | • I'd be more likely to visit [this social media site] if I knew it contained interesting new postings.<br>• I'd be more likely to visit [this social media site] if there were more activities that allowed me to contribute to the spirit of the site.<br>• I'd be more likely to visit [this social media site] if there were more fun things to do while there. |
| Identification with winning | • I'd be more likely to visit [this social media site] consistently if it had better coverage in other media.<br>• I'd be more likely to visit [this social media site] if it were more exciting. |
| Self-defining experience | • When I participate in [this social media site], I imagine myself influencing events.<br>• I feel a sense of accomplishment when [this social media site] changes the world around me.<br>• Participating with a social media site of the caliber of [this social media site] appeals to me. |
| Unique, self-expressive experience | • [This social media site] allows me to spend a few hours in a different atmosphere than where I otherwise spend my time.<br>• Visiting [this social media site] is more exciting than hearing about it somewhere else. |
| Internalization | • I enjoy participating in "the site" at [this social media site].<br>• I consider myself more knowledgeable about [this social media site] than most other people.<br>• [This social media site] is good entertainment. |

of Values), the most advanced means-end chains described in Chapter 8, and the functional methodology described in this chapter. We also encourage researchers to gather relevant demographic variables and information about topic-specific and product-specific phenomena. Then, think about what all the data mean and attempt to develop and test structural equation models that describe what you, the researcher, are attempting to understand. Careful theory and comprehensive research usually result in the best understanding of topics of interest in social science—and the topic of lifestyle phenomena is no exception.

# 10

# General Conclusions

Following this detailed overview of approaches to lifestyle studies, results need to be placed in a balanced perspective. For several years, lifestyles have given rise to numerous discussions and commentary. For the new light they claim to shed on behavior patterns and sociocultural society, lifestyle studies fascinated businesspeople and practitioners—at least at first.

A closer analysis quickly highlights the contradictions of different proposed approaches. In this final chapter, we review the different methods of analysis and decision making as they apply to theoretical studies of lifestyles. We will summarize the research, identify trends, and look at prospects for development in the field.

## A World of Theoretical Approaches to Lifestyles

Except for a brief examination by Cathelat (1990), to our knowledge the first marketing attempt at describing the realm of lifestyles came from Askegaard (1991). His design of three poles (psychological, sociological, and psychosocial), however, seems incomplete. To truly understand the entire realm of lifestyles, it seems preferable to extend its study to four areas: psychological, sociological, cultural, and homoeconomics (see Figure 10.1).

Thus, a study of individuality that characterizes the psychological component may clash with the sociological approach. Likewise, we can also consider the phenomena of acculturation, that is to say, the study of diffusion and interpretation between cultures, and instead adopt a more objective view—a view based on the tracking of economic data and the subsequent analysis of the accuracy (*homo economicus*) of specific behavioral studies. The realm of lifestyles is summed up in the tetrahedron pictured in Figure 10.1.

Each side of the tetrahedron represents a tradition of investigation that, more or less, has followed the historical development of studies and approaches to lifestyles. For the psychosocial tradition, we can see that in all

Figure 10.1 **Lifestyle Domains**

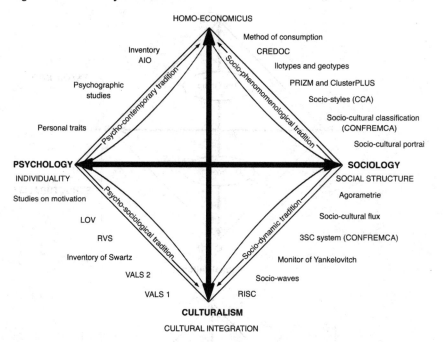

studies, the initial identification of personal traits has quickly turned to a more detailed analysis of behavior (known as *psychographic studies*), and has gone through an extensive inventory tracking of activities, including the interests and opinions of individuals. Similarly, the psychosociological tradition turns to highlighting motivations of individuals and tracking their adherence to values and social standards within an international context. Note that this shift is about the development of measuring instruments, drawn largely from the work of Rokeach (e.g., 1973). It also follows the psychosociological tradition, measured in the United States by innovative instruments such as the VALS 1 and 2 approaches, whose purpose is to define values a priori by a theoretical analysis and a structuring of American society. In addition, this approach has been applied successfully in the European context (Mitchell, 1983). It is interesting to note that these two traditions—psychobehavioral and psychosociological (Figure 10.2)—grew out of academics, as opposed to empirical-deductive approaches that stem from sociophenomenological or sociodynamic traditions. Figure 10.2 gives two overlays of Figure 10.1 to depict dimensions in the Figure's conceptualization.

The difference between these two orientations lies in the basis of the studies. The emphasis in the sociophenomenological tradition is on the taxonomic

Figure 10.2  **Design and Formalizations of Lifestyle Theories**

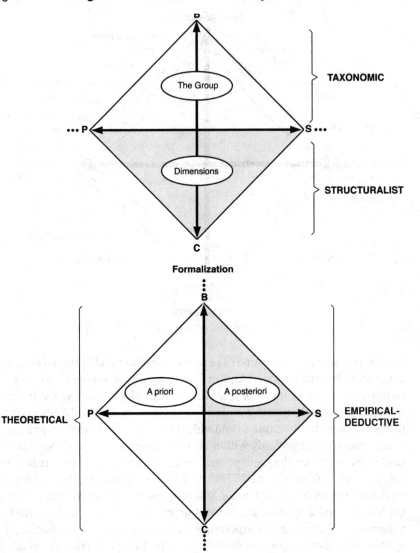

aspect, which forms groups of individuals based on their psychosocial behavioral identity. Traditional sociodynamics is characterized by a structuralist orientation, whose purpose is to study the structure of mainstream sociocultural factors that modulate our society. Under this second approach, the sociological method has evolved considerably, with the development of measurement tools that take studies to the international level. Examples of the developments include the

RISC (Research Institute on Social Change) network, created in the 1970s by COFREMCA to study memberships in various international trends, and the creation of *sociowaves* that extend the CCA's work on sociocultural trends. The Yankelovich Monitor, the system of the CCA, COFREMCA, and the systematic survey conducted each year by the Agorametrics association—all of these reflect a desire to expand upon the various traditions of lifestyle studies. A more behavioral and sociological orientation informs some of the approaches toward the modes of consumption: The analysis proposed by CREDOC and COREF in France or PRIZM and Cluster Plus in the United States differentiate their methods from sociological portraits such as sociocultural factors, but in different ways than the CCA or COFREMCA.

As we already stated, Figure 10.2 allows us to define the differences in these approaches. For instance, a design taxonomy of the behaviorist approach may oppose the structurally culturalist approach. Indeed, this latter line of analysis has always been more interested in the identification of certain values and, in fact, focuses on lists of values or sociocultural trends that were established before the formation of groups of individuals. The main feature of this approach is centered on the study of *homo economicus*. Similarly, it may oppose a theoretical formalization, approaching the university studies that tried to define a priori a conceptual framework to fit the instruments they advocate, such as empirical-specific deductions to corporations that have developed tracking tools currently utilized in sociocultural typologies and sometimes subsequent attempts to formalize their approach on a theoretical plan.

In addition, the interest in such a description of the theoretical realm of lifestyles allows us to quickly identify how traditional social science fits approaches that are currently available on the operation of marketing research. Note also that some agencies, such as CCA or COFREMCA, nevertheless try to have a more comprehensive approach, opting to have both the identification of sociocultural fluxes or types of lifestyles. After the presentation of the domain of lifestyles, it seems now possible to provide more detail in the various fields of application.

## CURRENT TRENDS

Despite the variety of investigative procedures and possible approaches to lifestyle studies (see Figure 10.1), along with the extent of the criticism they encounter, approaches to lifestyles are still numerous and deserve attention.

### The Principle Guidelines

The study of lifestyles in France is largely the result of two companies: the COFREMCA and the CCA; however, their guidelines seem somewhat different. COFREMCA dedicated itself to the specific study of a product or the marketing of a product to a particular segment (e.g., launching "Black Magic" by Lancôme). The CCA, although it has conducted specific product-area studies (e.g., electronics or furniture), chose instead to develop a comprehensive approach to the presentation of its findings, specifically in the form of maps. The CCA's popular books provide biannual portraits of the French sociocultural landscape (e.g., Mermet, 1985; Cathelat, 1985a, b, 1990). Overall, two approaches seem to emerge: The first is oriented toward the internationalization of lifestyles studies, while the second is oriented to new modes of investigation.

*Transcultural Studies*

The increasing openness of markets and the increasing mobility of consumers have prompted an internationalization of lifestyle studies to account for the growing diversity in cultural backgrounds. In this context, there are two key considerations: (1) the international memberships in various sociocultural categories, and (2) the creation of a typology of styles of international life, whether created from scratch (e.g., CCA) or incorporated from an existing structure (e.g., VALS).

The first structural orientation (cf. Figure 10.2) is found, for example, in the international use of Yankelovich's inventory, or in the identification of the major international cultural trends (e.g., Naisbitt, 1982). In Europe, the RISC network, developed by De Vulpian (1974), has examined the changing trends of ten general sociocultural issues presented in Table 10.1.

The Center for Advanced Communication has proposed the concept of sociowaves as an extension of the sociocultural trends (see Chapter 4) that are already in use in France. The differences with the latter concern their formulation, their operation, and their number:

- The number of waves is overrepresented as concrete sociocultural trends. Each sociowave is measured in a way that is relevant to the item through both a psychological formula in terms of principles of life (private life), as well as a sociological formula in terms of collective life (social life).
- Guidance for each (sociological or psychological intricacies) of the sociowaves appears to be measured by a single proposal leading to a choice between two competing values, and more of a choice is often necessary to understand sociocultural trends, captured by several items on the practices of everyday life (Cathelat and Cathelat, 1991);
- Although there are thirteen sociocultural trends, the sociowaves are structured in eighteen bipolar orientations, measuring thirty-six specific values.

Table 10.1

**Ten General Sociocultural Issues from RISC**

1. The complexity of consumption
2. "Tailor-made"
3. Convenience
4. Social communication of consumption
5. Conspicuous consumption
6. Personal relationship with the consumer
7. Awareness of the body
8. Consumption in "piecemeal"
9. Consumerism
10. The consumer environment

*Source:* Codeluppi, V., and Weber, D. (1989), The Ten C's: How to Use Socio-Trends Analysis in Marketing Strategy. In *Seminar on Is Marketing Keeping Up With the Consumer?* ESOMAR (European Society for Opinion and Market Research), Vienna, pp. 293–313.

Sociocultural trends measure serious, long-term, crystallizing tendencies. On the other hand, the phenomena of collective psychology, the sociowaves, are more operational in the short and medium terms, embodying the collective dynamics in a sociocultural environment at a given time. This distinction is not always obvious (Cathelat, 1990). Indeed, the differences are hardly noticeable because, as shown in Table 10.2, the titles remain nearly the same with only two exceptions: Commonality/Transcendence replaced with Confidence/Humanity/Faith in God and Symbolism/Realism replaced with Intuition/Relationality. The only real innovation affects their numbers, which rose from thirteen for each trend to eighteen for sociowaves, and for those last implementations, which are apparently more simplified, faster, and less costly.

Regarding taxonomy (see Figure 10.2), a typology must be extended to international lifestyles. One way to do this is simply to substitute a structure that has been validated in a given country in a different cultural context. This approach is advocated by VALS (see Table 10.3), which has successfully tested its classification at a European level (Mitchell, 1983).

A more ambitious perspective seeks to propose an original typology consisting of many cultural backgrounds at once. This approach is pursued by the CCA view, through a detailed investigation,. It offers sixteen social and European styles, divided into six major families. These styles are structured around a horizontal axis, between the values of movement to those of stability, and a vertical axis, between the research and personal immaterial values (spirituality) and possession of tangible assets and value (the materials), see Table 10.4 and Figure 10.3. A third axis exists juxtaposing the imaginary from the serious.

Conducted in fifteen countries and fifty-eight regions, this study led to the identification of European sociostyles that varied in relevance according to specific

Table 10.2

**Center for Advanced Communication—Sociocultural Trends vs. Sociowaves**

| Sociocultural trends | | Sociowaves | |
|---|---|---|---|
| 1 | Dynamic/Passivity | 1 | Dynamic/Passivity |
| 2 | Extension/Refocusing | 2 | Extension/Refocusing |
| 4 | Integration/Individualism | 4 | Integration/Individualism |
| 6 | Hierarchy/Cooperation | 5 | Hierarchy/Cooperation |
| 7 | Originality/*Modeling* | 7 | Originality/*Standardization* |
| 8 | *Liberalism*/Discipline | 6 | *Tolerance*/Discipline |
| 9 | Monolithic/Mosaic | 3 | Monolithic/Mosaic |
| 10 | Nature/*Technology* | 8 | Nature/*Technology* |
| 11 | Hedonism/Functionalism | 14 | Hedonism/Functionalism |
| 12 | Being self/Materials | 11 | Being self/Materials |
| 13 | Metamorphosis/Permanence | 10 | Metamorphosis/Permanence |
| 3 | *Commonality/Transcendence* | 16 | *Confidence/Humanity/Faith in God* |
| 5 | *Symbolism/Realism* | 9 | *Intuition/Rationality* |
| | | 12 | **Puritanism/Sexuality** |
| | | 13 | **Economic Liberalism/Social Contract** |
| | | 15 | **Liberation of Women/Women Traditional** |
| | | 17 | **Showing off/Discretion** |
| | | 18 | **Monitoring Health/Health Risk** |

*Source:* Adapted from Cathelat (1990).
*Note:* Italics indicate shifted words from trends to sociowaves. Bold type indicates additional categories of sociowaves.

regions. This method is in fact advocating a vision of a unified world (Cathelat, 1987). CCA research also has undertaken an analysis of national and regional disparities within Europe. Such a project represents a great marketing challenge in the years to come (Cathelat, 1987). Nevertheless, it is not easy to reconcile the broader European approach with the one already proposed in France, where the number of sociostyles and corresponding families are different. The nature of lifestyle typologies tends to vary with the type of measurement tool employed by researchers. Kahle, Beatty, and Homer (1986) show the superiority of one approach exclusively centered on values, as is the List of Values (LOV), also presented in Chapter 2.

*Other Modes of Investigation*

In the United States, researchers have moved away from the strict use of AIO inventories, focusing instead on using values as the main tool of sociocultural analysis. American studies have given rise to several publications that describe the theoretical foundations and the methods of operation (Yankelovich, 1971 and 1974; Mitchell, 1983).

Based on this work, two companies perform continuing surveys of lifestyles: the Yankelovich, Skelly, and White Monitor Service and the Stanford

Table 10.3

**VALS at the European Level**

| | Necessities | | | Oriented Toward the Exterior | |
| --- | --- | --- | --- | --- | --- |
| | Survivors | Laborious | Affiliate | Young | Director |
| United States | Aged, extremely poor, depressed, marginally lost. | At the edge of poverty, embittered, survive by doing odd jobs. | Aging, conservative, patriotic, sentimental, stable, traditional, middle class. | Ambitious young macho, posers, pushy, demanding of themselves and others; dream of being in charge. | Middle-aged, prosperous, leaders, self-confident, materialistic, satisfied, defenders of the order. |
| France | Few remain but they are similar to Americans and share the same traits. | Retirement age and older people living in the countryside; poorly educated; oppose change. | Aged, have family ties, financial security, appear to be in good health. | Young, but a bit older and more reserved than those in the United States, better educated, suspicious of ideologies, concerned about their health. | Two groups: the first group is more like the Americans, the second is younger, more intuitive and concerned about the environment. |
| Italy | Similar to American survivors; live in shanty-towns in the North. | Aging; poorly educated; from rural areas; assisted living. | Aging, authoritarian, fatalistic, investors, reflect the society and its problems. | Young, male, well educated, have distanced themselves from the family; materialists; read a lot. | Middle-aged; in touch with their family and religion (especially women); preoccupied with their success. |

*continued*

Table 10.3 (continued)

| | | | | | |
|---|---|---|---|---|---|
| Sweden | Divided into two categories: an older group, which is similar to the one in the U.S., and a group of unemployed young people who failed in school. | Richer than in other countries. Anxious for their children, critical of institutions, concerned for their security and their retirement. | Like in the U.S., but more critical of institutions and political affairs. | A little bit older, preoccupied with their prestige. Hoping for a comfortable house and a calm lifestyle. | As interested in their social standing as in money; buy goods that their children will inherit; have middle-class values. |
| United Kingdom | As in Sweden, the younger group is more aggressive and organizes itself into groups of delinquents. | Traditional working class values; centered on the family; critical of institutions; mostly women. | Two groups: one similar to the U.S., the other more active and demanding. | Older, often women. Very worried about style and their social status. | Very few; rich; the oldest are fairly traditional. |
| West Germany | More affected psychologically than materially; often hypochondriacs. | Negative and pessimistic, resigned and apathetic, more affected psychologically than materially; often hypochondriacs. | Like in the U.S., although richer and better educated. Preoccupied with their social standing and prestige. | Very young, educated, preoccupied with their social standing and physical security. | Like in the U.S., although more politically active and more concerned with the environmental movement. |

*Source:* Adapted from Dubois (1990).

Table 10.4

**The Euro-Sociostyles of the CCA**

| European Sociostyles | Mindsets | % in France | Dominant features in France | |
| --- | --- | --- | --- | --- |
| | | | Priorities | Sociodemographic characteristics |
| Dandy Rugged Business | Ambitious | 29 | Succeed socially | Young, spendthrift, living in large cities, conspicuous consumption. |
| Team Romantic | Dreamers | 9 | The children and the house | Middle class, employees, officials, towns with fewer than 20,000 inhabitants. |
| Forgotten Vigilante Prudent Defense | Entrenched | 25 | Need support | People who are old and live quite modestly. |
| Protest Pioneer | Protesters | 8 | Social tolerance, consumerism, and protection of the environment | Young, active, very independent character. |
| Scout Citizen | Militant | 18 | Efficiency and social contract | Opinion leaders, executives of average age, responsible economically and socially. |
| Moralist Gentry Strict | Notables | 25 | Return to order and values | Executives, profession- als, seeking high-quality consumables. |

*Source:* Adapted from Dubois and Jolibert (1992) and Brochand and Lendrevie (1983).

Figure 10.3   **A Map of Eurostyles**

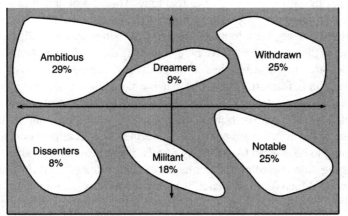

*Source:* Brochand and Lendrevie (1983), p. 159.

Research Institutes Value and Lifestyle Survey (VALS). As indicated in Chapter 2, more than 100 companies, including CBS, General Foods, and General Electric, have used the services of Yankelovich and associates. The VALS approach is also in widespread usage; for example, Avon has used the VALS study to develop its advertising strategies and campaigns, and companies such as AT&T (Veltri and Schiffman, 1984), the *New York Times,* Boeing, and Chrysler have used this approach for many years.

More so than in Europe, U.S. researchers have taken a structured approach to lifestyle studies. Verifiable results have strengthened the legitimacy of the values-based theory, to the detriment of AIO inventories, whose empirical nature has been shown to be problematic. The emergence of the concept of values is reflected in the renewed interest it arouses outside of recent academic research (Beatty et al., 1985; Kahle and Xie, 2008; Munson and McQuarrie, 1987; Wong and Tse, 1987; Perkins and Reynolds, 1987). In addition, identification of values found in the instrument developed by Schwartz (1992) reinforces the solid theoretical foundation and international validation of values-based studies. Therefore, it may serve as a powerful substitute for the current methods used in analyzing international lifestyles.

Note, finally, that the development of such studies is based on the analysis of consumption practices. For now, specific companies in France (Trois Suisses, La Redoute, etc.) have implemented their own unique tools. This approach allows them to better understand the profile of their clientele based on purchasing patterns, and such information then assists in the identification of major consumer trends. Interesting prospects also appear with the development of scanning systems in supermarkets. By providing an accurate reflection of consumption, this method is very useful for ongoing management of inventory, supplies, and the measurement of profits. It is also interesting to note major consumer trends as they evolve in real time. The data obtained can then be successfully used not only by department heads at the local level, but also by centralized management to make informed decisions on purchasing policy.

Besides the food industry, we note in passing that such management functions are growing in a number of other diverse companies as well (News Galerles, Etam, Damart, Andre, just to name a few). Most famously, Walmart has used scanner data very effectively. Admittedly, the use of scanning data is limited by cost, time restraints, and the capacity to process and make suitable use of the information provided. Nevertheless, specialized data are also beginning to be offered by company panels, while providing producers with interesting data regarding the evolution of sales numbers and the nature of production. Much of this research is highly proprietary, and much of it is apparently relatively atheoretical, with insufficient lifestyle and psychographic input to ascertain consumer motives.

## The Current Landscape of Lifestyles

After these long developments on the theme of lifestyles, what is the outcome of the current realm of studies and their corresponding fields of investigation? Researchers and practitioners need to have an instrument to guide the selection of different approaches that are currently in use. That issue is why Table 10.5 makes a point of presenting the different aspects of lifestyles. Related to the structured studies of lifestyles, it illustrates whether the corresponding approaches pertain to different ideas that were presented throughout the book. Similarly, the origin, the scope, and the accessibility of the results are also shown. Through the factor analysis of multiple matches, we see in Figure 10.4 the current universe of lifestyles. It appears in three lines that can account substantially for the relevant information. It should be noted that the first axis, which is by far the largest, contrasts the academic approaches with the entrepreneurial research companies, while the second axis contrasts the identification of the trends with the identification of groups. This information clearly shows the respective positioning of the different methods proposed. For example, we can see that the objective of the RISC network approach is to highlight social trends. In addition, a culturalist analysis (as contrasted on the third axis) studies these trends across many different cultural backgrounds. On the other hand, we observe that the VALS 1 and 2 approaches are easily accessible, focus primarily on the study of groups, and belong to a more theoretical tradition of psychological origin. The VALS approaches have also been taking an academically inspired look at the dissemination of these different groups in different cultural settings. Similarly, the CCA has an entrepreneurial, original, and international approach, but it is also imbued with a strong empirical and trend-oriented tradition. It mirrors COFREMCA but is more global in scope (unlike COFREMCA, which is dedicated to a single country, France).

## PROSPECTS FOR CHANGE

In France, studies of lifestyle types and sociocultural trends focus largely on the identification of values common to the members of each group. This approach gives more weight to the importance of individuals' motivations than do studies of American origin. However, the development of approaches is essentially empirical; thus, the disparity of conclusions and the resulting methodological questions have led to a reevaluation of the importance of observed social behavior, particularly its low predictive power. Moreover, one of the most important criticisms concerns the willful ignorance of sociological behavior and its impact. It is this failure to address sociological

Table 10.5

**Different Aspects of Lifestyle Systems**

| Study | Psycho-logical | Socio-logical | Behav-iorist | Cultural-ist | Struc-turalist | Taxo-nomic | Theo-retical | Empiri-cal | Public | Com-mercial | Aisle | Plot | Single Country | Interna-tional |
|---|---|---|---|---|---|---|---|---|---|---|---|---|---|---|
| CCA | 0 | 1[a] | 1[b] | 1[c] | 1 | 1 | 0 | 1 | 0 | 1 | 0 | 1 | 1 | 1[l] |
| COFREMCA | 0 | 1 | 0 | 0 | 1 | 1[d] | 0 | 1 | 0 | 1 | 0 | 1 | 1 | 0 |
| AGORAMETRICS | 0 | 0 | 1 | 0 | 1 | 0 | 0 | 1 | 1 | 1[h] | 1 | 0 | 1 | 0 |
| CREDOC | 0 | 0 | 1 | 0 | 1 | 1[e] | 0 | 1 | 1 | 1[i] | 1 | 0 | 1 | 0 |
| COREF | 0 | 0 | 1 | 0 | 0 | 1 | 0 | 1 | 1 | 1 | 0 | 1 | 1 | 1[m] |
| PRIZM | 0 | 0 | 1 | 1 | 0 | 1 | 0 | 1 | 0 | 1 | 0 | 1 | 1 | 0 |
| VALS 1 AND 2 | 1 | 0 | 0 | 0 | 0 | 0 | 1[f] | 0 | 1[j] | 1 | 1[j] | 0 | 1 | 1[n] |
| RVS | 1 | 0 | 0 | 0 | 1 | 0 | 1 | 0 | 1 | 0 | 1 | 1 | 1 | 1[o] |
| LOV | 1 | 0 | 0 | 0 | 1 | 0 | 1 | 0 | 1 | 0 | 1 | 0 | 1 | 1[o] |
| SCHWARTZ | 1 | 0 | 0 | 1 | 1 | 0 | 1 | 0 | 1 | 0 | 1 | 0 | 0 | 1 |
| AIO | 0 | 0 | 1 | 0 | 1 | 1 | 1[g] | 1 | 1 | 1[k] | 1 | 1[k] | 1 | 1[p] |
| RISC | 0 | 1 | 0 | 1 | 1 | 0 | 0 | 1 | 0 | 1 | 0 | 1 | 0 | 1 |
| YANKELOVICH | 0 | 1 | 0 | 0 | 1 | 0 | 0 | 1 | 0 | 1 | 0 | 0 | 1 | 0 |

[a] Sociocultural fluxes
[b] Sociostyles
[c] Sociowaves
[d] Sociocultural sociography
[e] Typology on opinions
[f] A priori typology
[g] In the case of timely studies
[h] Studies realized to account for public enterprises
[i] Public bodies, CREDOC also has commercial activity
[j] Stanford Research Institute (SRI) has a vocation for conceptual study of lifestyles
[k] These are used by private firms
[l] With Eurostyles
[m] With European partners
[n] For VALS 1 study realized thanks to RISC network
[o] In an intercultural research setting
[p] In an intercultural research context

Figure 10.4  **The Current Universe of Structure of Lifestyles**

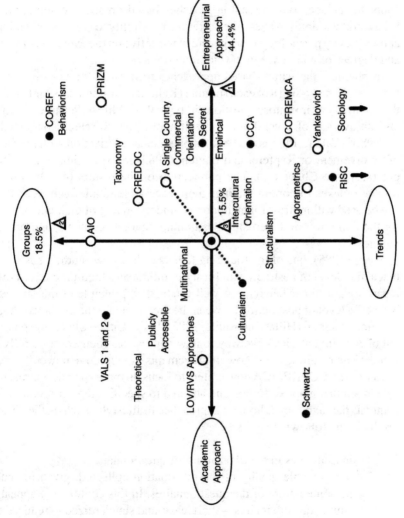

concepts that has led some critics to question the adequacy of the proceedings of lifestyles in the European and French context. Market fragmentation,
cultural differences from one country another, and social disparities cannot
be examined in a vacuum: They must be viewed in the context of belonging
to a social group.

Thus, systems using AIO inventory of American or French design cannot
claim to replace conventional approaches based on sociodemographic or
behavioral variables. At best, they offer the possibility to enrich conventional
approaches by providing a more general perspective on the evolution of values
and degrees of adherence to the cultural norms of a society.

In practice, the values-based approaches to lifestyle studies offer many
benefits. At thirty-six (Rokeach) or nine (Kahle), their number is far less than
the hundreds of inventory questions in typical AIO lifestyle surveys, which
take an average of several hours to self-administer. Research conducted in
the 1980s (Valette-Florence, 1988a) shows a clear connection with the facets
of involvement of Kapferer and Laurent (1983) in explaining consumption
practices (see Chapter 7). The publication of the results of values-based
research makes important findings more accessible to all. Such an analysis
can be used within firms for an improved understanding of their clientele and
for the definition of advertising positioning, market segments, and product
policies.

Wells (1985), one of the founding fathers of lifestyles studies, has shown
that a high level of abstraction in lifestyles diminishes their predictive power
regarding consumer behavior. A well-established principle of measurement
is that the level of abstraction between the predictor and the predicted should
be commensurate (Hilles and Kahle, 1985). In the United States, the phasing
out of AIO inventories gave way to new approaches focused more fully on
values. The resulting data show improvements in predictive power.

In France, COFREMCA now prefers to focus on more specific approaches,
developed in a maplike format and adapted to specific steps or problems. In
contrast, the taxonomic, holistic approaches to lifestyle, such as the CCA's,
results in the following issues:

1. inaccuracies in the translations of questionnaires;
2. questionable quality of the information collected, given the cum-
   bersome nature of the questionnaires. In this context, the appeal of
   simple questionnaires—short, easy, and standardized— reduced the
   possible bias; a low transparency of the systems used is beneficial.

We must emphasize that the following prospects seem most interesting
in the future:

• It will be possible to obtain a detailed analysis of specific consumption practices. Apart from their sociological interest, the current typologies are too general to have satisfactory predictive value regarding purchasing behavior. It is the same elsewhere, but to a lesser degree, on current inventories of values. It is in the field that studies cognitive chaining applications we find their most striking results. This approach has shown significant prediction ($R^2 = 20$ percent). (See Aurifeille and Valette-Florence, 1992b, for a detailed presentation.) Yet based on the values of Kahle in the same vein, perhaps it is beneficial, particularly in advertising, for explicit consideration of values.

• For those who continue to seek an overview of lifestyles, it might be advisable to opt for a new approach—one that would be easy to work with, such as the semiometrics proposal. This method also offers the dual advantage of transparency (known issues) and objectivity (the motives of the investigation are never revealed by the explicit method). It has already shown impressive applications for characterizing various types of consumption and understanding how different media draw different audiences. Advertising (especially the marketing side of advertising) is one of last fields of application that benefits from classical lifestyles studies. Now, the major remaining problem is finding a true conceptual basis for its instructive value and power to explain consumption behavior. Finally, new advances may spring from methodologies that strive to model the nature of behavior that has already been studied. Similarly, the VALS method of the United States has looked for trends between groups of lifestyles (even incorporating the effect of generations) (Mitchell, 1983). A more precise analysis of the temporal evolution of lifestyles seems necessary to truly anticipate the future sociological change. Preliminary tests have already been proposed in the political world in particular.

Regardless of whether these studies or analyses were based on lifestyles, we should remind users that a few precautions should be taken to ensure the quality and relevance of their results (see Valette-Florence and Rapacchi, 1990b, for an illustration).

1. First, researchers and consumers must know the questions in the questionnaire through which information is collected or, at least, how to revert to the different issues: attitudes, behaviors, opinions, interests, etc. Who, nowadays, would buy a car without knowing about the engine specs, safety rating, and average fuel consumption?

2. Then, researchers and consumers must know how the statistics are linked and connected. To reiterate the previous point, who would drive a car without knowing what type of gas to put into it?

3. Researchers and consumers must find out, by discriminant bias analysis, the quality of the preceding chaining (the sequence analysis). If this approach

is correct, it is vital to identify the initial variables on which recurring information is expected to affect subsequent groupings. We recall in this connection that an inferior allocation rate of 50 percent is not acceptable (since random assignment could then have superior predictive power).

4. The researchers and consumers must verify the reliability and validity of measurement scales used. A good range in one cultural environment may not be suitable in another, and vice versa. Without going into technical details, the coefficient of Cronbach (1951) often allows us to appreciate the quality of the scales used—that is to say, if they really measure what they purport to measure. This coefficient allows for testing in such a way that the consistency of responses to various questions should be at least equal to 0.7 and never be lower than 0.6.

5. The researchers and consumers must examine the predictive quality of the typologies proposed. In this regard, it is important to clarify the fundamental difference between descriptive and explanatory analysis. The descriptive analysis (factor analysis, connections, etc.) merely relate to the characteristics of various classifications. In this sense, they offer no insights into the causes and effects that regulate them. Consider an example: Assuming that lifestyle types match certain purchasing patterns, it seems logical that the choice of laundry detergent would vary from one lifestyle group to another. To make this inference, we must use a predictive analysis (logistic regression, logit models, etc.). We are only able to state whether membership of lifestyles categories can predict with any degree of accuracy the consumption of a provided product.

Such research transparency could only benefit providers of education and users:

- This would hurt the recruitment of clients sometimes. In the United States, for example, companies have not hesitated to attack the Yankelovich company due to lack of operational validity of results.
- This change to transparency would also relocate the exact focus of lifestyles studies. These changes are presented as alternatives to classic sociodemographics; however, they are superseded by those exact variables, which are important to the predictive analysis of consumption practices.
- Finally, we need to advance our knowledge through an improved analysis of the evolution of values and degrees of adherence to cultural norms in a given society (Kahle et al., 2000; Kahle, Marshall, and Kropp, 2003).

Can lifestyles reveal consumption patterns? A priori, no, they cannot, or at least not currently. Bourdieu (1987) rejects lifestyle studies because he believes that the scientific analysis of retailers and products is a largely intuitive process. Lifestyles were established very mysteriously, and developers have no incentive to tell their clients that their questions are not interesting or, worse, irrelevant. This honesty would deprive them of complex instruments, but may provide a new perspective on society, its evolution, and major trends that characterize lifestyles. Researchers should refine methodologies and improve their conceptual foundations.

Approaches focused on cultural values may be preferable (Solomon, 1983). Aligned with other variables, value studies offer insights that are vital to the study of behavior. And we know that social values do influence consumer choice (e.g., Kahle, 1996; Pitts, Canty, and Tsalikis, 1985; Reynolds and Olson, 2001).

One enormous change in the world—the development of social media—has created a demand for renewed research on lifestyles (and provides proof that Bourdieu was wrong). That change is why we developed Chapter 9, and it is why we have great optimism about lifestyle research going forward.

## FINAL THOUGHT

Finally, as Gregory (1986) so aptly notes, the major business users can influence the study of lifestyles positively, acting as rational and prudent consumers who compare products and require relevant results. May this work encourage such an orientation. He develops theoretical justifications for the definitions he proposes, the conclusions that were reached, the suggested guidelines and the debates—all of which might permit students, teachers, researchers, and especially professional practitioners to better identify the scope and impact of lifestyles. All approaches resting on solid theoretical and methodological foundations should provide a new direction and worthy interest for segmentation techniques and communication strategies. We also hope that between myth and reality, lifestyle research permits key decision makers, today and tomorrow, to make the right choices.

# References

Aaker, J. (1997). Dimensions of Brand Personality. *Journal of Marketing Research,* 34, 347–356.

Adler, A. (1912). *Über den nervösen Charakter.* Wiesbaden, Germany: Bergmann. Translated as *The Neurotic Constitution.* New York: Moffat, Yard, 1917.

———. (1919). *Praxis und Theorie der Individual-Psychologie.* Wiesbaden, Germany: Bergmann. Translated by P. Radin as *The Practice and Theory of Individual Psychology.* London: Routledge and Kegan Paul, 1925.

———. (1926). *Liebesbeziehungen und deren Störungen* ("Love Relationships and Their Disorders"). Vienna, Austria: Moritz Perles.

———. (1929). *The Science of Living.* New York: Greenburg.

Adler, F. (1956). The Value Concept in Sociology. *American Journal of Sociology,* 62, 272–279.

———. (1960). On Values and Value Theory. *American Sociological Review,* 25, 85–88.

Agostini, J., and Boss, J. (1973). Classifying Informants in Consumers' Surveys According to Their Areas of Interest. *European Research,* 1, 20–25.

Agresti, A. (1990). *Categorical Data Analysis.* New York: Wiley.

Allen, M.W., and Ng, S.H. (1999). The Direct and Indirect Influences of Human Values on Product Ownership. *Journal of Economic Psychology,* 20, 5–39.

Allport, G. (1935). Attitudes. In C. Murchison (ed.), *A Handbook of Social Psychology.* Winchester, MA: Clark University Press, 798–844.

———. (1961). *Pattern and Growth in Personality.* New York: Holt, Rinehart, and Winston.

Allport, G., Vernon, P., and Lindsey, G. (1961). *A Study of Values.* Boston: Houghton Mifflin.

Alpert, L., and Gatty, R. (1969). Product Positioning by Behavioral Lifestyles. *Journal of Marketing,* 33, 65–69.

Alreck, P. (1976). Time Orientation and Behavior. Unpublished doctoral dissertation, San Diego State University.

Anderson, J.C., and Gerbing, D.W. (1988). Structural Equation Modeling in Practice: A Review and Recommended Two-Step Approach. *Psychological Bulletin,* 103, 411–423.

Anderson, W.T., Jr., and Golden, L.L. (1983). Lifestyle and Psychographics: A Critical Review and Recommendation. In T.C. Kinnear (ed.), *Advances in Consumer Research,* 11. Provo, UT: Association for Consumer Research, 405–411.

Antoine, J. (1986). Styles de vie des français. *Futuribles*, 95, 75–80.

Arabie, P., Caroll, J., De Sarbo, W., and Wind, Y.C. (1981). Overlapping Clustering: A New Method for Product Positioning. *Journal of Marketing Research*, 18(3), 310–317.

Arellano, R. (1983). Le comportement de consommation d'énergie domestique. Thèse de doctorat d'état ès sciences de gestion, Institut d'études commerciales, Université des sciences sociales de Grenoble.

Arellano, R., Valette-Florence, P., and Jolibert, A. (1988). Le comportement du consommateur d'énergie domestique: une analyse causale. *Actes du 4th congrès de l'association française du marketing*, Montpellier, 5–6 mai.

Arndt, J. (1976). Reflections on Research in Consumer Behavior. In B. Anderson (ed.), *Advances in Consumer Research*, 3. Cincinnati, OH: Association for Consumer Research, 213–321.

Arndt, J., and Uusitalo, L. (1980). Backward Segmentation by Consumption Style: A Sociological Approach. In R. Bagozzi et al. (eds.), *Combined Proceedings: Marketing in the 80s*. Chicago: American Marketing Association, 126–130.

Arnoux, P., and Malet, E. du. (1984). La fin du prêt à penser. *L'Express*, du 5 au 11 octobre, 24–31.

Askegaard, S. (1991). What Do Life-Styles Studies Study? Toward a Universe of Life-Style Methodologies. In *Proceedings of the Workshop on Value and Lifestyle Research in Marketing*. Brussels, Belgium: EIASM.

Assael, H. (1984). *Consumer Behavior and Marketing Action*, 2d ed. Boston: Kent Publishing.

Aurifeille, J.M. (1991). Contribution of "Instrumental Values" to Means-End Chain Analysis and to Advertising Conceptualization. In *Proceedings of the Workshop on Value and Lifestyle Research in Marketing*. Brussels, Belgium: EIASM.

———. (1992). Les chaînes moyens-fins: concepts mèthodes et champs d'application, *Mémoire d'habilitation à diriger des recherches*, non publié, IAE de Poitiers, France.

Aurifeille, J.M., and Valette-Florence, P. (1992a). A "Chain-Constrained" Clustering Approach in Means-End Analysis: An Empirical Illustration, Marketing for Europe–Marketing for the Future. In *Proceedings of the EMAC Annual Conference*. Aarhus, Denmark: EMAC, 49–64.

———. (1992b). An Empirical Investigation of the Predictive Validity of Micro Versus Macro Approaches in Consumer Value Research, Marketing for Europe–Marketing for the Future. In *Proceedings of the EMAC Annual Conference*. Aarhus, Denmark: EMAC, 65–81.

———. (1992c). L'implication influe-t-elle sur les chaînes moyens-fins? *Actes du colloque de l'association française du marketing*, 8, 311–321.

———. (1995). Determination of the Dominant Means-End Chains: A Constrained Clustering Approach, *International Journal of Research in Marketing,* 12, 267–278.

Bales, R. (1950). *Interaction Process Analysis*. Chicago: University of Chicago Press.

———. (1970). *Personality and Interpersonal Behavior*. New York: Holt, Rinehart, and Winston.

Bales, R., Cohen, S., and Williamson, S. (1979). *SYMLOG: A System for the Multiple Level Observation of Groups*. New York: The Free Press.

Bales, R., and Couch, A. (1969). The Value Profile. *Sociological Inquiry*, 39, 3–18.

Bandura, A. (1988). Self-Regulation of Motivation and Action Through Goal Systems. In V. Hamilton, G.H. Bower, N.A. Frijda (eds.), *Cognitive Perspectives on Emotion and Motivation*. Boston: Kluwer Academic, 37–61.

Bardi, A., and Schwartz, S.H. (2003). Values and Behavior: Strength and Structure of Relations. *Personality and Social Psychology Bulletin*, 29, 1207–1220.

Barthélémy, B. (1980). Les styles de vie, dix ans après. *Stratégies*, 247, 44–53.

Basford, K., and McLachlan, G. (1985). The Mixture Method of Clustering Applied to Three-Way Data. *Journal of Classification*, 2(4), 109–125.

Batra, R., Homer, P., and Kahle, L. (2001). Values, Susceptibility to Interpersonal Influence, and Attribute Importance Weights: A Nomological Analysis. *Journal of Consumer Psychology*, 11(2), 115–128.

Baudrillard, J. (1970). *La société de consommation*. Paris: Gallimard.

———. (1986a). *Amérique*. Paris: Grasset.

———. (1986b). Naissance et influence des modes. *Restons simples*, 2.

Bearden, W., Teel, J., and Durand, R. (1978). Media Usage, Psychographic and Demographic Dimensions of Retail Shoppers. *Journal of Retailing*, 54(1), 65–74.

Bearden, W., Woodside, A., and Ronkainen, L. (1978). Contributions of Demographic and Consumer Beliefs on Buyer Behavior Research. *Actes du 5th séminaire international de recherche en marketing*, 112–127.

Beatty, S.E., Homer, P.M., and Kahle, L.R. (1988). Problems with VALS in International Marketing Research: An Example from an Application of the Empirical Mirror Technique. In M.J. Houston (ed.), *Advances in Consumer Research*, 15. Provo, UT: Association for Consumer Research, 375–380.

Beatty, S., Kahle, L., Homer, P., and Misra, S. (1985). Alternative Measurement Approaches to Consumer Values: The List of Values and the Rokeach Value Survey. *Psychology and Marketing*, 2, 181–200.

Becker, B., and Connor, P. (1981). Personal Values of the Heavy User of Mass Media. *Journal of Advertising Research*, 21, 37–43.

Becker, H. (1941). Supreme Values and the Sociologist. *American Sociological Review*, 6, 155–172.

———. (1950). *Through Values to Social Interpretation*. Durham, NC: Duke University Press.

Bee, C.C., and Kahle, L.R. (2006). Relationship Marketing in Sports: A Functional Approach. *Sport Marketing Quarterly*, 15, 101–110.

Benedict, R. (1934). *Patterns of Culture*. New York: Houghton Mifflin.

Benguigui, A. (1980). Styles de vie, sociologie et marketing. *Changements socioculturels et styles de vie, bilan des expériences, réflexion prospective*. Paris: IREP, 1er et 2 octobre, 5–13.

Bentham, J. (1789). *An Introduction to the Principles of Morals and Legislation*. Oxford: Clarendon Press. Reprinted. Rye Brook, NY: Adamant Media Corporation, 2005.

———. (1815). A Table of the Springs of Action. In A. Goldworth (ed.), *Deontology, Together with A Table of the Springs of Action and the Article on Utilitarianism*. Oxford: Clarendon Press, 1983.

Bergadaa, M. (1989). Temporal Orientation: Perception of Destiny, Personal Projects and Consumer Behavior. In G. Avlonitis et al. (eds.), *Marketing Thought and Practice in the 1990s*, Vol. 2, 1677–1679.

———. (1990). The Role of Time in the Action of the Consumer. *Journal of Consumer Research*, 17 (December), 239–302.

————. (1991). Cognitive Temporal System of the Consumer: Structures and Organizations. Papier de recherche no. 91023, Cergy-Pontoise, France: ESSEC.

Berlyne, D. (1967). Arousal and Reinforcement. In D. Levine (ed.), *Nebraska Symposium on Motivation*. Lincoln: University of Nebraska Press, 15, 1–110.

Bernard-Becharies, J.F. (1980). Le signe et le style, recherche épistémologique et théorique d'un concept de style de vie. *Revue française du marketing*, 80, 9–47.

————. (1985). La notion de révolution scientifique en économie. *Colloque de l'association Charles-Gide*, Montpellier, septembre.

Bernard-Becharies, J.F., and Pinson, C.H. (1981). Mode de vie et styles de vie. Quatre observations sur le fonctionnement des termes. *Consommation*, 4, 73–90.

Bernay, E. (1971). Life Style Analysis as a Basis for Media Selection. In C. Wing and D. Tigert (eds.), *Attitude Research Reaches New Heights*. Chicago: American Marketing Association, 189–195.

Blake, J., and Davis, K. (1964). Norms, Values, and Sanctions. In R. Faris (ed.), *Handbook of Modern Sociology*. Chicago: Rand McNally, 456–484.

Blau, P. (1964). *Exchange and Power in Social Life*. New York: Wiley.

Boas, F. (1911). *The Mind of Primitive Man*. New York: Macmillan.

Boltanski, L. (1982). *Les cadres, la formation d'un groupe social*. Paris: Éd. de Minuit.

Bolton, L.E., Reed II, A., Volpp, K., and Armstrong, K. (2008). How Does Drug and Supplemental Marketing Affect a Healthy Lifestyle? *Journal of Consumer Research*, 34, 71–81.

Boudon, R., and Bourricaud, F. (1982). *Dictionnaire critique de la sociologie*, 2d ed. Paris: PUF.

Bouffard, L., Lens, W., and Nuttin, J. (1983). Extension de la perspective temporelle future en relation avec la frustration. *International Journal of Psychology*, 18, 429–442.

Bourdieu, P. (1982). *La Distinction*. Paris: Éd. de Minuit.

————. (1987). Les sondages, une "science" sans savant. In *Choses dites*. Paris: Éd. de Minuit.

Bourdieu, P., and Passeron, J.E. (1964). *Les héritiers, les étudiants et la culture*. Paris: Éd. de Minuit.

Boush, D.M., and Kahle, L.R. (2001). Evaluating Negative Information in Online Consumer Discussions: From Qualitative Analysis to Signal Detection. *Journal of EuroMarketing*, 11(2), 89–105.

————. (2005). What, and How, We Can Learn from Online Consumer Discussion Groups. In C. Haugtvedt, K. Machleit, and R. Yalch (eds.), *Online Consumer Psychology: Understanding and Influencing Behavior in the Virtual World*. Mahwah, NJ: Lawrence Erlbaum Associates, 101–121.

Bozinoff, L., and Cohen, R. (1982). The Effects of Personal Values on Attitude and Store Choice Behavior. In J. Walker et al. (eds.), *An Assessment of Marketing Thought and Practice*. Chicago: American Marketing Association, 25–29.

Brochand, B., and Lendrevie, J. (1983). *Le Publicitor*. Dalloz Gestion.

Budillon, J.P., and Valette-Florence, P. (1990). Pratiques sportives: une approche par les systèmes de valeurs. *Revue des sciences et techniques des activités physiques et sportives*, 21, 9–23.

Burke, M. (1987). *À chacun son style d'entreprise*. Paris: InterÉditions.

Burke, M., and Cathelat, B. (1980). Bilan rétrospectif des styles de vie: les grandes étapes de leur évolution. *Changements socio-culturels et styles de vie, bilan des expériences et réflexion prospective*. Paris: IREP, 1er et 2 octobre, 47–57.

Buss, A., and Strauss, N. (2009). *Online Communities Handbook: Building Your Business and Brand on the Web.* Indianapolis, IN: New Riders.

Cahill, D.J. (2006). *Lifestyle Market Segmentation.* New York: Haworth.

Calabresi, R., and Cohen, J. (1968). Personality and Time Attitudes. *Journal of Abnormal Psychology,* 73(5), 431–439.

Caroll, J., Green, P., and Schaffer, C. (1986). Interpoint Distance Comparisons in Correspondence Analysis. *Journal of Marketing Research,* 23(3), 271–280.

———. (1987). Comparing Interpoint Distances in Correspondence Analysis: A Clarification. *Journal of Marketing Research,* 24(4), 445–450.

———. (1989). Reply to Greenacre's Commentary on the Caroll Green-Schaffer Scaling of a Two-Way Correspondence Analysis Solution. *Journal of Marketing Research,* 26(3), 366–368.

Cathelat, B. (1977). *Les styles de vie des français.* Montreal, Quebec: Éd. Stanké.

———. (1985a). *Styles de vie, courants et scénarios,* Vol. 1. Paris: Les Éditions d'Organisation.

———. (1985b). *Styles de vie, courants et scénarios,* Vol. 2. Paris: Les Éditions d'Organisation.

———. (1987). Il faut repenser profondément le marketing. *Marketing-Mix,* 15, 33–36.

———. (1990). *Socio-Styles systèmes.* Paris: Les Éditions d'Organisation.

Cathelat, B., and Cathelat, M. (1991). *Panorama des styles de vie: 1960–1990.* Paris: Les Éditions d'Organisation.

Cathelat, B., and Ebguy, R. (1987). *Styles de pub, 60 manières de communiquer.* Paris: Les Éditions d'Organisation.

Cathelat, B., and Matricon, C. (1976). Communication et innovation dans une société en mutation les styles de vie en France en 1976. *Revue française du marketing,* 62, 41–52.

Cathelat, B., and Mermet, G. (1985). *Vous et les français.* Paris: Flammarion.

Catton, W. (1954). Exploring Techniques for Measuring Human Values. *American Sociology Review,* 19, 49–55.

———. (1959). A Theory of Values. *American Sociology Review,* 24, 310–317.

Cerha, J. (1974). The Limits of Influence. *European Research,* 2, 141–151.

Clawson, C. (1946). *Psychology in Action.* New York: Macmillan.

Clawson, C., and Vinson, D. (1977). Human Values: A Historical and Interdisciplinary Analysis. In *Advances in Consumer Research,* 5. Ann Arbor, MI: Association for Consumer Research, 396–402.

Cochrane, R., Billig, M., and Huggs, M. (1979). British Politics and the Two-Value Model. In M. Rokeach (ed.), *Understanding Human Values.* New York: The Free Press, 179–191.

Cohen, J.B. (1967). An Interpersonal Orientation to the Study of Consumer Behavior. *Journal of Marketing Research,* 7, 270–278.

Comm, J. (2009). *Twitter Power: How to Dominate Your Market One Tweet at a Time.* Hoboken, NJ: Wiley.

Copeland, M. (1924). *Principles of Merchandising.* Chicago: A.W. Shaw Co.

Cosmas, C. (1982). Lifestyles and Consumption Patterns. *Journal of Consumer Research,* 8, 453–455.

Crask, M., and Reynolds, F. (1978). An In-Depth Profile of the Department Store Shopper. *Journal of Retailing,* 54, 23–32.

Cronbach, J. (1951). Coefficient Alpha and the Internal Structure of Tests. *Psychometricka,* 16 (September), 297–334.

Daniel, E., Scheifer, D., and Knafo, A. (2012). One and Not the Same: The Consistency of Values Across Contexts Among Majority and Minority Members in Israel and Germany. *Journal of Cross-Cultural Psychology,* forthcoming.

Darden, W., and Reynolds, F. (1974). Backward Profiling of Male Innovators. *Journal of Marketing Research,* 11, 79–85.

Daudin, J., and Trécourt, P. (1980). Analyse factorielle des correspondances et modèle log-linéaire: comparaison des deux méthodes sur un exemple. *Revue de statistiques appliquées,* 1, 5–24.

Davidov, E. (2008). A Cross-Country and Cross-Time Comparison of the Human Values Measurement with the Second Round of the European Social Survey. *Survey Research Methods,* 2(1), 33–46.

Davidov, E., Schmidt, P., and Schwartz, S.H. (2008). Bringing Values Back In: The Adequacy of the European Social Survey to Measure Values in 20 Countries. *Public Opinion Quarterly,* 72(3), 420–445.

Deci, E., and Ryan, R. (1985). *Intrinsic Motivation and Self-Determination in Human Behavior.* New York: Plenum.

Delbès, R., and Teyssonniere de Gramont, E. (1991). *Études de marché.* Paris: Éditions Delmas.

De Leeuw, J. (1984). *Canonical Analysis of Categorical Data.* Leiden, The Netherlands: DSWO Press.

Demuth, G. (1978). Profil socio-culturel des consommateurs et implication socio-culturelle des messages publicitaires. *IREP,* avril, 187–210.

———. (1980). Approches socio-culturelles et ajustement des stratégies de marketing. *IREP,* octobre, 15–45.

Demuth, G., and Neirac, J.N. (1976). Typologie socio-culturelle et fréquentation média-supports. *Revue française du marketing,* 62, 99–105.

De Sarbo, W. (1982). GENNCLUS: New Models for General Nonhierarchical Clustering Analysis. *Psychometrika,* 47(4), 449–476.

De Sarbo, W., and Cron, W.C. (1988). A Maximum Likehood Methodology for Clusterwise Linear Regression. *Journal of Classification,* 5(4), 249–282.

Deutsch, E. (1989). Sémiométrie: une nouvelle approche de positionnement et de segmentation. *Revue française du marketing,* 125, 5–16.

De Vulpian, A. (1974). Détection et suivi périodique des courants socio-culturels en France. *Compte rendu des journées de l'IREP,* 27 mai, 117–162.

———. (1976). Caractéristiques socio-culturelles et sympathies politiques. *Revue française du marketing,* 62, 81–91.

Dillon, W., and Goldstein, M. (1984). *Multivariate Analysis: Methods and Application.* New York: Wiley.

Dizambourg, G. (1983). Style de vie et fréquentation des points de vente. Thèse de doctorat de troisième cycle ès sciences de gestion, Université de Paris-I, Panthéon-Sorbonne.

Dolich, I. (1967). Congruence Relationships Between Self-Images and Product Brands. *Journal of Marketing Research,* 7, 80–84.

Douglas, S. (1978). L'analyse du style de vie et des courants socio-culturels: problemes actuels et perspecitves futures. *Encyclopedie du marketing,* Vol 1. *Le comportement du consommateur.* Editions Techniques, p. 3.

Douglas, S., and Craig, C. (1983). *International Marketing Research.* Englewood Cliffs, NJ: Prentice-Hall.

Douglas, S., and Le Maire, P. (1973). Les styles de vie et le positionnement des produits. *IREP*, mai, 7–40.

———. (1976). Le style de vie: la mesure des styles de vie à travers les activités, les attitudes et les opinions. *Revue française du marketing*, 62, 61–79.

Douglas, S., and Urban, C. (1977). Using Lifestyle Analysis to Profile Women in International Markets. *Journal of Marketing*, 14, 46–54.

Dubois, B. (1987). Culture et marketing. *Recherche et applications en marketing*, 1, 43–64.

———. (1990). *Comprendre le consommateur*. Paris: Dalloz.

Dubois, B., and Douglas, S. (1977). Culture et comportement d'achat. *Encyclopédie du marketing*, Vol. 1, *Le comportement du consommateur*. Paris: Éditions Techniques, 1–21.

Dubois, P.L, and Jolibert, A. (1992). Le Marketing: fundaments et pratique. Eonometrica.

Duncan, O. (1966). Methodological Issues in the Analysis of Social Mobility. In N. Smelser and S. Lipset (eds.), *Social Structure and Mobility in Economic Development*. Chicago: Aldine Publishing.

Dunn, T. (1971). Attitude Research Reaches New Heights. In C.W. King and D.J. Tigert (eds.), *Attitude Research Reaches New Heights*. Chicago: American Marketing Association, 202–205.

Durand, J., Pages, J.P., Brenot, J., and Barny, M.H. (1990). Public Opinion and Conflicts: A Theory and System of Opinion Polls. *International Journal of Public Opinion Research*, 2(1), 30–52.

Durkheim, E. (1893). *De la division du travail social*. Paris: Alcan.

Dutta-Bergman, M.J., and Wells, W.D. (2002). The Values and Lifestyles of Idiocentrics and Allocentrics in an Individualist Culture: A Descriptive Approach. *Journal of Consumer Psychology*, 12, 231–242.

Eagly, A.H., and Chaiken, S. (1993). *The Psychology of Attitudes*. New York: Harcourt Brace Jovanovich.

Engel, J., Blackwell, R., and Kollat, D. (1978). *Consumer Behavior*, 3d ed. Hinsdale, IL: Dryden Press.

Enriquez, E. (1983). *De la horde à l'état*. Paris: Gallimard.

Erikson, E.H. (1968). *Identity: Youth and Crisis*. New York: Norton.

Escofier, B. (1987). Analyse des correspondances multiple conditionnelle. *Cinquièmes journées d'analyse des données et informatique*, INRIA, 2, 13–22.

Evans, D. (2008). *Social Media Marketing*. Hoboken, NJ: Wiley.

Evans, R. (1952). Personal Values as Factors in Anti-Semitism. *Journal of Abnormal and Social Psychology*, 47, 749–756.

Evrard, Y., and Laurent, G. (1983). Les modèles log-linéaires: applications en marketing. *Cahier de recherche*, M 911 N 83. Jouy-en-Josas, France: Centre HEC-ISA.

Evrard, Y., and Le Maire, P. (1976). *Modèles et décisions en marketing*. Paris: Dalloz.

Evrard, Y., and Tissier-Desbordes, E. (1985). Les systèmes de valeurs et les lectures dans la famille. *Actes du 12e séminaire international de recherche en marketing*, Aix-en-Provence.

Faivre, J.P., and Le Maire, P. (1982). Les styles de vie. *APEREC*, 17–18 mai, Paris.

Fabrigar, L.R., Wegener, D.T., MacCallum, R.C., and Strahan, Erin J. (1999). Evaluating the use of exploratory factor analysis in psychological research. *Psychological Methods*, 4, 272–299.

Falcy, S. (1992). Les chemins de la persuasion: de nouvelles propositions théoriques. *Actes du colloque de l'association française du marketing*, 8, 110–130.

Feather, N. (1975). *Values in Education and Society*. New York: The Free Press.

Feather, N., and Bond, M. (1983). Time Structure and Purposeful Activities Among Employed and Unemployed University Graduates. *Journal of Occupational Psychology*, 56, 241–254.

Feldman, L., and Hornik, J. (1981). The Use of Time: An Integrated Conceptual Model. *Journal of Consumer Research*, 7, 407–419.

Festinger, L. (1957). *A Theory of Cognitive Dissonance*. Evanston, IL: Row, Petersen.

Fischer, R., Vauclair, J., Fontaine, J.R.J., and Schwartz, S.H. (2010). Are Individual-Level and Country-Level Value Structures Different? Testing Hofstede's Legacy with the Schwartz Value Survey. *Journal of Cross-Cultural Psychology*, 41, 135–151.

Fishbein, M., and Ajzen, I. (1975). *Belief, Attitude, Intention: An Introduction to Theory and Research*. Reading, MA: Addison Wesley.

Florenthal, B., and Shoham, A. (2000). Value Differences Between Risky Sports Participants and Nonparticipants. *Sport Marketing Quarterly*, 9, 26–33.

Fornell, C., ed. (1982). *A Second Generation of Multivariate Analysis*. 2 vols. New York: Praeger.

Fornell, C., and Yi, D. (1992). Assumptions of the Two-Step Approach to Latent Variable Modeling. *Sociological Methods & Research*, 20, 291–320.

Fornell, C., and Westbrook, R.A. (1979). Identification of Consumer Information Gathering Approaches: Application of Functional/Structural Segmentation Methodology. In *Proceedings of the Annual Meeting of the European Academy for Advanced Research in Marketing*. Stockholm.

Frank, R.E., and Strain, C.E. (1972). A Segmentation Research Design Using Consumer Panel Data. *Journal of Marketing Research*, 9, 385–390.

Frankena, W. (1967). Value and Evaluation. In P. Edwards (ed.), *The Encyclopedia of Philosophy*, Vol. 3. New York: Macmillan.

Frye, R., and Klein, G. (1974). Psychographies and Industrial Design. In W. Wells (ed.), *Life Style and Psychographics*. Chicago: American Marketing Association, 225–232.

Gabilliet, P. (1987). Les styles de vie des vendeurs en 1999. *Action commerciale*, 58, première partie, 17–19; 59, deuxième partie, 15–17; 60, troisième partie, 16–18; 61, quatrième partie, 20–22; 62, cinquième partie, 22–23.

Genzel, D. (1983). *De la publicité a la communication*. Paris: Rochevignes.

Gillin, P. (2007). *The New Influencers: A Marketer's Guide to the New Social Media*. Sanger, CA: Quill Driver Books.

———. (2009). *Secrets of Social Media Marketing*. Sanger, CA: Quill Driver Books.

Goldberg, L.R. (1993). The Structure of Phenotypic Personality Types. *American Psychologist*, 48, 26–34.

Goldberg, M. (1976). Identifying Relevant Psychographics Segments: How Specifying Product Functions Can Help. *Journal of Consumer Research*, 3, 163–169.

Goldberger, A., and Gamaletsos, T. (1970). A Cross-Country Comparison of Consumer Expenditure Patterns. *European Economic Review*, 2, 357–380.

Gordon, L. (1960). *Survey of Interpersonal Values*. Chicago: Science Research Associates.

Gottlieb, M. (1959). Segmentation by Personality Types. In L. Stockman (ed.), *Advancing Marketing Efficiency*. Chicago: American Marketing Association, 148–158.

Grandjean, M. (1978). Les styles de vie en média-planning, problèmes et perspectives. *IREP*, 18–32.

Green, E., Maheshwari, A., and Rao, V. (1969). Self-Concept and Brand Preference: An Empirical Application of Multidimensional Scaling. *Journal of the Market Research Society*, 11, 25–78.

Greenacre, M. (1989). The Caroll-Green-Schaffer Scaling in Correspondence Analysis: A Theoretical and Empirical Appraisal. *Journal of Marketing Research*, 26(3), 358–365.

Gregory, P. (1986). Recentrés, décalés ou passéistes? Faut-il croire aux "styles de vie"? *Commentaires*, 35, 526–531.

Grover, R., and Dillon, W. (1988). Understanding Market Characteristics from Aggregated Brand Switching Data by the Method of Spectral Decomposition. *International Journal of Research in Marketing*, 5, 77–89.

Grubb, E., and Grathwohl, H. (1967). Consumer Self-Concept, Symbolism, and Market Behavior: A Theoretical Approach. *Journal of Marketing*, 31, 22–27.

Grube, J., Weir, L., Getzlaf, S., and Rokeach, M. (1984). Own Value System, Value Images, and Cigarette Smoking. *Personality and Social Psychology Bulletin*, 10, 306–313.

Grunert, K.G., and Grunert, S.C. (1991). Measuring Subjective Meaning Structures by the Laddering Method: Theoretical Considerations and Methodological Problems. In *Proceedings of the Workshop on Value and Lifestyle Research in Marketing*. Brussels, Belgium: EIASM.

Grunert, S. and Juhl, H. (1991). Values, Environmental Attitudes, and Buying of Organic Foods: Their Relationships in a Sample of Danish Teachers. In *Proceedings of the Workshop on Value and Lifestyle Research in Marketing*. Brussels, Belgium: EIASM.

Gurel-Atay, E., Xie, G., Chen, J., and Kahle, L.R. (2010). Changes in Social Values in the United States: 1976–2007. *Journal of Advertising Research*, 50(1), 57–67.

Gutman, J. (1982). A Means-End Chain Model Based on Consumer Categorization Processes. *Journal of Marketing*, 46, 60–72.

———. (1986). Analyzing Consumer Orientations Toward Beverages Through Means-End Chain Analysis. *Psychology and Marketing*, 3, 28–42.

———. (1997). Means-End Chains as Goal Hierarchies. *Psychology & Marketing*, 14(6), 545–560.

Haley, R. (1968). Benefit Segmentation: A Decision-Oriented Tool. *Journal of Marketing*, 8, 3–8.

———. (1971). Beyond Benefit Segmentation. *Journal of Advertising Research*, 11, 3–8.

Hall, E. (1959). *The Silent Language*. Garden City, NY: Doubleday.

———. (1976). *Beyond Culture*. Garden City, NY: Anchor Press.

———. (1983). *The Dance of Life*. Garden City, NY: Anchor Press.

Hall, S., and Lindzey, G. (1970). *Theories of Personality*. New York: Wiley.

Haney, L. (1936). *History of Economic Thought*, 3d ed. New York: Macmillan.

Hartman, R. (1967). *The Structure of Value: Foundations of Scientific Axiology*. Carbondale, IL: Southern Illinois University Press.

Heller, H. (1970). Defining Target Market by Their Attitudes Profiles. In L. Adler and I. Crespi (eds.), *Attitude Research on the Rocks*. Chicago: American Marketing Association, 45–47.

Henault, G. (1973). *Le comportement des consommateurs*. Québec: Presses Universitaires du Québec.

Henry, W. (1976). Cultural Values Do Correlate with Consumer Behavior. *Journal of Marketing Research,* 13, 121–127.

Herpin, N. (1986a). L'habillement, la classe sociale et la mode. *Économic et statistiques,* 188, 35–54.

———. (l986b). Socio-style. *Revue française de sociologie,* 27, 265–272.

Hilles, W.S., and Kahle, L.R. (1985). Social Contract and Social Integration in Adolescent Development. *Journal of Personality and Social Psychology,* 49, 1114–1121.

Hodock, H. (1974). The Use of Psychographics in the Analysis of Channel of Distribution. In W.D. Wells (ed.), *Life Style and Psychographics.* Chicago: American Marketing Association, 205–221.

Hofstede, G. (1980). *Culture's Consequences: International Differences in Work Related Values.* Thousand Oaks, CA: Sage.

Holman, R. (1981). The Imagination of the Future: A Hidden Concept in the Study of Consumer Decision Making. In *Advances in Consumer Research,* 8. Ann Arbor, MI: Association for Consumer Research, 187–191.

———. (1984). A Values and Life Styles Perspective on Human Behavior. In R. Pitts and A. Woodside (eds.), *Personal Values and Consumer Psychology.* Lexington, MA: Lexington Books, 35–54.

Holtz, S., and Havens, J.C. (2009). *Tactical Transparency: How Leaders Can Leverage Social Media to Maximize Value and Build Their Brand.* San Francisco: Jossey-Bass.

Holzner, S. (2009). *Facebook Marketing: Leveraging Social Media to Grow Your Business.* Indianapolis, IN: Que.

Homer, P., and Kahle, L. (1988). A Structural Equation Test of the Value-Attitude-Behavior Hierarchy. *Journal of Personality and Social Psychology,* 54(4), 638–646.

Hu, L., and Bentler, P.M. (1999). Cutoff Criteria for Fit Indexes in Covariance Structure Analysis: Conventional Criteria Versus New Alternatives. *Structural Equation Modeling,* 6(1), 1–55.

Hustad, P., and Pessemier, E. (1974). The Development and Application of Psychographic, Life Style, and Associated Activity and Attitude Measures. In W. Wells (ed.), *Life Style and Psychographics.* Chicago: American Marketing Association, 32–70.

Inoguchi, T., and Fujii, S. (2008). The AsiaBarometer: Its Aim, Its Scope, and Its Development. In V. Moller, D. Huschka, and A. Michalos (eds.), *Barometers of Quality of Life Around the Globe: How Are We Doing?* New York: Springer, 187–232.

Jacoby, J. (1971). Personality and Innovation Proneness. *Journal of Marketing Research,* 8, 244–247.

Jacoby, J., Szybillo, G., and Bering, C. (1976). Time and Consumer Behavior: An Interdisciplinary Overview. *Journal of Consumer Research,* 2, 320–339.

Jolibert, A., Nique, W., and Velasquez, M. (1987). L'influence de la culture et du pouvoir sur les résultats de la négociation commerciale: une étude empirique entre la France et le Brésil. *Actes du 3e congrès de l'association française du marketing,* Dinard, mai 1987.

Jones, A., Sensenig, J., and Ashmore, R. (1978). Systems of Values and Their Multidimensional Representations. *Multivariate Behavioral Research,* 13, 255–270.

Jones, S., Bee, C., Burton, R., and Kahle, L.R. (2004). Marketing Through Sports Entertainment: A Functional Approach. In L.J. Shrum (ed.), *The Psychology of Entertainment Media: Blurring the Lines Between Entertainment and Persuasion.* Mahwah, NJ: Lawrence Erlbaum Associates, 309–322.

Kaes, R. (1963). *Vivre dans les grands ensembles.* Paris: Éditions ouvrières.

Kahle, L.R. (1980). Stimulus Condition Self-Selection by Males in the Interaction of Locus of Control and Skill-Chance Situations. *Journal of Personality and Social Psychology,* 38, 50–56.

———. (1983). *Social Values and Social Change: Adaptation to Life in America.* New York: Praeger.

———. (1984). *Attitudes and Social Adaptation: A Person-Situation Interaction Approach.* New York: Pergamon.

———. (1986). The Nine Nations of North America and the Value Basis of Geographic Segmentation. *Journal of Marketing,* 50, 37–47.

———. (1996). Social Values and Consumer Behavior: Research from the List of Values. In Clive Seligman, James M. Olson, and Mark P. Zanna (eds.), *The Psychology of Values: The Ontario Symposium,* 8. Mahwah, NJ: Lawrence Erlbaum Associates, 135–151.

Kahle, L.R. and Beatty, S.E. (1987). The Task Situation and Habit in the Attitude-Behavior Relationship: A Social Adaptation View. *Journal of Social Behavior and Personality,* 2, 219–232.

Kahle, L.R., Beatty, S., and Homer, P. (1986). Alternative Measurement Approaches to Consumer Values: The List of Values (LOV) and Values and Life-Style (VALS). *Journal of Consumer Research,* 13, 405–409.

Kahle, L.R., and Berman, J.J. (1979). Attitudes Cause Behavior: A Cross-Lagged Panel Analysis. *Journal of Personality and Social Psychology,* 37, 315–321.

Kahle, L.R., and Close, A., eds. (2011). *Consumer Behavior Knowledge for Effective Sports and Event Marketing.* New York: Psychology Press.

Kahle, L.R., Duncan, M., Dalakas, V., and Aiken, D. (2001). The Social Values of Fans for Men's Versus Women's University Basketball. *Sport Marketing Quarterly,* 10(2), 156–162.

Kahle, L.R., and Eisert, D.C. (1986). Social Values and Adaptation in the American Workplace. In E.G. Flamholtz, Y. Randle, and S. Sackman (eds.), *Future Directions in Human Resource Management.* Los Angeles: UCLA Publications, 203–223.

Kahle, L.R., and Homer, P.M. (1985). Physical Attractiveness of the Celebrity Endorser: A Social Adaptation Perspective. *Journal of Consumer Research,* 11, 954–961.

Kahle, L.R., Homer, P.M., O'Brien, R.M., and Boush, D. (1997). Maslow's Hierarchy and Social Adaptation as Alternative Accounts of Value Structures. In L.R. Kahle and L. Chiagouris (eds.), *Values, Lifestyles, and Psychographics.* Mahwah, NJ: Lawrence Erlbaum Associates, 111–137.

Kahle, L.R., and Kahle, K.E. (2009). The Silence of the Lambdas: Science, Technology, and Public Knowledge. *International Journal of Technology, Knowledge, and Society,* 5(2), 137–142.

Kahle, L.R., Kambara, K.M., and Rose, G.M. (1996). A Functional Model of Fan Attendance Motivations for College Football. *Sport Marketing Quarterly,* 5 (December), 51–60.

Kahle, L.R., Liu, R., Rose, G.M., and Kim, W.-S. (2000). Dialectical Thinking in Consumer Decision Making. *Journal of Consumer Psychology,* 9(1), 53–58.

Kahle, L.R., Liu, R., and Watkins, H. (1991). Psychographic Variation Across United States Geographic Regions. In J. Sherry and B. Sternthal (eds.), *Advances in Consumer Research*, 19. Provo, UT: Association for Consumer Research, 375–380.

Kahle, L.R., Marshall, S., and Kropp, F. (2003). The New Paradigm Marketing Model. *Journal of Euromarketing*, 12(3–4), 99–121.

Kahle, L.R., Poulos, B., and Sukhdial, A. (1988). Changes in Social Values in the United States During the Past Decade. *Journal of Advertising Research*, 28 (February-March), 35–41.

Kahle, L.R., and Riley, C., eds. (2004). *Sports Marketing and the Psychology of Marketing Communication*. Mahwah, NJ: Lawrence Erlbaum.

Kahle, L.R., and Xie, G. (2008). Social Values in Consumer Psychology. In Curtis P. Haugtvedt, Paul M. Herr, and Frank R. Kardes (eds.), *Handbook of Consumer Psychology*. Mahwah, NJ: Lawrence Erlbaum Associates, 275–285.

Kamakura, W., and Mazzon, J. (1991). Values Segmentation: A Model for the Measurement of Values and Value Systems. *Journal of Consumer Research*, 18 (September), 208–218.

Kamakura, W., and Novak, T. (1992). Value-System Segmentation: Exploring the Meaning of LOV. *Journal of Consumer Research*, 19 (June), 119–132.

Kanter, D. (1977). The Europeanizing of America: A Study in Changing Values. In *Advances in Consumer Research*. Ann Arbor, MI: Association for Consumer Research, 408–410.

Kapferer, J.N. (1985). Publicité: une révolution des méthodes de travail. *Revue française de gestion*, sept.-déc., 102–111.

Kapferer, J.N., and Laurent, G. (1981a). Une analyse des relations entre les classifications socioculturelles et de styles de vie et l'achat des produits courants. *IREP*, La communication et son efficacité, 205–223.

———. (1981b). Les décalés et les jouisseurs n'ont pas enterré les cadres supérieurs et les cols bleus. *Stratégies*, 292, 52–53.

———. (1983). *La sensibilité aux marques: un nouveau concept pour gérer les marques*. Fondation jours de France pour la recherche en puhlicité.

———. (1985). *Le pouvoir prédictif des typologies de styles de vie et socioculturelles: choix qualitatifs du consommateur*. Congrès de l'association française du marketing, Le Touquet.

Kaplan, A.M., and Haenlein, M. (2010). Users of the World, Unite! The Challenges and Opportunities of Social Media. *Business Horizons*, 53(1), 59–68.

Kassarjian, H. (1971a). Personality and Consumer Behavior Research: A Review. *Journal of Marketing Research*, 8, 409–418.

———. (l971b). Incorporating Ecology into Marketing Strategy. *Journal of Marketing Research*, 8, 61–65.

Kau, A.K., Jung, K., Tambyah, S.K., and Tan, S.J. (2004). *Understanding Singaporeans: Values, Lifestyles, Aspirations, and Consumption Behaviors*. Singapore: World Scientific Publishing.

Kau, A.K., Tan, S.J., and Wirtz, J. (1998). *7 Faces of Singaporeans: Their Values, Aspirations, and Lifestyles*. New York: Prentice-Hall.

Kelley, E. (1963). Discussion. In S. Greyser (ed.), *Toward Scientific Marketing*. Chicago: American Marketing Association, 164–171.

Kelly, G. (1955). *The Psychology of Personal Constructs*. 2 vols. New York: Norton.

Kelly, J. (1975). Life Style and Leisure Choices. *The Family Coordinator*, 4, 185–190.

Kelman, H.C. (1958). Compliance, Identification, and Internalization: Three Processes of Attitude Change. *Journal of Conflict Resolution*, 2, 51–60.

———. (1961). Processes of Opinion Change. *Public Opinion Quarterly*, 25, 57–78.

———. (1974). Further Thoughts on the Processes of Compliance, Identification, and Internalization. In J.T. Tedeschi (ed.), *Perspectives on Social Power*. Chicago: Aldine, 125–171.

Kelman, H.C., and Eagly, A.H. (1965). Attitude Toward the Communicator, Perception of the Communication Content, and Attitude Change. *Journal of Personality and Social Psychology*, 1, 63–78.

Kets de Vries, M., and Miller, D. (1985). *L'entreprise névrosée*. Paris: McGraw-Hill.

Kilbourne, W., Grunhagen, M., and Foley, J. (2005). A Cross-Cultural Examination of the Relationship Between Materialism and Individual Values. *Journal of Economic Psychology*, 26, 624–641.

Kim, W.S., Boush, D.M., Marquardt, A. and Kahle, L.R. (2006). "Values, Brands, and Image." In L.R. Kahle and C.H. Kim (eds.), (2006). *Creating Images and the Psychology of Marketing Communication*. Mahwah, NJ: Lawrence Erlbaum, 279–290.

Klages, L. (1906). Das Persönliche Leitbild. In *Graphol. Monastshefte*. London: Ackermann.

Kluckhohn, C. (1951). Values and Value Orientation in the Theory of Action: An Exploration in Definition and Classification. In T. Parsons and E. Shils (eds.), *Toward a General Theory of Action*. Cambridge, MA: Harvard University Press, 388–433.

Kluckhohn, F. (1950). Dominant and Substitute Profiles of Cultural Orientations. *Social Forces*, 28, 376–393.

Kluckhohn, F., and Strodtbeck, F. (1961). *Variations in Value Orientations*. Evanston, IL: Row, Peterson.

Kohn, M. (1969). *Class and Conformity: A Study in Values*. Homewood, IL: Dorsey Press.

Kohn, M., and Schooler, C. (1969). Class, Occupation, and Orientation. *American Sociological Review*, 34, 659–678.

Koponen, A. (1960). Personality Characteristics of Purchasers. *Journal of Advertising Research*, 1, 6–12.

Kotler, P., and Keller, K. (2009). *Marketing Management*, 13th ed. Upper Saddle River, NJ: Prentice-Hall.

Krech, D., Crutchfield, R., and Ballachey, E. (1948). *Theory and Problems of Social Psychology*. New York: McGraw-Hill.

Krief, J., and Loiseau, M. (1979). Les styles de vie en question. *Stratégies*, 199, 30–68.

Kropp, F., Lavack, A.M., and Silvera, D. (2005). Values and Collective Self-Esteem as Predictors of Consumer Susceptibility to Interpersonal Influence Among University Students. *International Marketing Review*, 22, 7–33.

Kropp, F.G., Smith, M.C., Rose, G.M., and Kahle, L.R. (1992). Values and Lifestyles of Pet Owners. In T.J. Page, Jr., and S.E. Middlestadt (eds.), *Proceedings of the Society for Consumer Psychology*. Clemson, SC: CtC Press, 46–49.

Kurpis, L.H.V., Bozman, C.S., and Kahle, L.R. (2010). Distinguishing Between Amateur Sport Participants and Spectators: The List of Values Approach. *International Journal of Sports Marketing and Management,* 7(3–4), 190–201.

Lasch, C. (1982). *Le complexe de narcisse.* Paris: Laffont.

Lastovicka, J. (1982). On the Validation of Lifestyle Traits: A Review and Illustration. *Journal of Marketing Research,* 19, 126–138.

Lastovicka, J., Murry, J., and Joachimsthaler, E. (1990). Evaluating the Measurement Validity of Lifestyle Typologies with Qualitative Measures and Multiplicative Factoring. *Journal of Marketing Research,* 27(2), 11–23.

Laumann, E., and House, J. (1970). Living Room Styles and Social Attributes: The Patterning of Material Artifacts in a Modern Urban Community. *Sociology and Social Research,* 54, 321–342.

Lazarsfeld, P. (1935). The Art of Asking Why. *National Marketing Review,* 1, 26–38.

Lazer, W. (1963). Life Style Concepts and Marketing. In S.A. Greyser (ed.), *Toward Scientific Marketing.* Chicago: American Marketing Association, 130–139.

Lebart, L. (1986). Qui pense quoi? Evolution et structure des opions en France de 1978 a 1984. *Consommation,* 4, 3-22.

Lebart, L., et al. (1983). Conditions de vie et aspirations des français. *Futuribles,* février, 15–33.

Lebart, L., and Houzel-Van Effenterre, Y. (1980). Le système d'enquêtes sur les aspirations des français: une brève présentation. *Consommation,* 1, 3–25.

———. (1981). Conditions de vie et aspirations des français, 1978–1981. *Consommation,* 2, 15–33.

Lee, D. (1959). Culture and the Experience of Values. In A. Maslow (ed.), *New Knowledge in Human Values.* New York: Harper.

Le Maire, P. (1981). Styles de vie et courants socio-culturels: Pour quoi faire? *Consommation,* 2, 91–97.

Le Maire, P., Evrard, Y., and Douglas, S. (1973). Profiling Customers Based on Product Purchasing Characteristics. In *Proceedings of the XXIVth ESOMAR Congress,* 285–300.

Lemaitre, N. (1984). La culture de l'entreprise facteur de performance. *Revue française de gestion,* 47–48, 153–162.

Levinson, H. (1981). *The Executive.* Cambridge, MA: Harvard University Press.

Levitin, T. (1973). Values. In J. Robinson and P. Shaver (eds.), *Measures of Social Psychological Attitudes,* rev. ed. Ann Arbor, MI: Survey Research Center, Institute for Social Research, 489–585.

Levy, S. (1963). Symbolism and Lifestyle. In S.A. Greyser (ed.), *Toward Scientific Marketing.* Chicago: American Marketing Association, 140–149.

Lewin, K. (1951). *Field Theory in Social Science,* ed. D. Cartwright. New York: Harper.

Lhermie, C. (1984). Les styles de vie en matière commerciale (The Lifestyles Matter in Marketing). Thèse de doctorat d'état ès sciences de gestion, Institut d'études Université de Paris-I, Panthéon-Sorbonne.

Li, C., and Bernoff, J. (2008). *Groundswell: Winning in a World Transformed by Social Technologies.* Cambridge, MA: Harvard University Press.

Limon, Y., Kahle, L.R., and Orth, U. (2009). Package Design as a Communications Vehicle in Cross-Cultural Values Shopping. *Journal of International Marketing,* 17(34), 30–57.

Lindeman, M., and Verkasalo, M. (2005). Measuring Values with the Short Schwartz's Value Survey. *Journal of Personality Assessment*, 85(2), 170–178.

Lovell, M. (1974). European Developments in Psychographics. In W. Wells (ed.), *Life Style and Psychographics*. Chicago: American Marketing Association, 259–276.

Lunn, J. (1966). Psychological Classification. *Commentary*, 8, 161–173.

Lybeck, J. (1976). The Allocation of Consumer Expenditures in a Swedish Macroeconomic Model. *European Economic Review*, 8, 371–378.

Maio, G., and Olson, J.M. (1994). Value-Attitude-Behaviour Relations: The Moderating Role of Attitude Functions. *British Journal of Social Psychology*, 33, 301.

Malraux, André. (1951). *Les Voix du silence*, Paris: Gallimard.

Martineau, P. (1958). Social Classes and Spending Behavior. *Journal of Marketing*, 1, 18–23.

Maslow, A. (1954). *Motivation and Personality*. New York: Harper.

———. (1959). *New Knowledge in Human Values*. New York: Harper.

Matras, J. (1960). Comparison of Intergenerational Occupational Mobility Patterns. *Population Studies*, 14, 163–169.

Matricon, C., Burke, M., and Cathelat, B. (1974). L'importance de l'environnement socio-culturel. *Compte rendu des journees de l'IREP*, 27 mai, 40–94.

Mauduit, J. (1976). *Le premier grand prix publicité des lectrices d'Elle*. Paris: Espace Cardin.

Mauss, M. (1969). *Cohésion sociale et divisions de la sociologie: Oeuvres*, Vol. 3. Paris: Éd. de Minuit.

Mayer, R., and Nicosia, F. (1977). The Sociology of Consumption: Searching for Useful Perspectives on Society. *European Research*, 5, 143–152.

McClelland, D., Atkinson, J., Clark, R., and Lowell, E. (1953). *The Achievement Motive*. New York: Appleton-Century-Crofts.

McFarland, D. (1969). Measuring the Permeability of Occupational Structures: An Information Theoretic Approach. *American Journal of Sociology*, 75, 41–61.

———. (1981). Spectral Decomposition as a Tool in Comparative Mobility Research. *Sociological Methodology*, 12, 338–358.

McGuire, W. (1969). The Nature of Attitude and Attitude Change. In E. Lindzey and E. Aronson (eds.), *The Handbook of Social Psychology*, 2, vol. 3. Reading, MA: Addison Wesley, 136–314.

Mead, G.H. (1934). *Mind, Self, and Society: From the Standpoint of a Social Behaviorist*. Chicago: University of Chicago Press.

Meddin, J. (1975). Attitudes, Values, and Related Concepts. *Social Science Quarterly*, 55, 889–900.

Mermet, G. (1985). *Francoscopie. Les Français: Qui sont-ils? Où vont-ils?* Paris: Larousse.

Merton, R. (1949). *Social Theory and Social Structure*. Glencoe, IL: The Free Press.

Michaels, P. (1973). Lifestyle and Magazine Exposure. In V. Greer (ed.), *Conceptual and Methodological Foundation of Marketing*. Chicago: American Marketing Association, 324–331.

Michman, R.D., Mazze, E.M., and Greco, A.J. (2003). *Lifestyle Marketing: Reaching the New American Consumer*. Westport, CT: Praeger.

Midgley, D., and Dowling, G. (1978). Innovativeness: The Concept and Its Measurement. *Journal of Consumer Research*, 4, 229–242.

Millon, C. (1987). Phox fait flasher ses confrères. *Marketing-Mix*, 15, 30.

Mitchell, A. (1983). *The Nine American Lifestyles*. New York: Macmillan.

Mitchell, J. (1976). The Structure and Predictive Efficacy of an Empirical Model of the Value-Attitude System as Postulated by Rokeach. *Measurement Evaluation Guidance*, 8, 229–239.

Molt, W. (1982). Complex Decisions of Consumers and Aspects of Energy Consciousness and Price Sensitivity. Presented at the International Conference on Consumer Behavior and Energy Policy, Noordwijkerhout, Netherlands, September.

Moore, D. (1963). Lifestyle in Mobile Suburbia. In S.A. Greyser (ed.), *Toward Scientific Marketing*. Chicago: American Marketing Association, 151–164.

Moore, M. (1975). Rating Versus Ranking in the Rokeach Value Survey: An Israeli Comparison. *European Journal of Social Psychology*, 5, 405–408.

Morris, C. (1956). *Varieties of Human Value*. Chicago: University of Chicago Press.

———. (1964). *Signification and Significance*. Cambridge, MA: MIT Press.

Mukerjee, R. (1946). The Sociology of Values. *Sociological and Social Research*, 31, 101–109.

Munson, J.M. (1984). Personal Values: Consideration on Their Measurement and Application to Five Areas of Research Inquiry. In R. Pitts and A. Woodside (eds.), *Personal Values and Consumer Psychology*. Lexington, MA: Lexington Books, 13–33.

Munson, J.M., and McIntyre, S.H. (1977). Personal Values: A Cross-Cultural Assessment of Self Values and Values Attributed to a Distant Cultural Stereotype. In H. Hunt (ed.), *Contributions to Consumer Research*, 5. Chicago: Association for Consumer Research, 160–166.

———. (1979). Developing Practical Procedures for the Measurement of Personal Values in Cross-Cultural Marketing. *Journal of Marketing Research*, 16, 48–52.

Munson, J.M., and McQuarrie, E. (1987). Adaptation of the Rokeach Value Survey to Consumer Research, with Applications to International Marketing. In *Advances in Consumer Research*, 15. Provo, UT: Association for Consumer Research, 381–386.

Munson, J.M., and Spivey, W.A. (1981). Product and Brand User Stereotypes Among Social Classes. *Journal of Advertising Research*, 21, 37–46.

Murray, H. (1938). *Exploration in Personality: A Clinical and Experimental Study of Fifty Men of College Age*. New York: Oxford University Press.

Myers, J., and Gutman, J. (1974). Life Style: The Essence of Social Class. In W. Wells (ed.), *Life Style and Psychographics*. Chicago: American Marketing Association, 235–256.

Naisbitt, J. (1982). *Megatrends*. New York: Warner Books.

Ng, S., Hossain, A., Ball, P., Bond, M., Hayashi, K., Lim, S., O'Driscoll, M., Sinha, D., and Yang, K. (1982). Human Values in Nine Countries. In R. Roth, A. Ashana, D. Sinha, and J. Sinha (eds.), *Diversity and Unity in Cross-Cultural Psychology*. Lisse, Netherlands: Swets and Zeitlinger.

Nietzsche, F. (1872). *Wille Zur Macht: Eine Umwertung alter Werte*. English translation, *Will to Power: A revaluation of all values*. Bianquis, 1947–1948.

Nouzille, V. (1985). Qu'est-ce qui fait courir les vendeurs? *L'Usine Nouvelle*, 47, Nov. 21, p. 134.

Novak, J., and MacEvoy, B. (1990). On Comparing Alternative Segmentation Schemes: The List of Values (LOV) and Values and Life Styles (VALS). *Journal of Consumer Research*, 17 (June), 105–109.

Novak, T.P., and Hoffman, D. (2010). Roles and Goals: Consumer Motivations to Use the Social Web. Paper presented at the annual meeting of the INFORMS Marketing Science Conference, Cologne, Germany, June.

Nuttin, J. (1979). La perspective temporelle dans le comportement humain: étude théorique et revue de recherches. *Du temps biologique au temps psychologique.* Paris: PUF, 307–563.

Orth, U., and Kahle, L.R. (2008). Intrapersonal Variation in Consumer Susceptibility to Normative Influence: Toward a Better Understanding of Brand Choice Decisions. *Journal of Social Psychology*, 148(4), 423–447.

Pages, J.P., Barny, M.H., Bonnefous, S., and Iliakopoulos, A. (1987). *La structure des opinions en 1987.* Paris: Agoramétrie.

Pages, J.P., Brenot, J., Bonnefous, S., and Barny, M.H. (1991). Stabilité des structures dans les enquêtes de suivi des opinions. *La qualité de l'information dans les enquêtes.* Paris: École nationale supérieure des télécommunications, 451–473.

Pages, M., et al. (1979). *L'Emprise de l'organisations.* Paris: Presses Universitaires de France.

Parsons, T. (1939). *The Structure of Social Action,* 2d ed. Glencoe, IL: The Free Press.

Pearlin, L., and Kohn, M. (1966). Social Class, Occupation, and Parental Values. *American Sociological Review,* 31, 466-479.

Peltier, J.W., Schibrowski, J.A., Schultz, D.E., and Davis, J. (2002). Interactive Pychographics: Cross-Selling in the Banking Industry. *Journal of Advertising Research,* 42, 7–22.

Peninou, G. (1980). Réflexion critique sur les styles de vie et les courants socioculturels. *Changements socio-culturels et styles de vie, bilan des expériences et réflexions prospective.* IREP, 91–105.

Penner, L., and Anh, T. (1977). A Comparison of American and Vietnamese Value Systems. *Journal of Social Psychology,* 101, 187–204.

Perkins, W., and Reynolds, T. (1987). The Explanatory Power of Values in Preference Judgements: Validation of the Means-End Perspective. In *Advances in Consumer Research,* 15. Provo, UT: Association for Consumer Research, 122–126.

Perloe, S. (1977). *The Factorial Structure of the Social Values Questionnaire.* Ann Arbor, MI: Survey Research Center, Institute for Social Research.

Pernica, J. (1974). The Second Generation of Market Segmentation Study: An Audit of Buying Motivation. In W. Wells (ed.), *Life Style and Psychographics.* Chicago: American Marketing Association, 277–313.

Perrinjaquet, A., Furrer, O., Usunier, J.-C., Cestre, G., and Valette-Florence, P. (2007). A Test of the Quasi-Circumplex Structure of Human Values. *Journal of Research in Personality,* 41(4), 820–840.

Perry, W.B. (1970). *Forms of intellectual and ethical development in the college years.* New York: Holt, Rinehart, & Winston.

Pessemier, E., and Bruno, A. (1971). An Empirical Investigation of the Reliability and Stability of Selected Activity and Attitude Measures. In *Proceedings of the Second Annual Conference of the Association for Consumer Research.* Association for Consumer Research, 389–403.

Pessemier, E., and Tigert, D. (1966). Personality Activity and Attitude Predictors of Consumer Behavior. In J. Wright and J. Goldstucker (eds.), *New Ideas for Successful Marketing.* Chicago: American Marketing Association, 332–347.

Peterson, R. (1972). Psychographics and Media Exposure. *Journal of Advertising Research,* 12, 17–20.

Petry, G. (1987). Rôle et profils des vendeurs: contribution à une méthodologie du recrutement. *Recherche et applications en marketing,* 2(4), 53–90.

Phillips, J.M., Reynolds, T.J., and Reynolds, K. (2010). Decision-Based Voter Segmentation: Optimizing the Campaign Message Development Process. *European Journal of Marketing,* 44(3–4), 310–330.

Piirto, R. (1991). *Beyond Mind Games: The Marketing Power of Psychographics.* Ithaca, NY: American Demographic Books.

Pinter, R. (1933). A Comparison of Interests, Abilities, and Attitudes. *Journal of Abnormal and Social Psychology,* 27, 351–357.

Pitts, R.E., Canty, A.L., and Tsalikis, J. (1985). Exploring the Impact of Personal Values on Socially Oriented Communication. *Psychology and Marketing,* 2, 267–278.

Pitts, R.E., Jr., and Woodside, A.G., eds. (1984). *Personal Values and Consumer Psychology.* Lexington, MA: Lexington Books.

Plummer, J. (1971a). Learning About Consumers as Real People: The Application of Psychographic Data. Paper presented to the Montreal Chapter of the American Marketing Association, November.

———. (1971b). Lifestyles Patterns: A New Constraint for Mass Communications Research. *Journal of Broadcasting,* 16, 79–89.

———. (1971c). Lifestyles Patterns and Commercial Bank Credit Card Usage. *Journal of Marketing,* 35, 35–41.

———. (1974a). The Concept and Application of Lifestyle Research. *Journal of Marketing,* 38, 33–37.

———. (1974b). Applications of Lifestyle Research to the Creation of Advertising Campaigns. In W. Wells (ed.), *Life Style and Psychographics.* Chicago: American Marketing Association, 159–169.

Poulsen, C. (1990). Mixed Markov and Latent Markov Modelling Applied to Brand Choice Behaviour. *International Journal of Research in Marketing,* 7, 5–19.

Poumadère, M. (1985). SYMLOG et les valeurs de l'organisation. In R. Reitter and B. Ramanantsoa (eds.), *Pouvoir et Politique.* Paris: McGraw-Hill, 79–95.

Prais, S.J., and Houthakker, H.S. (1971). *The Analysis of Family Budgets.* Cambridge: Cambridge University Press.

Pras, B., and Tarondeau, J.C. (1981). *Comportement de l'acheteur.* Paris: Sirey.

Pugnet, A., and Coutin, J.-C. (1982). Application of a Lifestyle Customer Banking: A Specific Approach of Credit Agricole. *Revue francaise du marketing,* 90, 55–64.

Punj, G., and Stewart, R. (1983). An Interaction Framework of Consumer Decision Making. *Journal of Consumer Research,* 10, 181–196.

Radcliffe-Brown, A.R. (1922). *The Andaman Islanders.* Cambridge: Cambridge University Press.

Rankin, W., and Grube, J. (1980). A Comparison of Ranking and Rating Procedures for Value System Measurement. *European Journal of Social Psychology,* 10, 233–246.

Raynor, J., and Entin, E. (1983). The Function of Future Orientation as a Determinant of Human Behavior in Step-Path Theory of Action. *International Journal of Psychology,* 18, 463–487.

Rettig, S., and Pasamanick, B. (1959). Changes in Moral Values as a Function of Adult Socialization. *Social Problems,* 7, 117–125.

Reynolds, F., and Darden, W. (1972a). Intermarket Patronage: A Psychographic Study of Consumer Outshoppers. *Journal of Marketing,* 36, 50–54.

———. (1972b). An Operational Construction of Lifestyle. In *Proceedings of the Third Annual Conference of the Association for Consumer Research.* Association for Consumer Research, 475–489.

————. (1974). Construing Life Style and Psychographies. In W. Wells (ed.), *Life Style and Psychographics.* Chicago: American Marketing Association, 71–97.

Reynolds, T. (1985). Recent Developments in Means-End Chain Analysis. *Psychology and Marketing*, 2, 168–180.

Reynolds, T., and Gutman, J. (1984). Advertising Is Image Management: Translating Image Research to Image Strategy. *Journal of Advertising Research*, 24, 27–38.

————. (1988). Laddering theory, method, analysis, and interpretation. *Journal of Advertising Research*, 28, 11-31.

Reynolds, T., and Jolly, J. (1980). Measuring Personal Values: An Evaluation of Alternative Methods. *Journal of Marketing Research*, 17, 37–80.

Reynolds, T.J. (2006). Methodological and Strategy Development: Implications of Decision Segmentation. *Journal of Advertising Research*, December, 445–461.

Reynolds, T.J., and Olson, J.C. (2001). *Understanding Consumer Decision Making: The Means-End Approach to Marketing and Advertising Strategy.* Mahwah, NJ: Lawrence Erlbaum Associates.

Reynolds, T.J., and Phillips, J.M. (2008). A Review and Comparative Analysis of Laddering Research Methods: Recommendations for Quality Metrics. *Review of Marketing Research*, 5, 130–174.

Richins, M.L., and Dawson, S. (1992). A Consumer Values Orientation for Materialism and Its Measurement: Scale Development and Validation. *Journal of Consumer Research*, 19 (3), 303–316.

Riesman, D., Glazer, N., and Denney, R. (1950). *The Lonely Crowd.* New Haven, CT: Yale University Press.

Rigaux-Bricmont, B. (1986). L'avenir de la recherche en matière de décision collective d'achat. *Recherche et applications en marketing,* 1(2), 17–26.

Ring, L., Hofer, S., McGee, H., Hickey, A., and O'Boyle, C.A. (2007). Individual Quality of Life: Can It Be Accounted for by Psychological or Subjective Well Being? *Social Indicators Research,* 82(3), 443–461.

Ritchie, J. (1974). An Exploratory Analysis of the Nature and Extent of Individual Differences in Perception. *Journal of Marketing Research,* 11, 41–49.

Robinson, J., and Shaver, P. (1973). *Measures of Social Psychological Attitudes.* Ann Arbor, MI: Survey Research Center, Institute for Social Research.

Roehrich, G., and Valette-Florence, P. (1986). Besoin de stimulation, innovativité, implication et valeurs: test empirique d'un modèle structurel. *Actes du colloque de l'association française du marketing,* 2, 37–80.

————. (1987a). À la recherche des causes individuelles de l'achat des produits nouveaux. *Actes du 14e séminaire international de recherche en marketing,* 349–376.

————. (1987b). Une approche causale du comportement d'achat innovateur. *Publication de recherche du CERAG.* École supérieure des affaires, Université des sciences sociales de Grenoble.

————. (1991). A Weighted Cluster-Based Analysis of Direct and Indirect Connections in Means-End Analysis: An Application to Lingerie Retail. In *Proceedings of the Workshop on Value and Lifestyle Research in Marketing.* Brussels, Belgium: EIASM.

————. (1992). Apport des chaînages cognitifs à la segmentation des marchés. *Actes du colloqui de l'association française du marketing,* 8, 479–498.

Roehrich, G., Valette-Florence, P., and Rapacchi, B. (1989). Combined Influence of Personal Value Systems, Involvement, and Innovativeness on Innovative Consumer

Behaviour. In *Seminar on Is Marketing Keeping Up with the Consumer?* ESOMAR (European Society for Opinion and Market Research),Vienna, 261–279.

Rogers, C.R. (1961). *On Becoming a Person.* Boston: Houghton Mifflin.

Rogers, J.L. (2010). The Epistemology of Mathematical and Statistical Modeling: A Quiet Methodological Revolution. *American Psychologist,* 65, 1–12.

Rokeach, M. (1968a). *Beliefs, Attitudes, and Values.* San Francisco: Jossey-Bass.

———. (1968b). Role of Values in Public Opinion Research. *Public Opinion Quarterly,* 32, 547–560.

———. (1973). *The Nature of Human Values.* New York: The Free Press.

———. (1974). Change and Stability in American Value Systems. *Public Opinion Quarterly,* 38, 222–238.

Romana, J. (1975). Cross-National Comparisons and Consumer Stereotypes: A Case Study of Working and Non-Working Wives in the U.S. and France. Working Paper. Jouy-en-Josas, France: Centre HEC-ISA.

Ronsse, J.M. (1991). *Media Marketing.* Paris/Brussels: De Boeck Université Presse.

Rose, G., Shoham, A., Kahle, L.R., and Batra, R. (1994). Fashion, Dress, and Conformity. *Journal of Applied Social Psychology,* 24, 1501–1519.

Russell, B. (1925). *What I Believe.* London: K. Paul, Trench, Trübner.

Saporta, G. (1990). *Probabilités, analyse des données et statistique.* Paris: Éditions Technip.

Scardigli, V. (1976). Modes de vie et évolution de la société française. *Revue française du marketing,* 14, 107–118.

Schary, P. (1971). Consumption and the Problem of Time. *Journal of Marketing,* 35, 50–55.

Schiffman, L.G., and Kanuk, L.L. (1981). *Consumer Behavior,* 4th ed. Englewood Cliffs, NJ: Prentice Hall.

Schultz, P.W., Gouveia, V., Cameron, L.D., Tankha, G., Schmuck, P., and Franek, M. (2005). Values and Their Relationship to Environmental Concern and Conservation Behavior. *Journal of Cross-Cultural Psychology,* 36, 457–475.

Schwartz, S. (1992). Universals in the Content and Structure of Values: Theoretical Advance and Empirical Tests in 20 Countries. In M. Zanna (ed.), *Advances in Experimental Social Psychology,* 25. New York: Academic Press, 1–65.

Schwartz, S.H. (2007). Universalism Values and the Inclusiveness of Our Moral Universe. *Journal of Cross-Cultural Psychology,* 38, 711–728.

Schwartz, S., and Bilsky, W. (1987). Toward a Universal Psychological Structure of Human Values. *Journal of Personality and Social Psychology,* 53(3), 550–562.

———. (1990). Toward a Theory of the Universal Content and Structure of Values: Extensions and Cross-Cultural Replications. *Journal of Personality and Social Psychology,* 58(5), 878–89.

Schwartz, S. H. and Boehnke, K. (2004), Evaluating the structure of human values with confirmatory factor analysis, *Journal of Research in Personality,* 38, 230–255.

Schwartz, S.H., Melech, G., Lehmann, A., Burgess, S., Harris, M. and Owens, V. (2001). Extending the Cross-Cultural Validity of the Theory of Basic Human Values with a Different Method of Measurement. *Journal of Cross-Cultural Psychology,* 32, 519–542.

Schwartz, S. H., and Sagiv, L. (1995). Identifying Culture-specifics in the Content and Structure of Values. *Journal of Cross-Cultural Psychology,* 26, 91–116.

Scitovsky, T. (1976). *The Joyless Economy: An Inquiry into Human Satisfaction and Consumer Dissatisfaction*. New York: Oxford University Press.

Scott, D.M. (2009). *The New Rules of Marketing and PR: How to Use News Releases, Blogs, Podcasting, Viral Marketing, and Online Media to Reach Your Buyers Directly*. Hoboken, NJ: Wiley.

Scott, J., and Lamont, L. (1973). Relating Consumer Values to Consumer Behavior: A Model and Method for Investigation. In T. Green (ed.), *Increasing Marketing Productivity*. Chicago: American Marketing Association, 283–288.

Scott, W. (1959). Cognitive Consistency, Response Reinforcement, and Attitude Change. *Sociometry*, 22, 219–229.

———. (1965). *Values and Organizations: A Study of Fraternities and Sororities*. Chicago: Rand McNally.

Searing, D. (1979). A Study of Values in the British House of Commons. In M. Rokeach (ed.), *Understanding Human Values*. New York: The Free Press, 154–178.

Segnit, S., and Broadbent, S. (1974). Clustering by Product Usage: A Case History. In *Proceedings of the XXVth ESOMAR Congress*. Amsterdam, 118–124.

Settle, R., Alreck, P., and Glasheen, J. (1978). Individual Time Orientations and Consumer Life Styles. In H. Hunt (ed.), *Advances in Consumer Research*, 5. Ann Arbor, MI: Association for Consumer Research, 315–319.

Shavitt, S. (1990). The Role of Attitude Objects in Attitude Functions. *Journal of Experimental Social Psychology*, 26, 124–148.

Shepard, R., and Arabie, P. (1979). Additive Clustering: Representation of Similarities as Combinations of Discrete Overlapping Properties. *Psychological Review*, 86(2), 87–123.

Shimp, T.A. (2010). *Advertising, Promotion, and Other Aspects of Integrated Marketing Communications*, 8th ed. Mason, OH: South-Western Cengage Learning.

Shoham, A., Rose, G. M., and Kahle, L. R. (2004). Risky Sports: Making the Leap. In L. R. Kahle and C. Riley (eds), *Sports Marketing and the Psychology of Marketing Communication*. Mahwah, NJ: Lawrence Erlbaum, 87-104.

Silver, D. (2009). *The Social Network Business Plan*. Hoboken, NJ: Wiley.

Simmons, W. (1971). Overall Impressions on Psychographics. In C.W. King and D.J. Tigert (eds.), *Attitude Research Reaches New Heights*. Chicago: American Marketing Association, 215–219.

Sinka, P., and Sayeed, O. (1979). Value Systems. *Industrial Journal of Social Work*, 40, 139–145.

Skinner, B.F. (1974). *About Behaviorism*. New York: Alfred A. Knopf.

Small, A., and Vincent, G. (1894). *An Introduction to the Study of Society*. New York: American Book Co.

Smelser, N. (1959). *Social Change in the Industrial Revolution*. Chicago: University of Chicago Press.

Smith, P.B., Peterson, M.F., and Schwartz, S.H. (2002). Cultural Values, Sources of Guidance, and Their Relevance to Managerial Behavior: A 47-Nation Study. *Journal of Cross-Cultural Psychology*, 33(2), 188–208.

Solomon, M.R. (1983). The Role of Products as Social Stimuli: A Symbolic Interactionism Perspective. *Journal of Consumer Research*, 10, 319–329.

———. (2009). *Consumer Behavior: Buying, Having, Being*, 8th ed. Upper Saddle River, NJ: Pearson/Prentice-Hall.

Spini, D. (2003). Measurement Equivalence of 10 Value Types from the Schwartz Value Survey Across 21 Countries. *Journal of Cross-Cultural Psychology*, 34(1), 3–23.

Spranger, E. (1928). *Types of Men: The Psychology and Ethics of Personality,* trans. P.J.W. Pigors. Halle, Germany: Max Niemeyer.

Steiner, J.F., and Auliard, O. (1991). La sémiométrie: un outil de validation des réponses. *La qualité de l'information dans les enquêtes.* Paris: École nationale supérieure des télécommunications, 225–240.

Steinmetz, H., Schmidt, P., Tina-Booh, A., Wieczorek, S., and Schwartz, S.H. (2009). Testing Measurement Invariance Using Multigroup CFA: Difference Between Educational Groups in Human Values Measurement. *Quality and Quantity,* 43(4), 599–616.

Stemmelen, E. (1984). Symboliques et structures dans l'opinion publique. *Futuribles,* January, 65–81.

Stoetzel, J. (1960). A Factor Analysis of the Liquor Preferences of French Consumers. *Journal of Advertising Research,* 1, 7–11.

———. (1983). *Les valeurs du temps présent: une enquête européenne.* Paris: PUF.

Strategor, J. (1988). *Stratégie, structure, décision, identité, ouvrage collectif.* Paris: InterÉditions.

Sumner, W. (1906). *Folkways.* Boston: Ginn.

Sun, T., Horn, M., and Merritt, D. (2004). Values and Lifestyles of Individualists and Collectivists: A Study of Chinese, Japanese, British, and U.S. Consumers. *Journal of Consumer Marketing,* 21, 318–331.

Swiners, J.L. (1979). Les styles de vie sont morts, vive les styles de mort. *Stratégies,* 185, 30–34.

Tabachnick, B., and Fidell, L.C. (1989). *Using Multivariate Statistics,* 2d ed. New York: Harper & Row.

Tambyah, S.K., Tan, S.J., and Kau, A.K. (2009). *The Well-Being of Singaporeans: Values, Lifestyles, Satisfaction, and Quality of Life.* Singapore: World Scientific Publishing.

Thomas, W., and Znaniecki, F. (1921). *The Polish Peasant in Europe and America.* Chicago: University of Chicago Press.

Thompson, C., and Troester, M. (2002). Consumer Value Systems in the Age of Postmodern Fragmentation: The Case of the Natural Health Microculture. *Journal of Consumer Research,* 28, 550.

Thurstone, L. (1954). The Measurement of Values. *Psychological Review,* 6, 47–58.

Tigert, D. (1973). A Research Project in Creative Advertising Through Lifestyle Analysis. In W. King and D. Tigert (eds.), *Attitude Research Reaches New Heights.* Chicago: American Marketing Association, 223–227.

Tigert, D., and Arnold, S. (1971). Profiling Self-Designated Opinion Leaders and Self-Designated Innovators Through Life Style Research. In *Proceedings of the Second Annual Conference of the Association for Consumer Research.* Association for Consumer Research, 425–445.

Tönnies, F. (1957). *Community and Society,* trans. C.P. Loomis. East Lansing: Michigan State University Press.

Torelli, C., and Kaikati, A. (2009). Values as Predictors of Values and Behaviors: The Role of Concrete and Abstract Mindsets. *Journal of Personality and Social Psychology,* 96, 231.

Triandis, H. (1972). *The Analysis of Subjective Culture.* New York: Wiley.

———. (1979). *Attitude and Attitude Change.* New York: Wiley.

Tucker, L. (1958). An Inter-Battery Method of Factor Analysis. *Psychometrika,* 23, 111–137.

Tull, D.S., and Kahle, L.R. (1990). *Marketing Management.* New York: Macmillan.

Usunier, J.C. (1991). Business Time Perceptions and National Cultures: A Comparative Survey. *Management International Review,* 31(3), 197–217.

Usunier, J.C., and Valette-Florence, P. (1991). Perceptual Time Patterns (Time-Styles): Preliminary Findings. In J.C. Chebat and Van Venkatesan (eds.), *Proceedings of the Conference on Time and Consumer Behavior.* Montreal: UQAM.

Usunier, J.C., Valette-Florence, P., and Falcy, S. (1992). Systèmes de valeurs et styles de temps: une approche exploratoire de leur complémentarité. *Actes du colloque de l'association française du marketing,* 8, 271–295.

Uusitalo, L. (1979a). *Consumption Style and Way of Life: An Empirical Identification and Explanation of Consumption Style Dimensions.* Acta Oeconomiae Helsingiensis, Series A:27. Helsinki, Finland: Helsinki School of Economics.

———. (1979b). Identification of Consumption Style Segments on the Basis of Household Budget Allocation. In *Advances in Consumer Research,* 7. Ann Arbor, MI: Association for Consumer Research, 451–459.

Valette-Florence, P. (1985). Une évaluation empirique des effets des styles de vie sur la consommation. Thèse de 3e cycle ès sciences de gestion, Institut d'études commerciales, Université des sciences sociales de Grenoble.

———. (1986). Les démarches de styles de vie: concepts, champs d'investigation et problèmes actuels. *Recherche et applications en marketing,* 1, 94–109; 2, 42–58.

———. (1987). Comparaison de systèmes de valeurs selon Kahle et Rokeach. *Actes du colloque de l'association française du marketing,* 3, 1–21.

———. (1988a). L'Implication, variable médiatrice entre styles de vie, valeurs et modes de consommation. Thèse de doctorat d'état ès sciences de gestion, École supérieure des affaires, Université des sciences sociales de Grenoble.

———. (1988b). Analyse structurelle comparative des composantes des systèmes de valeurs selon Kahle et Rokeach. *Recherche et applications en marketing,* 3(1), 15–35.

———. (1988c). Spécificité et apport des méthodes d'analyse multivariée de la deuxième génération. *Recherche et applications en marketing,* 3(4), 23–57.

———. (1989a). Conceptualisation et mesure de l'implication. *Recherche et applications en marketing,* 4(1), 57–78.

———. (1989b). *Les styles de vie: fondements, méthodes et applications.* Paris: Economica.

———. (1990). Les styles de vie en question: mythes et réalitiés. *Revue française du marketing,* 125(5), 17–26.

———. (1991). A Causal Analysis of the Predictive Power of Selected Indicators. In *Proceedings of the Workshop on Value and Lifestyle Research in Marketing.* Brussels, Belgium: EIASM.

———. (1994). *Les styles de vie: bilan critique et perspectives.* Paris: Nathan.

Valette-Florence, P., Falcy, S., and Rapacchi, B. (1993). Optimum Stimulation Level and Means-End Hierarchies: Implications in Segmentation, Product Positioning, and Advertising Strategies. In *Proceedings of the ESOMAR/EMAC/AFM Symposium on Information-Based Decision Making in Marketing,* Paris, 167–190.

Valette-Florence, P., Ferrandi, J.-M., Roehrich, G. (2003). Apport des chaînages cognitifs à la segmentation des marchés. *Décisions marketing,* 32, 31–43.

Valette-Florence, P., Grunert, K., Grunert, S., and Beatty, J.C. (1991). Une comparaison franco-allemande de l'adhésion aux valeurs personnelles. *Recherche et applications en marketing,* 6(3l), 5–20.

Valette-Florence, P., and Jolibert, A. (1985). Un essai empirique de clarification des approches de styles de vie. *Actes de l'association française de marketing,* 1, 133–157.

———. (1987a). Life-Style: An Empirical Investigation of the Relationships Between Its Indicators. *Publication de recherche du CERAG.* École supérieure des affaires, Université des sciences sociales de Grenoble.

———. (1987b). Personal Values: A Validity Investigation. TIMS/ORSA Marketing Science Conference, June, Jouy-en-Josas, France: Centre HEC-ISA.

———. (1988). Life-Styles and Consumption Patterns, *Publication de recherche du CERAG.* École supérieure des affaires, Université des sciences sociales de Grenoble.

———. (1990). Social Values, AIO, and Consumption Patterns: Exploratory Findings. *Journal of Business Research,* 20(2), 109–122.

———. (1991). Measuring Social Values: An Exploratory Study of Alternative Methods. In T. Childers et al. (eds.), *Marketing Theory and Applications.* Chicago: American Marketing Association, 263–274.

Valette-Florence, P., Le Brun, C., Leclercq, S., and Nalpas, R. (1992). Pour un renouveau de la segmentation comportementate en milieu bancaire, *Actes du 2e séminaire international de recherche en management des activités de service,* Vol. 2, 645–664.

Valette-Florence, P., and Rapacchi, B. (1989). Value Analysis by Linear Representation and Appropriate Positioning: An Extension of Laddering Methodology. In *Proceedings of the EMAC Annual Conference.* Athens: EMAC, 2, 969–989.

———. (1990a). Application et extension de la théorie des graphes à l'analyse des chaînages cognitifs: une illustration pour l'achat de parfums et eaux de toilette. *Actes du colloque de l'association française du marketing,* 6, 485–511.

———. (1990b). Analyse structurelle et analyse typologique: illustration d'une démarche complémentaire. *Recherche et applications en marketing,* 5(1), 73–91.

———. (1991a). A Cross-Cultural Means-End Chain Analysis of Perfume Purchases. In *Proceedings of the Third Symposium on Cross-Cultural Consumer and Business Studies,* 161–173.

———. (1991b). Improving Means-End Chain Analysis Using Graph Theory and Correspondence Analysis. *Journal of Advertising Research,* 31(1), 30–45.

———. (1991c). Apport de la méthode de décomposition spectrale à l'analyse de l'évolution temporelle des styles de vie. *Actes du 7e colloque de l'association française du marketing,* 7, 165–182.

Valette-Florence, P., and Usunier, J.C. (1991). Personal Value Systems and Temporal Patterns (Time-Styles): Exploratory Findings. In *Proceedings of the Workshop on Value and Lifestyle Research in Marketing.* Brussels, Belgium: EIASM.

Van Der Burg, E. (1988). *Nonlinear Canonical Correlation and Some Related Techniques.* Leiden: DSWO Press.

Veblen, T. (1899). *The Theory of the Leisure Class.* New York: Macmillan.

Veltri, J., and Schiffman, L. (1984). Fifteen Years of Consumer Life Style and Value Research at AT&T. In R.E. Pitts, Jr., and A.G. Woodside (eds.), *Personal Values and Consumer Psychology.* Lexington, MA: Lexington Books, 271–285.

Verhallen, T., Van Onzenoort, A., and Barzilay, J. (1989). Typology Versus Segmentation: A Domain Specific Approach to Market Segmentation. In *Is Marketing Keeping Up with the Consumer?* Vienna: ESOMAR, 143–164.

Veroff, J., Douvan, E., and Kulka, R. (1981). *The Inner American.* New York: Basic Books.

Villani, K. (1975). Personality, Lifestyle, and Television Viewing Behavior. *Journal of Marketing Research,* 12, 432–439.

Villani, K., and Lehmann, D. (1975). An Examination of the Stability of AIO Measures. In E. Mazze (ed.), *1975 Combined Proceedings.* Chicago: American Marketing Association, 484–488.

Vinson, D., and Munson, J. (1976). Personal Values: An Approach to Market Segmentation. In K. Bernhardt (ed.), *Marketing: 1776–1976 and Beyond.* Chicago: American Marketing Association, 313–317.

Vinson, D., Scott, J., and Lamont, L. (1977). The Role of Personal Values in Marketing and Consumer Behavior. *Journal of Marketing,* 14, 44–50.

Vitt, L.A. (2004). Consumers' Financial Decisions and the Psychology of Values. *Journal of Financial Service Professionals,* 58, 68-77.

Walsh, J. (1991). Consumer Purchasing for Uncertain Future Tastes. Unpublished doctoral dissertation, Cornell University, Ithaca, NY.

Wang, W. (2010). Lay Theories of Medicine and a Healthy Lifestyle. *Journal of Consumer Research,* 37, 80–97.

Watson, J.B. (1913). Psychology as the Behaviorist Views It. *Psychological Review,* 20, 158–177.

———. (1925). *Behaviorism.* New York: The People's Institute Publishing Co.

Weber, L. (2009). *Marketing to the Social Web: How Digital Customer Communities Build Your Business*, 2d ed. Hoboken, NJ: Wiley.

Weber, M. (1922). *Wirtschaft und Gesellschaft.* Transl. English, *Economy and Society*, Plon, 1964.

———. (1948). *From Max Weber: Essays in Sociology*, trans. and ed. H. Gerth and C. Mills. London: Routledge and Kegan Paul.

Wedel, M., and Steenkamp, J.B. (1989a). Consumer Benefit Segmentation Using Clusterwise Linear Regression, *International Journal of Research in Marketing,* 6(1), 45–59.

———. (1989b). A Fuzzy Clustering Regression Approach to Benefit Segmentation, *International Journal of Research in Marketing,* 6(4), 241–258.

———. (1991). A Clusterwise Regression Method for Simultaneous Fuzzy Market Structuring and Benefit Segmentation. *Journal of Marketing Research,* 28(4), 385–390.

Weil, P. (1986). *Et moi, émoi. La communication publicitaire face à l'individualisme.* Paris: Les Éditions d'Organisation.

Weiss, M. J. (1987). *The Clustering of America.* New York: Harper and Row.

———. (2000). *The Clustered World: How We Live, What We Buy, and What It All Means About Who We Are.* Boston: Little, Brown.

Wells, W. (1968a). Backward Segmentation. In J. Arndt (ed.), *Insights into Consumer Behavior.* Boston: Allyn and Bacon, 85–100.

———. (1968b). Segmentation by Attitude Types. In R. King (ed.), *Proceedings: Marketing and the New Science of Planning.* Chicago: American Marketing Association, 124–126.

————. (1974). Life Style and Psychographics: Definitions, Uses, and Problems. In W. Wells (ed.), *Life Style and Psychographics.* Chicago: American Marketing Association, 317–363.

————. (1975). Psychographics: A Critical Review. *Journal of Marketing Research,* 12, 196–213.

————. (1985). Attitude and Behavior: Lessons from the Needham Life Style Study. *Journal of Advertising Research,* 25, 40–44.

Wells, W., and Beard, A. (1973). Personality and Consumer Behavior. In S. Ward and T. Robertson (eds.), *Consumer Behavior: Theoretical Sources.* Englewood Cliffs, NJ: Prentice-Hall, 74–92.

Wells, W., and Tigert, D. (1971). Activities, Interests, and Opinions. *Journal of Advertising Research,* 2(4), 27–35.

Werkmeister, W. (1967). *Man and His Values.* Lincoln: University of Nebraska Press.

Wind, Y., and Douglas, S. (1972). International Market Segmentation. *European Journal of Marketing,* 17–25.

Wind, Y., and Green, P. (1974). Some Conceptual, Measurement, and Analytical Problems in Life Style Research. In W. Wells (ed.), *Life Style and Psychographics.* Chicago: American Marketing Association, 97–126.

Windal, P. (1990). Pour un positionnement à la carte: un exemple automobile. *Recherche et applications en marketing,* 5(2), 45–63.

Wong, J., and Tse, D. (1987). Consumption Values in Selected Rim Countries. In *Advances in Consumer Research,* 15. Provo, UT: Association for Consumer Research, 387–396.

Wood, N.T., and Solomon, M.R. (2009). *Virtual Social Identity and Consumer Behavior.* Armonk, NY: M.E. Sharpe.

Wright, B. (1973). An Exploration of the Domain of Values and Value Change Through the Use of Projective and Semi-Projective Techniques. *Annual Meeting of Southern Sociological Society.*

Wrong, D. (1961). The Oversocialized Conception of Man in Modern Sociology. *American Sociological Review,* 26, 183–193.

Yankelovich, D. (1964). New Criteria for Market Segmentation. *Harvard Business Review,* 42, 83–90.

————. (1971). What Life Style Means to Market Planners. *Marketing Communications,* 6, 38–45.

————. (ed). (1974). The Yankelovich Monitor.

Yankelovich, D., Skelly, A., and White, E. (1981). Social Trends Measured. Yankelovich Monitor, #3.

Young, S. (1971). Psychographic Research and Market Relevancy. In C.W. King and D.J. Tigert (eds.), *Attitude Research Reaches New Heights.* Chicago: American Marketing Association, 220–222.

————. (1972). The Dynamics of Measuring Unchange. In R. Haley (ed.), *Attitude Research in Transition.* Chicago: American Marketing Association.

Zaleznik, A., and Kets de Vries, M. (1975). *Power and the Corporate Mind.* Boston: Houghton Mifflin.

Ziff, R. (1971). Psychographies for Market Segmentation. *Journal of Advertising Research,* 11, 3–9.

# Index

Values
  measurement procedures
    *(continued)*
    Value Inventory, 21
    Value Profile, 21
  research development, 13–38
    CIRCUM analysis, 33–34, 35*t*,
      36*t*, 37*f*, 38
    European Social Survey (ESS),
      32
    historic evolution, 13–19, 27,
      28*t*, 29–30
    measurement procedures, 19–23
    Portraits Value Questionnaire
      (PVQ), 31–33
    Rokeach Value Survey (RVS),
      18–19, 22, 29–30
    Schwartz Value Survey (SVS),
      30, 31*t*, 32*f*, 33–38
    value specification, 23–27
  research limitations, 164–65, 169,
    171
  summary, 56–57
  value specification, 23–27
    attitudes, 25–27
    interests, 25
    needs, 24
    personality traits, 24–25
    social norms, 25

Values and Lifestyle Survey (VALS).
  *See* VALS research
Veblen, Thorstein, 4
Vietnam, 19
*Vous et les Francais* (Mermet and
  Cathelat), 92

**W**

Way of life, 8–9
Way of living, 7
Weber, Max, 4
Wennington, William, 4

**Y**

Yankelovich, Skelly and White
  Monitor Service, 254, 258
Yankelovich Monitor
  current research trends, 254,
    258
  development of, 77–78
  sociocultural trends, 52, 53*t*
  theoretical approach
    research comparison, 260*t*
    research expansion, 251,
      252
    research structure, 261*f*
Young & Rubicam, 74

# About the Authors

**Lynn R. Kahle** is the Ehrman Giustina Professor of Marketing and Chair of the Department of Marketing at the University of Oregon, where he was founding director of the Warsaw Sports Marketing Center. His interests center on applications of social psychology to understanding consumers and sports fans. He has served as president of the Society for Consumer Psychology and chair of the Sports and Special Events Special Interest Group in the American Marketing Association. He also served as editor of *Sport Marketing Quarterly.* His ten previous books include *Creating Images and the Psychology of Marketing Communication; Sports Marketing and the Psychology of Marketing Communications; Social Values and Social Change: Adaptation to Life in America;* and *Values, Lifestyles, and Psychographics.*

**Pierre Valette-Florence** is Professor of Marketing and Quantitative Methods at the University of Grenoble and Distinguished Visiting Professor at Audencia School of Business. His research interests focus on structural equation modeling and mixture data analysis, along with brand relationships management. He has published extensively in scholarly journals as well as in top international marketing conferences. Recognized as an expert in quantitative analysis and methods of marketing research, Valette-Florence acts as a consultant in consumer behavior and branding fields for leading international companies such as Chanel, Mars, and Firmenich, to name just a few.